Tourism Management

TOURISM MANAGEMENT

Vivek Verma

CENTRUM PRESS
NEW DELHI-110002 (INDIA)

CENTRUM PRESS
H.O.: 4360/4, Ansari Road, Daryaganj,
New Delhi-110002 (India)
Tel: 23278000, 23261597, 23255577, 23286875
B.O.: No. 1015, Ist Main Road, BSK IIIrd Stage,
IIIrd Phase, IIIrd Block, Bengaluru-560085 (INDIA)
Tel: 080-41723429
Email: centrumpress@gmail.com
Visit us at: www.centrumpress.com

Tourism Management

First Edition, 2011

ISBN 978-93-81293-83-6

PRINTED IN INDIA

Printed at Tarun Offset, Delhi

Contents

Preface

Tourism is travel for recreational, leisure or business purposes. The World Tourism Organization defines tourists as people who "travel to and stay in places outside their usual environment for more than twenty-four hours and not more than one consecutive year for leisure, business and other purposes not related to the exercise of an activity remunerated from within the place visited."

Tourism Management will be necessary reading for anyone interested in tourism-including tourists-and who want to understand how the business works, how it makes proceeds and what are the effects of its activities on objectives. The book scrutinizes all the key trends now affecting the tourism industry from the impact of technology to the low-cost airlines have transformed the market for leisure travel.

We are all living in an age of major social and economic transformation, and tourism is part of that transformation. This book will at least help you understand what is driving these changes in tourism and what is likely to stimulate future changes. For the tourism manager, this book will undoubtedly spell out a few home truths. For the general reader, it will show how hard being a manager in tourism actually is -and the problems that we, the traveling public-the tourist-in fact facade for businesses-as well as the opportunities and challenges.

Author

1

Introduction

In this course you will learn about the essential features of tourism industry, definition and meaning of various concepts, how to make travel arrangements, travel management, tourism marketing, tourism in India including emerging dimensions. In this session you will understand the different perspectives on the study of tourism, know the meaning of the term 'tourism', 'visitor tourist', 'excursionist', 'inbound' and 'outbound tourist' and the difference between travel and tourism.

CHANGING FACETS OF TOURISM

From the very inception of life, travel has fascinated man. Travel and tourism have been important social activities of human beings from time immemorial. The urge to explore new places within one's own country or outside and seek a change of environment and experience has been experienced from ancient times. Tourism is one of the world's most rapidly growing industries. Much of its growth is due to higher disposable incomes, increased leisure time and falling costs of travel. As airports become more enjoyable places to pass through, as travel agency services become increasingly automated, and as tourists find it easier to get information on places they want to visit, tourism grows.

The Internet has fuelled the growth of the travel industry by providing on line booking facilities. It has also provided people with the power to explore destinations and cultures from their home personal computers and make informed choices before finalizing travel plans. With its immense information resources, the Internet allows tourists to scrutinise hotels, check weather forecasts, read up on local food and even talk to other tourists around the world about their travel experiences for a chosen destination. This new trend has made the tourism job very challenging. The holiday makers want a good rate of return on their investment. They are to be lured with value additions and improved customer service.

This also put emphasis on the regular flow of manpower with specific skills at the appropriate levels to match and cater to global standards. The success of the hospitality industry comes from provision of quality rooms, food, service and ambience. There is no doubt that fitness has increasingly become a larger part of everyone's life. And business and leisure travellers alike look to maintain their fitness goals while away from home. Awareness should be created about the environment and education.

A collective effort and co-operation with powerful networking are the need of the hour. People should be acting as the watchdogs of the society as far as environmental issues are concerned. Eco-tourists are a growing community and tourism promotions have to adopt such eco-practices which could fit this growing community. Another growing trend in the tourism scene is the Incentive Market and the scope of the destination to attract conferences and convention traffic. Here the prospects are better for those destinations where state of the art infrastructure has been developed along with a safe and clean image.

Tourism today is much more than just developing products. It is more about quality, insightful thinking and ability to have global information about technology, partners, contacts and responding quickly to global and regional trends. The fundamental task before tourism promotion is to facilitate integration of the various components in the tourism trade as active participants in the nation's social and cultural life. There is a long road ahead.

All must work towards a society where people can work and participate as equal partners. Tourism should be a vehicle for international cooperation and understanding of the various civilizations and a harbinger of peace. From the foregoing we can see how fast the face of tourism is changing and how challenging the job of travel agencies is now. There is therefore a need for proper training of the personnel working in the industry through thorough and a detailed study of the subject A unified approach to the subject is also needed since at present people from different fields have been studying tourism from different perspectives.

DIFFERENT PERSPECTIVES ON THE STUDY OF TOURISM

GEOGRAPHICAL PERSPECTIVE

Geographical Perspective—from a geographer's perspective the main concern of tourism is to look into aspects like the geographical location of a place, the climate, the landscape, the environment, the physical planning and the changes in these emerging from provisioning of tourism facilities and amenities. A geographer feels that it is the climate, landscape or physical attributes which draw the tourist to a destination, for example; if a person from Delhi goes to Shimla in the summer he does so because of the cooler climate which he cannot get in Delhi

SOCIOLOGICAL PERSPECTIVE

From a sociologist's perspective Tourism is a social activity; it is about interaction between different communities—hosts and guests—and encounter between different cultures. This approach studies social classes, habits and customs of both hosts and guests in terms of tourism behaviour of individuals or groups of people and the impact of tourism on society.

HISTORICAL PERSPECTIVE

An historian's perspective tourism is a study of the factors instrumental in the initiation of tourism to a particular destination, the order of happenings leading to tourism development, the reasons for happening of the occurrences in that order, beneficiaries of the tourist activity and an untimely and premature identification of negative effects. For example we all know that a lot of tourists visit Taj Mahal in Agra but a historian would be interested in studying the factors that bring the tourist there, *e.g.* the architecture, the story behind the monument, or something else that draws them there.

MANAGERIAL PERSPECTIVE

The management perspective tourism is an industry, and therefore needs managerial skills in order to be properly managed. As the industry grows we see continuous changes in various organisations and services linked with the industry, the tourism products and so on so this approach concentrates on management activities such as planning, research, pricing, marketing, control etc. as vital to the operation of a tourist establishment.

ECONOMIC PERSPECTIVE

From an economist's perspective tourism is a major source of foreign exchange earnings, a generator of personal and corporate incomes, a creator of employment and a contributor to government earnings. It is a dominant global activity surpassing even trade in oil and manufactured goods. Economists study the effects of tourism industry on the economy. This is a two way process.

THE IMPORTANCE OF MANAGERIAL AND ECONOMIC PERSPECTIVES OF TOURISM

Now due to higher disposable incomes, increased leisure time and falling cost of travel, the Tourism industry has shown a very high growth and since tourism is a service industry it comprises of a number of tangible and intangible components. The tangible elements include transport systems—air, rail, road, water and now, space; hospitality services—accommodation, food and beverage, tours, souvenirs; and related services such as banking, insurance and safety and security. The intangible elements include: rest and relaxation, culture, escape, adventure, new and different experiences. As there are number of bodies involved the need arises for a management of services related to this industry and so the study of Tourism acquires a great practical necessity and usefulness. Tourism industry is very fast growing and this industry involves activities and interests of Transport Undertakings, Owners of Tourist Sites and Attractions, Various tourist Service Providers at the tourist destinations and Central and Local Government, etc. Each of these serves both the resident population and the tourists and their management must reconcile the needs of tourists with the needs of the resident population. So it becomes important to study tourism from the perspective of Management, since the management of various bodies in this industry is invaded.

TOURISM IN INDIA—DEFINITION AND MEANING

Tourism is the largest service industry in India, with a contribution of 6.23% to the national GDP and 8.78% of the total employment in India. India witnesses more than 5 million annual foreign tourist arrivals and 562 million domestic tourism visits. The tourism industry in India generated about US$100 billion in 2008 and that is expected to increase to US$275.5 billion by 2018 at a 9.4% annual growth rate. The Ministry of Tourism is the nodal agency for the development and promotion of tourism in India and maintains the "Incredible India" campaign. World Travel and Tourism Council, India will be a tourism hotspot from 2009–2018, having the highest 10-year growth potential. The Travel and Tourism Competitiveness Report 2007 ranked tourism in India 6th in terms of price competitiveness and 39th in terms of safety and security. Despite short- and medium-term setbacks, such as shortage of hotel rooms, tourism revenues are expected to surge by 42% from 2007 to 2017. India has a growing medical tourism sector. The 2010 Commonwealth Games in Delhi are expected to significantly boost tourism in India.

TOURISM BY STATE

Andhra Pradesh

Andhra Pradesh has a rich cultural heritage and a variety of tourist attractions. The state of Andhra Pradesh comprises scenic hills, forests, beaches and temples. Also known as The City of Nizams and The City of Pearls, Hyderabad is today one of the most developed cities in the country and a modern hub of information technology, ITES, and biotechnology. Hyderabad is known for its rich history, culture and architecture representing its unique character as a meeting point for North and South India, and also its multilingual culture. Andhra Pradesh is the home of many religious pilgrim centres.

Tirupati, the abode of Lord Venkateswara, is the richest and most visited religious centre in the world. Srisailam, the abode of Sri Mallikarjuna, is one of twelve Jyothirlingalu in India, Amaravati's Siva temple is one of the Pancharamams, and Yadagirigutta, the abode of an avatara of Vishnu, Sri Lakshmi Narasimha. The Ramappa temple and Thousand Pillars temple in Warangal are famous for some fine temple carvings. The state has numerous Buddhist centres at Amaravati, Nagarjuna Konda, Bhattiprolu, Ghantasala, Nelakondapalli, Dhulikatta, Bavikonda, Thotlakonda, Shalihundam, Pavuralakonda, Sankaram, Phanigiri and Kolanpaka.

The golden beaches at Visakhapatnam, the one-million-year old limestone caves at Borra, picturesque Araku Valley, hill resorts of Horsley Hills, river Godavari racing through a narrow gorge at Papi Kondalu, waterfalls at Ettipotala, Kuntala and rich bio-diversity at Talakona, are some of the natural attractions of the state. Visakhapatnam is home to many tourist attactions such as the INS Karasura Submarine museum, Yarada Beach, Araku Valley, VUDA Park, Indira Gandhi Zoological Gardens. The weather in Andhra Pradesh is mostly tropical and the best time to visit is in November through to January. The monsoon season commences in June and ends in September, so travel would not be advisable during this period. Also worth visiting, the only Indian Buddhism Based Theme Park and Resorts on the Vijayawada—Guntur Highway—Agrigold Haailand.

Arunachal Pradesh

Arunachal Pradesh attracts tourists from many parts of the world. Tourist attractions include Tawang, a beautiful town famous for its Buddhist monastery, Ziro, famous for cultural festivals, the Namdapha tiger project in Changlang district and Sela lake near Bomdila with its bamboo bridges overhanging the river. Religious places of interest include Malinithan in Lekhabali, Rukhmininagar near Roing and Parshuram Kund in Lohit district. Rafting and trekking are common activities. A visitor's permit from the tourism department is required. Places like Tuting have wonderful, undiscovered scenic beauty.

Assam

Assam is the central state in the North-East Region of India and serves as the gateway to the rest of the Seven Sister States. Assam boasts of famous wildlife preserves–the Kaziranga National Park, which is home to the Great Indian One-Horned Rhinoceros and the Manas National Park, the largest river island Majuli, historic Sivasagar, famous for the ancient monuments of Ahom Kingdom, the city of eternal romance, Tezpur and tea-estates dating back to time of British Raj. The weather is mostly sub-tropical. Assam experiences the Indian monsoon and has one of the highest forest densities in India. The winter months are the best time to visit. Assam has a rich cultural heritage going back to the Ahom Kingdom, which governed the region for many centuries before the British occupation. Other notable features include the Brahmaputra River, the mystery of the bird suicides in Jatinga, numerous temples including Kamakhya of Tantric sect. 'Gurdwara Sri Guru Tegh Bahadur also known as Damdama Sahib at Dhubri '. This famous Gurudwara is situated in the heart of the Dhubri Town on the bank of the mighty Brahmaputra river in far north-east India. Guru Nanak the first Sikh Guru visited this place in 1505 and met Srimanta Sankardeva as the Guru travelled from Dhaka to Assam, ruins of palaces, etc. Guwahati, the capital city of Assam, boasts many bazaars, temples, and wildlife sanctuaries.

Bihar

Bihar is one of the oldest continuously inhabited places

in the world with history of 3000 years. The rich culture and heritage of Bihar is evident from the innumerable ancient monuments that are dotted all over this state in eastern India. This is the Place of Aryabhata, Great Ashoka, Chanakya and many more.

Attractions:

- *Patna*: The capital of Bihar, famous for its rich history and royal architecture. Golghar and Budha Smriti Park are famous lanmarks.
- *Gaya*: Known for Bodh Gaya the place at which Gautam Buddha attained enlightenment.Attraction for Buddhists across the globe.
- *Barauni*: Petrochemical work for national level
- *Muzaffarpur*: Famous for its education.
- *Kesariya*: World's largest Buddhist Stupa located here.
- *Nalanda*: World's oldest university remains here.
- *Sasaram*: Tomb of Sher Shah Suri, the great Emperor of Mughal age who defeated Humayun.
- *Sonpur*: The Sonepur Cattle Fair or Sonepur Mela,it is the biggest cattle fair of Asia and stretches on from fifteen days to one month.
- *Takht Sri Patna Sahib*: One of the famous Sikh pilgrimage known for the birth place of Sikh's Tenth Guru Sri Guru Gobind Singh Sahib.

Bihar is one of the most sacred places of various religions such as Hinduism, Buddhism, Jainism, Sikhism and Islam. Famous Attraction includes Mahabodhi Temple, a Buddhist shrine and UNESCO World Heritage Site is also situated in Bihar, Barabar Caves the oldest rockcut caves in India, Khuda Bakhsh Oriental Library the Oldest Library of India.

Delhi

Delhi is the capital city of India. A fine blend of old and new, ancient and modern, Delhi is a melting pot of cultures, religions. Delhi has been the capital of numerous empires that ruled India, making it rich in history. The rulers left behind their trademark architectural styles. Delhi currently has many renowned historic monuments and landmarks such as the

Tughlaqabad fort, Qutub Minar, Purana Quila, Lodhi Gardens, Jama Masjid, Humayun's tomb, Red Fort, and Safdarjung's Tomb. Modern monuments include Jantar Mantar, India Gate, Rashtrapati Bhavan, Laxminarayan Temple, Lotus temple and Akshardham Temple. New Delhi is famous for its British colonial architecture, wide roads, and tree-lined boulevards. Delhi is home to numerous political landmarks, national museums, Islamic shrines, Hindu temples, green parks, and trendy malls.

Goa

Goa is one of the most famous tourist destinations in India. A former colony of Portugal, Goa is famous for its excellent beaches, Portuguese churches, Hindu temples, and wildlife sanctuaries. The Basilica of Bom Jesus, Mangueshi Temple, Dudhsagar Falls, and Shantadurga are famous attractions in Goa. Recently a Wax Museum has also opened in Old Goa housing a number of wax personalities of Indian history, culture and heritage. The Goa Carnival is a world famous event, with colourful masks and floats, drums and reverberating music, and dance performances. The celebrations run three days culminating in a carnival parade on fat Tuesday.

Himachal Pradesh

Himachal Pradesh is famous for its Himalayan landscapes and popular hill-stations. Many outdoor activities such as rock climbing, mountain biking, paragliding, ice-skating, and heli-skiing are popular tourist attractions in Himachal Pradesh. Shimla, the state capital, is very popular among tourists. The Kalka-Shimla Railway is a Mountain railway which is a UNESCO World Heritage Site. Shimla is also a famous skiing attraction in India. Other popular hill stations include Manali and Kasauli. Dharamshala, home of the Dalai Lama, is known for its Tibetan monasteries and Buddhist temples. Many trekking expeditions also begin here.

Jammu and Kashmir

Jammu and Kashmir is the northernmost state of India.

Jammu is noted for its scenic landscape, ancient temples, Hindu shrines, castles, gardens and forts. The Hindu holy shrines of Amarnath in kashmir attracts about.4 million Hindu devotees every year. Vaishno Devi alsoattract tens of thousands of Hindu devotees every year. Jammu's historic monuments feature a unique blend of Islamic and Hindu architecture styles.

Tourism forms an integral part of the Kashmiri economy. Often dubbed "Paradise on Earth", Kashmir's mountainous landscape has attracted tourists for centuries. Notable places are Dal Lake, Srinagar Phalagam, Gulmarg, Yeusmarg and Mughal Gardens etc. Kashmir's natural landscape has made it one of the popular destinations for adventure tourism in South Asia.Marked by four distinct seasons,Ski enthusiasts can enjoy the exotic himalayan powder during winters. 7000000 tourists arrived in kashmir in the months of April,May and June alone In recent years, Ladakh has emerged as a major hub for adventure tourism. This part of Greater Himalaya called "moon on earth" comprising of naked peaks and deep gorges was once known for the silk route to High Asia from the subcontinent. Leh is also a growing tourist spot.

Karnataka

Karnataka has been ranked as fourth most popular destination for tourism among states of India. It has the second highest number of protected monuments in India, at 507. Kannada dynasties like Kadambas, Western Gangas, Chalukyas, Rashtrakutas, Hoysalas and Vijayanagaras, ruled Karnataka particularly North Karnataka. They built great monuments to Buddhism, Jainism, Shaivism.

The monuments are still present at Badami, Aihole, Pattadakal, Hampi, Lakshmeshwar, Sudi, Hooli, Mahadeva Temple, Dambal, Lakkundi, Gadag, Hangal, Halasi, Galaganatha, Chaudayyadanapura, Banavasi, Belur, Halebidu, Shravanabelagola, Sannąti and many more. Notable Islamic monuments are present at Bijapur, Bidar, Gulbarga, Raichur and other part of the state. Gol Gumbaz at Bijapur, has the second largest pre-modern dome in the world after the

Byzantine Hagia Sophia. Karnataka has two World heritage sites, at Hampi and Pattadakal, both are in North Karnataka. Karnataka is famous for its waterfalls. Jog falls of Shimoga District is one of the highest waterfalls in Asia. This state has 21 wildlife sanctuaries and five National parks and is home to more than 500 species of birds. Karnataka has many beaches at Karwar, Gokarna, Murdeshwara, Surathkal. Karnataka is a rock climbers paradise. Yana in Uttara Kannada, Fort in Chitradurga, Ramnagara near Bangalore district, Shivagange in Tumkur district and tekal in Kolar district are a rock climbers heaven.

Kerala

Kerala is a state on the tropical Malabar Coast of southwestern India. Nicknamed as one of the "10 paradises of the world" by National Geographic, Kerala is famous especially for its ecotourism initiatives. Its unique culture and traditions, coupled with its varied demography, has made it one of the most popular tourist destinations in India. Growing at a rate of 13.31%, the tourism industry significantly contributes to the state's economy. Kerala is known for its tropical backwaters and pristine beaches such as Kovalam.

Madhya Pradesh

Madhya Pradesh is called the "Heart of India" because of its location in the centre of the country. It has been home to the cultural heritage of Hinduism, Islam, Buddhism, Sikhism, Jainism. Innumerable monuments, exquisitely carved temples, stupas, forts and palaces are dotted all over the State. The temples of Khajuraho are world-famous for their erotic sculptures, and are a UNESCO World Heritage Site. Gwalior is famous for its forts, the Tomb of Rani Lakshmibai, and the Palace of Tansen. Madhya Pradesh is also known as Tiger State because of the tiger population. Famous national parks like Kanha, Bandhavgadh, Shivpuri, Sanjay, Pench are located in MP. Spectacular mountain ranges, meandering rivers and miles and miles of dense forests offering a unique and exciting panorama of wildlife in sylvan surroundings.

Maharashtra

Maharashtra is the second most visited state in India by foreign tourists, with more than 2 million foreign tourists arrivals annually. Maharashtra boasts of a large number of popular and revered religious venues that are heavily frequented by locals as well as out-of-state visitors. Ajanta Caves, Ellora Caves and Chhatrapati Shivaji Terminus are the three UNESCO World Heritage sites in Maharashtra and are highly responsible for the development of Tourism in the state. Mumbai is the most cosmopolitan city in India, and a great place to experience modern India.

Mumbai famous for Bollywood, the world's largest film industry. In addition, Mumbai is famous for its clubs, shopping, and upscale gastronomy. The city is known for its architecture, from the ancient Elephanta Caves, to the Islamic Haji Ali Mosque, to the colonial architecture of Bombay High Court and Chhatrapati Shivaji Terminus. Maharashtra also has numerous adventure tourism destinations, including paragliding, rock climbing, canoeing, kayaking, snorkeling, and scuba diving in places like Kolad, Tarkarli, Koyna, Manor. aharashtra also has several pristine national parks and reserves, some of the best ones are Tadoba with excellent accommodation and safari experiences besides little known by amazing wildlife destinations like Koyna, Nagzira, Melghat, Dajipur, Radhanagari and of course the only national park within metropolic city limits in the world—Sanjay Gandhi National Park.

The Bibi Ka Maqbara at Aurangabad the Mahalakshmi temple at Kolhapur, the cities of Nashik, Trimbak famous for religious importance and the city of Pune the seat of the Maratha Empire and the fantastic Ganesh Chaturthi celebrations together contribute for the Tourism sector of Mahrashtra.

Manipur

Manipur as the name suggest is a land of jewels. Its rich culture excels in every aspects as in martial arts, dance, theater and sculpture. The charm of the place is the greenery with the moderate climate making it a tourists' heaven. The beautiful and seasonal Shirui Lily at Ukhrul, Sangai and the floating islands at Loktak Lake are few of the rare things found in Manipur.

Polo, which can be called a royal game, also originated from Manipur.

Some of the main tourist attractions are:

- Imphal
- Churachandpur
- Keibul Lamjao National Park
- War cemeteries
- Loktak Lake
- Shree Govindajee Temple
- Moreh

Meghalaya

Meghalaya has some of the thickest surviving forests in the country and therefore constitutes one of the most important ecotourism circuits in the country today. The Meghalayan subtropical forests support a vast variety of flora and fauna. Meghalaya has 2 National Parks and 3 Wildlife Sanctuaries. Meghalaya also offers many adventure tourism opportunities in the form of mountaineering, rock climbing, trekking and hiking, water sports etc.

The state offers several trekking routes some of which also afford and opportunity to encounter some rare animals such as the slow loris, assorted deer and bear. The Umiam Lake has a water sports complex with facilities such as rowboats, paddleboats, sailing boats, cruise-boats, water-scooters and speedboats. Cherrapunjee is one of the most popular tourist spots in North East of India. It lies to the south of the capital Shillong. The town is very well known and needs little publicity. A rather scenic, 50 kilometer long road, connects Cherrapunjee with Shillong. The popular waterfalls in the state are the Elephant Falls, Shadthum Falls, Weinia falls, Bishop Falls, Nohkalikai Falls, Langshiang Falls and Sweet Falls. The hot springs at Jakrem near Mawsynram are believed to have curative and medicinal properties.

Orissa

Orissa has been a preferred destination from ancient days for people who have an interest in spirituality, religion, culture, art and natural beauty. Ancient and medieval architecture, pristine sea beaches, the classical and ethnic dance forms and a variety of festivals. Orissa has kept the religion of Buddhism alive. Rock-edicts that have challenged time stand huge and over-powering by the banks of the river Daya. The torch of Buddhism is still ablaze in the sublime triangle at Udayagiri, Lalitagiri and Ratnagiri, on the banks of river Birupa.

Precious fragments of a glorious past come alive in the shape of stupas, rock-cut caves, rock-edicts, excavated monasteries, viharas, chaityas and sacred relics in caskets and the Rock-edicts of Ashoka. Orissa is also famous for its well-preserved Hindu Temples, especially the Konark Sun Temple and The Leaning Temple of Huma. Orissa is the home for various tribal communities who have contributed uniquely to the multicultural and multilingual character of the state. Their handicrafts, different dance forms, jungle products and their unique life style blended with their healing practices have got world wide attention. The Sitalsasthi Carnival is a must see for everyone who wants to see a glimpse of the art and culture of Odisha at one place.

Puducherry

The Union Territory of Puducherry comprises four coastal regions viz- Puducherry, Karaikal, Mahe and Yanam. Puducherry is the Capital of this Union Territory and one of the most popular tourist destinations in South India. Puducherry has been described by National Geographic as "a glowing highlight of subcontinental sojourn". The city has many beautiful colonial buildings, churches, temples, and statues, which, combined with the systematic town planning and the well planned French style avenues, still preserve much of the colonial ambience.

Punjab

The state of Punjab is renowned for its cuisine, culture and history. Punjab has a vast public transportation and communication network. Some of the main cities in Punjab are Amritsar, Chandigarh, and Ludhiana. Punjab also has a rich religious history incorporating Sikhism and Hinduism. Tourism in Punjab is principally suited for the tourists interested in culture, ancient civilization, spirituality and epic history. Some of the villages in Punjab are also a must see for the person who wants to see the true Punjab, with their beautiful traditional Indian homes, farms and temples, this is a must see for any visitor that goes to Punjab. India-Pakistan border at Wagha is also a popular tourist attraction.

Rajasthan

Rajasthan, literally meaning "Land of the Kings", is one of the most attractive tourist destinations in Northern India. The vast sand dunes of the Thar Desert attract millions of tourists from around the globe every year.

Attractions:

- *Jaipur*: The capital of Rajasthan, famous for its rich history and royal architecture and motidungari lord ganesha temple.
- *Jodhpur*: Fortress-city at the edge of the Thar Desert, famous for its blue homes and architecture.
- *Udaipur*: Known as the "Venice" of India.
- *Jaisalmer*: Famous for its golden fortress.
- *Barmer*: Barmer and surrounding areas offer perfect picture of typical Rajasthani villages.
- *Bikaner*: Famous for its medieval history as a trade route outpost.
- *Mount Abu*: Is the highest peak in the Aravalli Range of Rajasthan.
- *Pushkar*: It has the first and one of the very Brahma temples in the world.
- *Keoladeo Bird Sanctuary*: A UNESCO world heritage site
- *Nathdwara*: This town near Udaipur hosts the famous temple of Shrinathji.
- *Ranthambore*: Situated near Sawai Madhopur, this town has one of the largest and most famous national parks in India.

Sikkim

Originally known as Suk-Heem, which in the local language means "peaceful home", Sikkim was an independent kingdom till the year 1974, when it became a part of the Republic of India. The capital of Sikkim is Gangtok, located approximately 105 kilometers from New Jalpaiguri, the nearest railway station to Sikkim. Although, an airport is under construction at Dekiling in East Sikkim, the nearest airport to Sikkim would be Bagdogra. Sikkim is considered as the land of Orchids and mystic cultures and colourful traditions. Sikkim is well known among trekkers and adventure lovers, as West Sikkim has a lot to give them.

Places near Sikkim include Darjeeling also known as the Queen of hills and Kalimpong. Darjeeling, other than its world famous "Darjeeling tea" is also famous for its refined "Prep schools" founded during the British Raj. Kalimpong is also famous for its flora cultivation and is home to many internationally known Nurseries.

Tamil Nadu

Tamil Nadu is the top state in attracting the maximum number of foreign tourists in India. Tamil Nadu. Marina Beach, Carnatic music, Bharata Natyam dance and country's largest Shopping locality. This city is also famous for Medical tourism and houses Asia's largest hospital. Archaeological sites with civilization dating back to 3800 years are found in Tamil Nadu. With more than 34000 temples this state also holds the credit of having maximum number of UNESCO heritage sites in India which includes Great Living Chola Temples and Mahabalipuram.

Country's largest temple srirangam and Pichavaram the world's Second largest Mangrove forest are located in this state. Tamilnadu has some great temples like Madurai Meenakshi Amman Temple, Tanjore Brihadeeswarar Temple, Srirangam Ranganathaswamy Temple and all the mentioned temples has world class architecture that really mesmerize everyone. Kanyakumari is the southernmost tip of India provides sceneic view of sunset and sunshine over the Indian ocean.Hill stations like Yercaud, Kodaikanal, Ooty, Valparai, Yelagiri are widely visited. Velankanni Church and Nagoor Dharga are visited by people of all religion.Water Falls and Wildlife sanctuaries are located across the state.

Uttarakhand

Uttarakhand, the 27th state of the Republic of India, is called "the abode of the Gods". It contains glaciers, snow-clad mountains, valley of flowers, skiing slopes and dense forests, and many shrines and places of pilgrimage. Char-dhams, the four most sacred and revered Hindu temples: Badrinath, Kedarnath, Gangotri and Yamunotri are nestled in the Himalayas. Haridwar which means Gateway to God is the only place on the plains. It holds the watershed for Gangetic River System spanning 300 km from Satluj in the west to Kali river in the east. Nanda Devi is the second highest peak in India after Kanchenjunga. Dunagiri, Neelkanth, Chaukhamba, Panchachuli, Trisul are other peaks above 23000 Ft. It is considered the abode of Devtas, Yakashyas, Kinners, Fairies and Sages. It boasts of some old hill-stations developed during British era like Mussoorie, Almora and Nainital.

Uttar Pradesh

Situated in the northern part of India, Uttar Pradesh is important with its wealth of monuments and religious fervour. Geographically, Uttar Pradesh is very diverse, with Himalayan foothills in the extreme north and the Gangetic Plain in the centre. It is also home of India's most visited site, the Taj Mahal, and Hinduism's holiest city, Varanasi. The most populous state of the Indian Union also has a rich cultural heritage, and at the heart of North India, Uttar Pradesh has much to offer. Places of interest include Varanasi, Agra, Kanpur, Lucknow, Mathura, Jhansi, Prayag, Sarnath, Ayodhya, Dudhwa National Park and Fatehpur Sikri.

West Bengal

Kolkata, one of the many cities in the state of West Bengal has been nicknamed the City of Palaces. This comes from the numerous palatial mansions built all over the city. Unlike many north Indian cities, whose construction stresses minimalism, the layout of much of the architectural variety in Kolkata owes its origins to European styles and tastes imported by the British and, to a much lesser extent, the Portuguese and French. The buildings were designed and inspired by the tastes of the English gentleman around and the aspiring Bengali Babu. Today, many of these structures are in various stages of decay.

Some of the major buildings of this period are well maintained and several buildings have been declared as heritage structures. From historical point of view, the story of West Bengal begins from Gour and Pandua situated close to the present district town of Malda. The twin medieval cities had been sacked at least once by changing powers in the 15th century. However, ruins from the period still remain, and several architectural specimens still retain the glory and shin of those times. The Hindu architecture of Bishnupur in terracotta and laterite sandstone are renowned world over. Towards the British colonial period came the architecture of Murshidabad and Coochbehar.

NATURE TOURISM

India has geographical diversity, which resulted in varieties of nature tourism.

- Water falls in Western Ghats including Jog falls.
- Western Ghats
- Hill Stations
- Wildlife reserves
- Deserts

Wildlife in India

India is home to several well known large mammals including the Asian Elephant, Bengal Tiger, Asiatic Lion, Leopard and Indian Rhinoceros, often engrained culturally and religiously often being associated with deities. Other well known large Indian mammals include ungulates such as the domestic Asian Water buffalo, wild Asian Water buffalo, Nilgai,

Gaur and several species of deer and antelope. Some members of the dog family such as the Indian Wolf, Bengal Fox, Golden Jackal and the Dhole or Wild Dogs are also widely distributed.

It is also home to the Striped Hyaena, Macaques, Langurs and Mongoose species. India also has a large variety of protected wildlife. The country's protected forest consists of 75 National parks of India and 421 Sanctuaries, of which 19 fall under the purview of Project Tiger. Its climatic and geographic diversity makes it the home of over 350 mammals and 1200 bird species, many of which are unique to the subcontinent. Some well known national wildlife sanctuaries include Bharatpur, Corbett, Kanha, Kaziranga, Periyar, Ranthambore, Manas and Sariska. The world's largest mangrove forest Sundarbans is located in southern West Bengal. The Kaziranga National Park,Manas National Park, Sundarbans and Keoladeo National Park is UNESCO World Heritage Site.

Hill Stations

Several hill stations served as summer capitals of Indian provinces, princely states, or, in the case of Shimla, of British India itself. Since Indian Independence, the role of these hill stations as summer capitals has largely ended, but many hill stations remain popular summer resorts.

Most famous hill stations are:

- Mount Abu, Rajasthan
- Pachmarhi, Madhya Pradesh—It is also known as The Queen of Satpura.
- Araku, Andhra Pradesh
- Gulmarg, Srinagar and Ladakh in Jammu and Kashmir
- Darjeeling in West Bengal
- Munnar in Kerala
- Ooty, Yercaud and Kodaikanal in Tamil Nadu
- Shillong in Meghalaya
- Shimla, Kullu in Himachal Pradesh
- Nainital in Uttarakhand
- Gangtok in Sikkim

- Mussoorie in Uttarakhand
- Manali in Himachal Pradesh
- Tawang in Arunachal Pradesh
- Mahabaleshwar in Maharashtra
- Haflong in Assam

In addition to the bustling hill stations and summer capitals of yore, there are several serene and peaceful nature retreats and places of interest to visit for a nature lover. These range from the stunning moonscapes of Leh and Ladhak, to small, exclusive nature retreats such as Dunagiri, Binsar, Mukteshwar in the Himalayas, to rolling vistas of Western Ghats to numerous private retreats in the rolling hills of Kerala.

Beaches

India offers a wide range of tropical beaches with silver/ golden sand to coral beaches of Lakshadweep. States like Kerala and Goa have exploited the potential of beaches to the fullest. However, there are a lot many unexploited beaches in the states of Andhra Pradesh, Gujarat, Maharastra, Tamil Nadu and Karnataka. These states have very high potential to be develop them as future destinations for prospective tourists. Some of the famous tourist beaches are:

- Beaches of Vizag, Andhra Pradesh
- Beaches of Puri, Orissa
- Beaches of Digha, West Bengal
- Beaches of Goa
- Kovalam Beach, Kerala
- Marina Beach, Chennai
- City Beach, Puducherry
- Beaches of Mahabalipuram
- Beaches in Mumbai
- Beaches of Diu
- Beaches of Midnapore, West Bengal
- Beaches of Andaman and Nicobar Islands
- Beaches of Lakshadweep Islands

Adventure Tourism

- River rafting and kayaking in Himalayas

- Mountain climbing in Himalayas
- Rock climbing in Madhya Pradesh
- Skiing in Gulmarg or Auli
- Boat racing in Bhopal
- Paragliding in Maharashtra

DIFFERENCES BETWEEN TRAVEL AND TOURISM

Though the words Travel and Tourism are synonymised and used interchangeably but Tourism is a wider concept and encompasses a lot more than travel alone. Travel implies journeys undertaken from one place to another for any purpose including journeys to work and as a part of employment, as a part of leisure and to take up residence; whereas Tourism includes the journey to a destination and also the stay at a destination outside one's usual place of residence and the activities undertaken for leisure and recreation. All tourism includes some travel, but not all travel is tourism.A person may often travel for a wide variety of purposes of which tourism is only one.

However if properly handled, a part of the travel for non tourism purposes can be motivated into travel for tourism as an additional purpose.For example a person on a journey as a part of employment to a place with one or more tourist attractions –like a spot of scenic beauty or historical significance, a pilgrimage, a lake, etc. can be induced to spare some time and money for a short visit and or stay for tourism purposes alone.In this sense every traveller is a 'potential' tourist and is upto the managers of the industry to tap this 'potential' and convert the traveller into an 'actual' tourist.

Some of the characteristics that distinguish tourism:

- Temporary, to distinguish it from the permanent travel of the tramp and nomad
- Voluntary, to distinguish it from the forced travel of the exile and refugee
- Round up, to distinguish it from the one-way journey of the migrant
- Relatively long, to distinguish it from the recurrent trips of the holiday house owner

DEFINITIONS

The term Tourist is believed to have been derived from the Latin word 'TORNUS' which means a tool, a circle or a turner's wheel. In the sense of the word of the origin, tourist is a person who undertakes a circular trip, *i.e.*, ultimately comes back to the place from where he sets about his journey.

Based on the various definitions of a Tourist here are some of the characteristics of a Tourist:

- He takes up his journey of his own free will.
- He takes up the journey primarily in search of enjoyment.
- The money spent on the visit is the money derived from home, not money earned in the places of visit.
- He finally returns to his original starting point.

We now proceed to discuss the definition of Tourist as given by WTO.But since WTO considers a tourist a type of a Visitor. As suggested, first discuss the definition of a Visitor. The WTO in a conference held in 1963 introduced the term 'Visitor'. A Visitor is defined as 'Any person visiting a country other than that in which he has his usual place of residence for any reason other than being interested in an occupation remunerated from within the country visited.

The term includes two types of visitors:

- *Tourist*: Tourist is a temporary visitor staying for a period of at least 24 hours in the country visited and the purpose of whose journey can be classified under one of the following heads:
  - Leisure
  - Business, family, mission, meeting.
  - *As per the WTO's definition following persons are to be regarded as tourists*:
    a. Persons travelling for pleasure, for domestic reasons, for health etc.
    b. Persons travelling for meetings or in representative capacity of any kind
    c. Persons travelling for business purposes.
    d. Persons arriving in the course of sea cruises, even when they stay for less than 24 hours

in respect of this category of persons the condition of usual place of residence is waived off.

– *However persons belonging to the following categories are not considered as tourists*:
  a. Persons arriving with or without a contract to take up an occupation or engage in any business activity in that country.
  b. Residents in a frontier zone and persons domiciled in one country and working in an adjoining country.
  c. Students and young persons in boarding establishments of schools/colleges.
  d. Travellers passing through a country without stopping, even if the journey takes more than 24 hours.

- *Excursionist*: Excursionist is a temporary visitor staying for a period of less than 24hours in the country visited..

The drawback of the definition of a Visitor as per WTO is that it does not talk about the Visits made within the country. For these purposes a distinction is drawn between a Domestic and an International Visitor.

DOMESTIC VISITOR

A person who travels within the country he is residing in, outside the place of his usual environment for a period not exceeding 12 months.

INTERNATIONAL VISITOR

A person who travels to a country other than the one in which he has his usual residence for a period not exceeding 12 months.

After we have discussed the definition of a visitor, tourist, and excursionist as per WTO and made a distinction between a Domestic and an International Visitor, we now come to definitions used in India for the purpose of collecting tourism statistics.

SUMMARY

In this session we have seen how travel and tourism has changed over time and acquired new dimensions with the development of various facilities and infrastructure. From this we understand that in the present scenario tourism is considered a service industry, and this industry is the highest foreign exchange earner and employment generator. It is therefore very important to have proper planning and management of this industry and thereby arises the need and the importance of tourism statistics.

We have read also in this session, the definition of Tourism, Tourist, Excursionist and the forms of tourism as given by WTO and also the definitions followed in India.We know the difference between travel and tourism; tourist and an excursionist; domestic and International Tourist and the difference between WTO and Indian definitions. As Tourism is considered to be an Industry, it also has a product, the product that comes out of it is known as Tourism Product.

2

Tourism Products: Characteristics and Forms

INTRODUCTION

Along with this you already know by now the various perspectives of tourism. In this current session, we discuss what is a tourism product. As suggested, look at the characteristics and the forms of the tourism product. There will be a discussion on the forms like natural and man made tourism products. We go on to reading about the symbiotic, event based and site based products as well. We also see the new tourism products that have developed. In the end you can answer questions that will assess your understanding of the topic we have discussed.

DEFINITION OF TOURISM PRODUCT

A tourism product can be defined as the sum of the physical and psychological satisfaction it provides to tourists during their travelling en route to the destination. The tourist product focuses on facilities and services designed to meet the needs of the tourist. It can be seen as a composite product, as the sum total of a country's tourist attractions, transport, and accommodation and of entertainment which result in customer satisfaction. Each of the components of a tourist product is supplied by individual providers of services like hotel companies, airlines, travel agencies, etc. The tourist product can be analysed in terms of its attraction, accessibility and accommodation.

ATTRACTIONS

Of the three basic components of a tourist product, attractions are very important. Unless there is an attraction, the tourist will not be motivated to go to a particular place. Attractions are those elements in a product which determine the choice made by particular tourist to visit one particular destination rather than another.

The attractions could be cultural, like sites and areas of archaeological interest, historical buildings and monuments, flora and fauna, beach resorts, mountains, national parks or events like trade fairs, exhibitions, arts and music festivals, games, etc.

Tourist demands are also very much susceptible to changes in fashion. Fashion is an important factor in the demand for various tourist attractions and amenities. The tourist who visits a particular place for its natural beauty may decide to visit some other attractions due to a change in fashion. Peter has drawn up an inventory of the various attractions which are of significance in tourism. However, the attractions of tourism are, to a very large extent, geographical in character.

Location and accessibility (whether a place has a coastal or inland position and the ease with which a given place can be reached) are important. Physical space may be thought of as a component for those who seek the wilderness and solitude. Scenery or landscape is a compound of landforms; water and the vegetation and has an aesthetic and recreative value. Climate conditions, especially in relation to the amount of sunshine, temperature and precipitation (snow as well as rain), are of special significance.

Animal life may be an important attraction, firstly in relation to, bird watching or viewing game in their natural habitat and secondly, for sports purposes, eg. fishing and hunting. Man's impact on the natural landscape in the form of his settlements, historical monuments and archaeological remains is also a major attraction. Finally, a variety of cultural features-ways of life, folklore, artistic expressions, etc. provide valuable attractions to many.

ACCESSIBILITY

It is a means by which a tourist can reach the area where attractions are located. Tourist attractions of whatever type would be of little importance if their locations are inaccessible by the normal means of transport. A Tourist in order to get to his destination needs some mode of transport. This mode may be a motor car, a coach, an aeroplane, a ship or a train which enables him to reach his predetermined destination. If tourist destinations are located at places where no transport can reach or where there are inadequate transport facilities, they become of little value.

The tourist attractions, which are located near the tourist-generating markets and are linked by a network of efficient means of transport, receive the maximum number of tourists. The distance factor also plays an important role in determining a tourist's choice of a destination. Longer distances cost much more in the way of expenses on travel as compared to short distances. An example can be that of India. About two and a half million tourist arrivals for a country of the size of India may look rather unimpressive. However if one looks at certain factors like the country's distance from the affluent tourist markets of the world such as the United States, Europe, Canada, Japan and Australia, one may conclude that the long distance is one of the factors responsible for low arrivals.

It costs a visitor from these countries, quite a substantial amount, to visit India for a holiday. It has been stated earlier that Europe and North America continue to be the main generating and receiving areas for international tourism, accounting for as much as 70% and 20% respectively, of international tourist arrivals. Easy accessibility, thus is a key factor for the growth and development of tourist movements.

ACCOMMODATION

The accommodation and other facilities complement the attractions. Accommodation plays a central role and is very basic to tourist destinations. World Tourism Organization in its definition of a tourist has stated that he must spend at least one night in the destination visited, to qualify as a tourist. This presupposes availability of some kind of accommodation. The demand for accommodation away from one's home is met by a variety of facilities. The range and type of accommodation is quite varied and has undergone considerable change since the last half century. There has been a decline in the use of boarding houses and small private hotels.

Larger hotels are increasing their share of holiday trade, especially in big metropolitan areas and popular spots. In more traditional holiday and sea-side resorts in Europe and elsewhere, big hotels are keeping their share of holiday resorts. In recent years, some changes have been reflected in the type of accommodation. There has been an increasing demand for more non- traditional and informal types of accommodation. The latest trends in accommodation are holiday villages. In recent years there has been an increase in the popularity of such accommodation.

Accommodation may in itself be an important tourist attraction. In fact, a large number of tourists visit a particular destination or town simply because there is a first class luxury hotel or resort which provides excellent services and facilities. Some countries like Switzerland, Holland, France, Austria, and Belgium have gained a reputation for providing excellent accommodation with good cuisine. Many hotel establishments elsewhere in various countries, especially the resort hotels, have gained a reputation for their excellent cuisine, services and facilities. The French government for instance, paved the way for tourist development of Corsica by launching a big hotel development programme.

CHARACTERISTICS OF TOURISM PRODUCT

By now, you must have understood what a tourism product is. Now let us look at some of its characteristics:-

INTANGIBLE

Unlike a tangible product, say, a motor car or refrigerator, no transfer of ownership of goods is involved in tourism. The product here cannot be seen or inspected before its purchase. Instead, certain facilities, installations, items of equipment are made available for a specified time and for a specified use. For example, a seat in an aeroplane is provided only for a specified time.

PSYCHOLOGICAL

A large component of tourism product is the satisfaction the consumer derives from its use. A tourist acquires experiences while interacting with the new environment and his experiences help to attract and motivate potential customers.

HIGHLY PERISHABLE

A travel agent or tour operator who sells a tourism product cannot store it. Production can only take place if the customer is actually present. And once consumption begins, it cannot be stopped, interrupted or modified. If the product remains unused, the chances are lost *i.e.* if tourists do not visit a particular place, the opportunity at that time is lost. It is due to this reason that heavy discount is offered by hotels and transport generating organisations during off season.

COMPOSITE PRODUCT

The tourist product cannot be provided by a single enterprise unlike a manufactured product. The tourist product covers the complete experience of a visit to a particular place. And many providers contribute to this experience. For instance, airline supplies seats, a hotel provides rooms and restaurants, travel agents make bookings for stay and sightseeing, etc.

UNSTABLE DEMAND

Tourism demand is influenced by seasonal, economic political and others such factors. There are certain times of the year which see a greater demand than others. At these times there is a greater strain on services like hotel bookings, employment, the transport system, etc.

FIXED SUPPLY IN THE SHORT RUN

The tourism product unlike a manufactured product

cannot be brought to the consumer; the consumer must go to the product. This requires an in-depth study of users' behaviour, taste preferences, likes and dislikes so that expectations and realities coincide for the maximum satisfaction of the consumer. The supply of a tourism product is fixed in the short run and can only be increased in the long run following increased demand patterns.

ABSENCE OF OWNERSHIP

When you buy a car, the ownership of the car is transferred to you, but when you hire a taxi you buy the right to be transported to a predetermined destination at a predetermined price (fare). You neither own the automobile nor the driver of the vehicle. Similarly, hotel rooms, airline tickets, etc. can be used but not owned. These services can be bought for consumption but ownership remains with the provider of the service. So, a dance can be enjoyed by viewing it, but the dancer cannot be owned.

HETEROGENEOUS

Tourism is not a homogeneous product since it tends to vary in standard and quality over time, unlike a T.V set or any other manufactured product. A package tour or even a flight on an aircraft can't be consistent at all times. The reason is that this product is a service and services are people based. Due to this, there is variability in this product. All individuals vary and even the same individual may not perform the same every time. For instance, all air hostesses cannot provide the same quality of service and even the same air hostess may not perform uniformly in the morning and evening. Thus, services cannot be standardised.

RISKY

The risk involved in the use of a tourism product is heightened since it has to be purchased before its consumption. An element of chance is always present in its consumption. Like, a show might not be as entertaining as it promises to be or a beach holiday might be disappointing due to heavy rain.

MARKETABLE

Tourism product is marketed at two levels. At the first level, national and regional organisations engage in persuading potential tourists to visit the country or a certain region. These official tourist organisations first create knowledge of its country in tourist -generating markets and persuade visitors in these markets to visit the country. At the second level, the various individual firms providing tourist services, market their own components of the total tourist product to persuade potential tourists to visit that region for which they are responsible.

FORMS OF TOURISM PRODUCT

By now you must be aware of what a tourism product is and what its peculiar features are. It is necessary to understand the components of the tourist product from the point of view of the consumer. The product for the tourist covers the complete experience from the time he leaves home to the time he returns. The tourist product today is developed to meet the needs of the consumer and techniques like direct sales, publicity and advertising are employed to bring this product to the consumer.

The tourist product is the basic raw material, be it the country's natural beauty, climate, history, culture and the people, or other facilities necessary for comfortable living such as water supply, electricity, roads, transport, communication and other essentials. The tourist product can be entirely a man-made one or nature's creation improved upon by man. A consumer can combine individual products in a large number of ways.

There would be many possible destinations, each with a number of hotels, each to be reached by more than one airline. Thus, the potential choice facing the consumer is very large. The large number of tourist destinations have placed at the disposal of a tourist a very large variety of tourist products in abundant quantity from a large number of competing destinations. This eventually, has led to the adoption of the new concept *i.e.*, the marketing concept in tourism by various countries promoting tourism. Tourism, basically, is an infrastructure based service product. The nature of the service here is highly intangible and perishable offering a limited scope for creating and maintaining the distinctive competitive edge.

The effective marketing of tourism needs constant gearing up of infrastructure to international standards and presupposes in its coordination with the tourism suppliers. In strategic terms, it calls for the action of an integrated approach to management and marketing. In operational terms, it means the implementation of a better defined, better targeted market-driven strategy for realizing the defined objectives. The important point to note here is that marketing is applied to situations where the choice can be limited to a relatively small number of brands giving the consumer a reasonable choice. The process of selection thus becomes easier. In the field of tourism this process is taking place by the increased use of 'package tours'.

A package tour is a travel plan which includes most elements of vacation, such as transportation, accommodation, sight- seeing and entertainment. The tourist product is a composite product, whether it is sold as a package or assembled by the individual himself or his travel agent. There are many tourism products that are available to the consumer today.

In modern times these products, whether traditional in nature like culture and pilgrimage, or modern like adventure, conventions and conferences, health, medical, etc. are being packaged, promoted and priced appropriately to woo as many tourists as possible. Tourism products can be classified as under for a better understanding of each of their peculiar characteristics.

NATURAL TOURISM PRODUCTS

These include natural resources such as areas, climate and its setting, landscape and natural environment. Natural resources are frequently the key elements in a destination's attraction.

Let us look at some examples:

- Countryside
- Climate- temperature, rains, snowfall, days of sunshine
- Natural Beauty- landforms, hills, rocks, gorges, terrain
- Water- lakes, ponds, rivers, waterfalls, springs
- Flora and Fauna
- Wildlife
- Beaches
- Islands
- Spas
- Scenic Attractions

The climate of a tourist destination is often an important attraction. Good weather plays an important role in making a holiday. Millions of tourists from countries with extreme climates visit beaches in search of fine weather and sunshine. The sunshine and clear sea breeze at the beaches have attracted many people for a very long time. In fact, development of spas and resorts along the sea coasts in many countries were a result of the travellers. urge to enjoy good weather and sunshine. In Europe, countries like France, Italy, Spain and Greece have developed beautiful beach resorts. North Europeans visit the Mediterranean coast searching for older resorts like Monte Carlo, Nice and Cannes on the Riviera and new resorts in Spain and Italy.

Beautiful beaches of India, Sri Lanka, and Thailand, Indonesia and Australia and some other new destinations are more examples of how good weather can attract tourists. All these areas capitalise on good weather. Destinations with attractive winter climates, winter warmth and sunshine are also important centres of tourist attraction. Many areas have become important winter holiday resorts attracting a large number of tourists. Around these winter resorts, winter sport facilities have been installed to cater to the increasing needs of tourists. People from warm climates travel especially to see snowfall and enjoy the cold climate. In countries with tropical climates, many upland cool areas have been developed as 'hill stations'. Hence climate is of great significance as a tourism product. The scenery and natural beauty of places has always attracted tourists.

Tourists enjoy nature in all its various forms. There are land forms like mountains, canyons, coral reefs, cliffs, etc. One of the great all time favourite tourist destination is the Grand Canyon, Arizona. Mountain ranges like the Himalayas, Kilimanjaro, and Swiss Alps, etc. There are water forms like rivers, lakes waterfalls, geysers, glaciers, etc. The Niagara Falls shared by Canada and the United States is an example of how scenic waterfalls attract tourists. Lake Tahoe in California and the, deserts of Egypt are other examples of great tourist products.

Other great natural wonders that attract tourists are the Giants Causeway of Northern Ireland, the Geysers of Iceland, the glaciers of the Alps, the forests of Africa etc. Vegetation like forests, grasslands, moors deserts, etc. has all been developed as tourist products. Flora and Fauna attract many a tourist. Tourists like to know the various types of plants and trees that they see and which trees are seen in which seasons. There are many plants which are specific to certain regions and many times students and travellers visit those areas especially to see those varieties of plants.

Thick forest covers, attract tourists who enjoy trekking and hunting activities. Fauna attracts tourists who like to watch birds, wild mammals, reptiles and other exotic and rare animals. Countries in South East Asia have crocodile gardens, bird sanctuaries, and other tourist products that display the fauna of their region. Spas are gaining popularity as modern tourism products all over the world.

While most parts of the world have their own therapies and treatments that are effective in restoring the wellness and beauty of people. New kinds of health tours that are gaining popularity are spa tours. Spas offer the unique advantages of taking the best from the West and the East, combining them with the indigenous system and offering best of the two worlds. For example Swedish massages work well with the Javanese Mandy, lulur, aromatherapy, reflexology and traditional ayurvedic procedures. Now various spa products are being combined with yoga, meditation, and pranayama, giving a holistic experience to tourists. Spa treatments are now combined with other medical treatments to treat blood pressure, insomnia, depression, paralysis and some other diseases.

People are now travelling to spas and clinics for curative baths and medical treatment. In some countries like Italy, Austria and Germany, great importance is given to spa treatments. In Russia along the Black Sea coast and in the foothills of the Caucasus Mountains, there are many world famous sanatoria where millions of Russians and international tourists throng every year. Beach tourism is very popular among the tourists today. Tourists of all age groups, backgrounds, cultures and countries enjoy this tourism product. Besides attraction and saleability, beach holidaying has lead to overall development of tourism in many parts of the world.

The basic importance of beaches is that they provide aesthetic and environmental value of the beach such as beautiful natural scenery with golden sands, lush green vegetation and bright blue sky. The water should be clear, free of currents and underwater rocks. Beach tourism activities include water and land resource use. The water usage involves swimming, surfing, sailing, wind surfing, water scootering, Para- sailing, motorboat rides, etc.

The land use has multifacets like sunbathing, recreational areas for tourists (parks, playgrounds, clubs, theatre, amusement parks, casinos, cultural museums, etc.), accommodation facilities (hotels, cottages, villas, camping sites, etc.), car and bus parking areas, entertainment and shopping complexes, access roads and transportation network. Due to its multidimensional requirements the beach product needs special care. A beach resort needs to be developed as an integrated complex to function as a self-contained community. Environmental management should also ensure the availability of necessary infrastructure in the immediate hinterland to the coastal region in support of the development on the coast to maintain its ecosystem. Islands abound with natural beauty, with the rare flora and fauna and tribes. This makes islands an ideal place for adventure, nature and culture lovers to visit.

This tourist product has great scope as these islands are being developed as tourist paradises. For example, Hawaii, Maldives, Mauritius, Tahiti, Andaman and Nicobar Islands, etc. has developed with tourism activity over the past few decades. The topography is generally undulating and they offer natural scenic beauty with exotic flora and fauna. Most of these islands have places of worship like churches, temples, etc. As an added attraction some of these islands have developed as tax havens thereby encouraging commercial development of these economies.

They offer social and cultural attractions as tourists can experience the local lifestyle, local food, fairs and festivals, etc. Scenic attractions, like good weather, are very important factors in the development of tourism. Breath-taking mountain scenery and the coastal stretches exert a strong fascination on the tourist the magnificent mountain ranges provide an atmosphere of peace and tranquillity. Tourists visiting the northern slopes of the Alps in Switzerland and Austria and the southern slopes in Italy and also the Himalayan slopes of India and Nepal for the first time, cannot but be charmed by their physical magnificence.

MAN- MADE TOURISM PRODUCTS

Man- made tourism products are created by man for pleasure, leisure or business.

Man- made tourism products include:

CULTURE

- Sites and areas of archaeological interest
- Historical buildings and monuments
- Places of historical significance
- Museums and art galleries
- Political and educational institutions
- Religious institutions

Cultural tourism is based on the mosaic of places, traditions, art forms, celebrations and experiences that portray the nation and its people, reflecting the diversity and character of a country. Garrison Keillor, in an address to the 1995 White House Conference on Travel and Tourism, best described cultural tourism by saying, "We need to think about cultural tourism because really there is no other kind of tourism. It's what tourism is...People don't come to America for our airports, people don't come to America for our hotels, or the recreation facilities....They come for our culture: high culture, low culture, middle culture, right, left, real or imagined—they come here to see America." Two significant travel trends will dominate the tourism market in the next decade.

- Mass marketing is giving way to one-to-one marketing with travel being tailored to the interests of the individual consumer.
- A growing number of visitors are becoming special interest travellers who rank the arts, heritage and/or other cultural activities as one of the top five reasons for travelling.

The combination of these two trends is being fuelled by technology, through the proliferation of online services and tools, making it easier for the traveller to choose destinations and customise their itineraries based on their interests. Today we can witness large masses of people travelling to foreign countries to become acquainted with the usages and customs, to visit the museums and to admire works of art. One way of hastening the beneficial effects resulting from tourism is to bring the cultural heritage into the economic circuit, thus justifying the investments made at the cost of the national community, for its preservation.

Taking an economic view of the cultural heritage of a nation may not altogether be justified, considering that the preservation of its culture is one of the basic responsibilities of any community.

But considering the financial obstacles especially for the developing countries, this may appear to be a rational approach. Hence mass tourism can contribute unique benefits to the exploiting of the cultural heritage of a nation and can serve indirectly to improve the individual cultural levels of both citizens and travellers. Cultural resources have another specific characteristic, which many tourists want to experience the exotic.

There will be a great urge on the part of the tourist to visit and become acquainted with the ancient civilization in their quest for novel human knowledge. Culture means the prospect of contact with other civilizations, their original and varied customs and tradition with their distinct characteristics. This entire process creates a powerful motivator towards travel. Various Museums also attract tourists like Madame Tussauds Museum in London, the Louvre Museum in Paris, Smithsonian Washington Museum, Museums of famous painters like Salvador Dali, Pablo Picasso, Natural History Museum, British Museum, Museum of Modern Art are also popular tourist products. Sites of archeological interest like remains of Mohenjodaro and Harrapan civilizations, museums for fossils and dinosaurs.

Sites for historical interest like city of Hiroshima and Nagasaki, sites of holocaust in Germany, tombs of various leaders and emperors. Historical buildings like Warwick Castle, Tower of London, Stratford-on-Avon which is Shakespeare's birthplace, the Roman Baths are all popular with tourists. Even historical cities like Varanasi in India get a lot of tourists due to its status as one of the oldest cities of the world. Stonehenge in United Kingdom, The White House, Buckingham Palace and other places of political significance, are also great tourist draws.

TRADITIONS

- Pilgrimages
- Fairs and festivals
- Arts and handicrafts
- Dance
- Music
- Folklore
- Native life and customs

A pilgrimage is a term primarily used for a journey or a search of great moral significance. Sometimes, it is a journey to a sacred place or shrine of importance to a person's beliefs and faith. Members of every religion participate in pilgrimages. A person who makes such a journey is called a pilgrim. Secular and civic pilgrimages are also practiced, without regard for religion but rather of importance to a particular society. For example, many people throughout the world travel to the City of Washington in the United States for a pilgrimage to see the Declaration of Independence and the Constitution of the United States. British people often make pilgrimages to London to witness the public appearances of the monarch of the United Kingdom.

A large number of people have been making pilgrimages to sacred religious places or holy places. This practice is widespread in many parts of the world. In the Christian world, for instance, a visit to Jerusalem or the Vatican is considered auspicious. Among Muslims, a pilgrimage to Mecca is considered a great act of faith. In India there are many pilgrimage centres and holy places belonging to all major religions of the world. India is among the richest countries in the world as far as the field of art and craft is concerned. Tourists like to visit and see the creative and artistic treasures of various countries.

Every country has certain traditional arts like soap sculptures and batik of Thailand; gems and jewellery, tie and dye works, wood and marble carving in Indonesia; ivory, glasswork, hand block printing, sandalwood, inlay work; are some of the examples of traditional art that attract tourists. There are many forms of dance in the world like Salsa, Hip-Hop, Jazz, Flamingo, Ballet and Traditional Dances. People who travel like to watch these dance performances and sometimes even take some introductory classes.

Music can be either traditional or modern. Traditional music like folk music and classical and country music is specific to every region and country. Modern forms include Blues, Rock, Pop, Jazz, Rap, Techno and Hip- Hop. Music also adds to the attraction of a destination. Fairs and Festivals capture the fun loving side and bring out the joyous celebrations of the community. Festivals like Christmas, Easter, Thanksgiving, Eid, Ramadan, Diwali, and Holi and so on, also bring people to destinations where the celebration can be enjoyed. Some popular Fairs which cater to fun and work are Pushkar Mela in Rajasthan, Prêt fair in Paris, Magic Fair in Vegas for garments, Hong Kong Fashion Week and various job fairs where people are recruited.

ENTERTAINMENT

- Amusement and recreation parks
- Sporting events
- Zoos and oceanariums
- Cinemas and theatre
- Night life
- Cuisine

Tourist products that have entertainment as their main characteristic are many. Just to name a few there are amusement and recreational parks like Disneyworld in United States, Hong Kong, Paris, Singapore and theme parks in various countries and cities like Appu Ghar and Fun and Food Village in Delhi, Essel World in Mumbai and so on. Tourists may come to attend sports events and it is also an opportunity to explore the country. The fundamental concept is that all tourist activities have an influence on providing economic benefits and have a powerful influence in some definite locality, like the Olympics in Athens has given immense benefit to all in tourism business in Athens in particular and Greece in general.

Many countries organise year round sports events like swimming meets, athletic meets, weight lifting events, cricket matches, baseball and football events and many more such events which encourage tourism. India will be hosting the Common-Wealth Games on 2010 and it is anticipated to give the tourism industry a big boost. Night Life is one of the prime attractions in a holiday. Tourists like to especially visit areas in cities where the night life activity is promoted. These areas are usually lit up with street stalls like flea markets and food areas. Bars, night clubs, casinos and very often open air bands attract and add to the psychological satisfaction and experience of tourists.

Cuisine is very often an understated but highly important part of any holiday. Now-a-days there is cuisine from all areas of the world which is found at most tourist destinations. Specialty restaurants serve Indian, Continental, Chinese, Italian, Japanese, Thai, Indonesian, Fast food, Mexican, Mediterranean, and Arabic and so on. However, tourists usually like to eat the local food of the areas they visit.

BUSINESS

- Conventions
- Conferences

People who travel in relation to their work come under the category of business tourism. However such travel for business purposes is also linked with tourist activity like visiting places of tourist attraction at the destination, sight seeing and excursion trips. Business travel is also related to what is termed today as convention business, which is a rapidly growing industry in hospitality and tourism. A business traveller is important to the tourism industry as it involves the usage of all the components of tourism. He travels because of different business reasons- attending conventions and conferences, meetings, workshops etc. Participants have a lot of leisure time at their disposal.

The conference organisers make this leisure time very rewarding for participants by organising many activities for their pleasure and relaxation. The spouses and families accompanying the participants are also well looked after by the organisers. The organisers plan sight seeing tours and shopping tours for the participants and their families. In India, cooking classes for learning Indian food cooking from the various states, visits to the craft bazaars where tourists see how artisans make clay pots and other handicrafts, they visit tie and dye units to see Indian printing eg. Batik printing etc. Women tourists enjoy henna demonstrations. Conferences are events which require meticulous planning and efficient implementation, co-coordinating various activities so that the right things happen at the right time.

There are a number of players in the convention business. On one hand are the customers or the consumers and on the other hand are the principle suppliers like hotels, transporters, convention centres, tour operators and travel agencies, tourism departments, exhibition organisers, sponsors etc.

SYMBIOTIC TOURISM PRODUCTS

Wildlife sanctuary, Marine parks, Aero products and Water sports, Flower festivals are the example of tourism products which are a blending of nature and man. Nature has provided the resource and man has converted them into a tourism product by managing them. National parks for example, are left in their natural state of beauty as far as possible, but still need to be managed, through provision of access, parking facilities, limited accommodation, litter bins etc.

Yet the core attraction is still nature in this category of product. These products are symbiosis of nature and man. In case of adventure sports tourists can be participants. The basic element of adventure is the satisfaction of having complete command over one's body, a sense of risk in the process, an awareness of beauty and the exploration of the unknown. Adventure tourism can be classified into aerial, water based and land based.

Aerial adventure sports include the following activities:

- Parachuting, which involves jumping off from an aircraft or balloon and descending by means of a parachute. The infrastructure required, includes an aircraft, parachutes and large landing zones
- Sky Diving, which involves a sky diver jumping off an aircraft or balloon at a much greater height without deploying his parachute initially and opening it after some interval at a pre determined height.
- Hang Gliding, which involves running off a mountain or being towed by a winch and essentially

flying like a glider where the directional control is achieved by a shift in his own weight by the pilot.

- Para Gliding, is the latest aero-sport which has taken the world by storm. A Para Glider is a specially designed square parachute, along with a harness attached by lines.
- Para Sailing is a simple sport that involves towing a parachutist to a height of a few hundred feet in the air and then descending by means of a parachute. As a year round activity, Para sailing can be done on land and water.
- Bungee Jumping, which requires no equipment except a 'bungee cord' made of nylon fibre of enough elasticity to be able to absorb the shock at the end of the jump. The jumper makes a headlong jump into empty space and the resultant rush of adrenalin makes the experience very exhilarating.
- Ballooning, where a balloon is attached to a basket by steel wire ropes. By regulating hot and cold air, the pilot can steer the balloon along any charted course.

Water based adventure sports include the following:

- White water rafting which is one of the most important and exciting water sports, which involves riding down water rapids in an inflatable raft which is used to negotiate fast flowing rivers.
- Canoeing and Kayaking are adventure sports which begin upstream where the water is wild and white. The gradient best suited for canoeing is the stage near the river's entry into the plains where the trip can be combined with a natural holiday in a forest. Kayaking is appealing as it enables innovation on the river by one or two oarsman seated in tandem.
- Adventure sports in the waters of the sea like wind surfing, scuba diving, snorkeling, yachting, water skiing, etc. also offer thrilling activities to the tourists.

Land based adventure tourist products include the following:

- Rock climbing which originated as a means of

practicing techniques for ascending high mountains. It was earlier provided as training to mountaineers but has now evolved into a highly developed sport. The climber moves up, using knowledge of rope handling, climbing, securing one to another, etc. Very sophisticated techniques and equipments are used nowadays to ascend or descend on very steep terrain.

- Mountaineering requires trained physical ability and suitable equipment. The higher peaks need better equipment which is also costly. The challenges which mountains like the Indian Himalayas pose attract mountaineers from various countries.
- Trekking the mighty Himalayas which spread across five Indian states form a sweeping arc and compress in its expanse a wide geographical variety and contrasting cultures.
- Skiing is the practice of sliding over snow on runners, called skis, attached to each foot. There are three types of ski resorts, the first are large town's, second type are alpine villages and the third resorts built for skiing.
- Heli skiing is a type of alpine skiing where the skier is dropped to the top of a mountain by a helicopter and then he slides down on his own.
- Motor Rally is a sport that tests the navigational skills of man and his endurance with the machine. Motor rallies, grand prix racing, hill climbing rallies, vintage car rallies, sports car racing, etc. are some forms of this tourism product.
- Safaris were earlier taken on camel, horse and elephants as an excursion for hunting or a journey. As a modern tourist product now safaris are taken on jeeps and in the form of caravans. Viewing and enjoying nature, meeting the local villagers, seeing their traditions, customs and lifestyle, entertainment and camp fires are some of the characteristics of modern safaris. Eg, Egypt desert safaris. Horse and elephant safaris are arranged in most of the national parks and wildlife sanctuaries.

EVENT BASED TOURISM PRODUCTS

Where an event is an attraction, it as an event based tourist product. Events attract tourists as spectators and also as participants in the events, sometimes for both. The Ocktoberfest organised in Germany, Dubai and Singapore shopping festivals, the camel polo at Jaisalmer, Kite flying in Ahmedabad attracts tourists, both as spectators and participants.

Whereas in case of the Snake Boat race of Kerala can be enjoyed witnessing it. Event attractions are temporary, and are often mounted in order to increase the number of tourists to a particular destination. Some events have a short time scale, such as the Republic Day Parade, others may last for many days, for example Khajuraho Dance Festival or even months like the Kumbh Mela. A destination which may have little to commend it to the tourist can nevertheless succeed in drawing tourists by mounting an event such as an unusual exhibition.

SITE BASED TOURISM PRODUCTS

When an attraction is a place or site then it is called a site based tourist product. Site attractions are permanent by nature, for example Taj Mahal, The Great Wall of China, The Grand Canyon in Arizona, Eiffel Tower, Statue of Liberty, Temples of Khajuraho, etc. A site destination can extend its season by mounting an off season event or festival. A large number of tourists are attracted every year by the great drawing power of Stratford on Avon in England because of its association with Shakespeare, the city of Agra in India with its famous Taj Mahal, Pisa in Italy for its famous Leaning Tower. Some new features have been added to the same product to keep the tourist interest alive in the products. For example now visitors can see Taj by night, music shows have been organised with Taj as the backdrop so that there are repeat tourists.

OTHER TOURISM PRODUCTS

HEALTH TOURISM

Holidaying is generally considered as an investment in

health, a subject that presents opportunities of cost- benefit analysis. The medical expertise of various countries has added a new product to the existing tourism products. People are travelling to various countries for treatment of various ailments and medical procedures like Cardio care, Bone Marrow Transplant, Dialysis and Kidney transplant, Neuro surgery, Joint Replacement Surgery, Urology, Osteoporosis, and numerous other diseases.

Even cosmetic surgery, alternative medicines like homeopathy, acupressure, ayurvedic medicines and naturopathy are also becoming tourism products wherein travel companies are offering Yoga and Rejuvenation packages. Tourists travel for what is illegal in one's own country, *e.g.* abortion, euthanasia; for instance, euthanasia for noncitizens is provided by Dignitas in Switzerland. Tourists travel also for advanced care that is not available in one's own country, in the case that there are long waiting lists in one's own country or for use of free or cheap health care organisations.

ECO-TOURISM

Tourism that combines local economic development, protection of the quality of the environment and promotion of the natural advantages and the history of an area. The combination of all or some of the above kinds of tourism could contribute significantly to the development of tourism in any country. The availability of tourist packages involving gastronomy, entertainment and information about the cultural wealth of a country should be regarded as a priority issue for tourist agents, as it will reduce the concentration of tourist activity in certain areas and will improve and enrich the tourist.

RURAL TOURISM

Any form of tourism that showcases the rural life, art, culture and heritage at rural locations, thereby, benefiting the local community economically and socially as well as enabling interaction between the tourists and the locals for a more enriching tourism experience an be termed as rural tourism. It is multifaceted and may entail farm/agricultural tourism, cultural tourism, nature tourism, adventure tourism, and eco-tourism.

The stresses of urban lifestyles have lead to this counter-urbanisation approach to tourism. There are various factors that have lead to this changing trend towards rural tourism like increasing levels of awareness, growing interest in heritage and culture and improved accessibility and environmental consciousness, Tourists like to visit villages to experience and live a relaxed and healthy lifestyle.

ETHNIC TOURISM

Ethnic tourism is travelling for the purpose of observing the cultural expressions of lifestyles of truly exotic people. Such tourism is exemplified by travel to Panama to study the San Blas Indians or to India to observe the isolated hill tribes of Assam. Typical destination activities would include visits to native homes, attending traditional ceremonies and dances, and possibly participating in religious rituals.

SENIOR CITIZEN TOURISM

A newly emerging trend in tourism, basically for senior citizens or old people who live in isolation, especially in the west, because of daily busy schedules of their children and more importantly the attitudes. The characteristic feature of this type of tourism is that the senior people are less demanding in the form of facilities and services, besides leaving minimum impact on the destination community and their main consideration is on personalised service.

SPIRITUAL TOURISM

Many people when living under conditions of stress turn to spirituality. The Eastern world is considered to be very spiritual with many of the new age Gurus and their hermitages. This takes the form of another tourism product, that is, spiritual tourism. Tourists visit places to attend spiritual discourses and meditation workshops. For example, The Osho

Foundation, Art of Living Foundation which have centres all over the world, Buddhist Monasteries and Ashrams.

GOLF TOURISM

Golf has been enjoyed by many for a long time. Earlier it was enjoyed as a sport but in recent times it has developed into a hot tourism product. Many tourist organizations plan promotional packages to woo the golf tourist especially from Japan where the green fees are very high. These tourists take exclusive golfing holidays wherein their accommodation is also arranged near the course and they return after serious golf playing.

CONCLUSION

You must be now clear about what really is a tourism product along with its unique and distinguishing features. We have discussed in the various forms of tourism products. By now you know natural, man-made, symbiotic, event based and site based tourist products. Now when you look around you, in any newspaper, magazine or even T.V. programmes, you will see the various tourism products and will be able to identify their forms. At this stage it's important for you to understand and identify how each tourism product has a distinguishing feature and its marketing strategy must highlight this feature.

Advertising, publicity, sales promotion, brochures, pamphlets, posters, direct mailing, personal selling and advertorial are some of these strategies. The tourism product has to be packaged and priced keeping in mind the target customer. Without any doubt, tourism is the main sector that can play a significant part in achieving rapid economic growth and drastically reducing unemployment in our country. Currently, it is the largest foreign exchange earner for our country. The development of the tourism industry on a priority basis is the need of the hour. You will study about Tourism as an industry and the economic impact of tourism.

3

Types and Forms of Tourism

RELIGIOUS TOURISM

Religious tourism, also commonly referred to as faith tourism, is a form of tourism whereby people of faith travel individually or in groups for pilgrimage, missionary, or leisure purposes.

The International Conference on Religious Tourism estimates the worldwide faith tourism industry at $18 billion. North American religious tourists comprise an estimated $10 billion of this industry.

TOURISM SEGMENTS

Religious tourism comprises many facets of the travel industry including:

- Christian and faith-based camps
- Crusades, conventions, and rallies
- Faith-based cruising
- Leisure vacations
- Missionary travel
- Monastery visits and guest-stays
- Pilgrimages
- Religious tourist attractions
- Retreats

STATISTICS

Although no definitive study has been completed on worldwide religious tourism, some segments of the industry have been measured,

- The Religious Conference Management Association, in 2006 more than 14.7 million people attended religious meetings, an increase of more than 10 million from 1994 with 4.4 million attendees.
- The U.S. Office of Travel and Tourism Industries, Americans traveling overseas for "religious or pilgrimage" purposes has increased from 491,000 travellers in 2002 to 633,000 travellers in 2005.
- The World Tourism Organization, an estimated 300 to 330 million pilgrim's visit the world's key religious sites every year.
- One-quarter of travellers said they were currently interested in taking a spiritual vacation. More than one in ten travellers said they were more interested now compared to five years ago in taking a spiritual vacation. The appeal of a spiritual vacation spans the ages, with approximately one-third of each age group expressing current interest in taking such a vacation.
- Religious attractions including Sight and Sound Theatre attracts 800,000 visitors a year while the Holy Land Experience and Focus on the Family Welcome Centre each receives about 250,000 guests annually. Religious tourism, also commonly referred to as faith tourism, is a form of tourism whereby people of faith travel individually or in groups for pilgrimage, missionary, or leisure purposes. The International Conference on Religious Tourism estimates the worldwide faith tourism industry at $18 billion.
- The 50,000 churches in the United States with religious travel programmes
- The Christian Camp and Conference Association states that more than eight million people are involved in CCCA member camps and conferences, including more than 120,000 churches.
- The United Methodist Church experienced an increase of 455% in mission volunteers from 1992 with almost 20,000 volunteers compared to 110,000 volunteers in 2006.

COUNTRIES, TOURIST BOARDS AND RELIGIOUS TOURISM

- *Bahamas*: One of the few countries with a Director of Religious Tourism and staff dedicated to attracting faith-based visitors
- *Cypress*: Launching new marketing efforts to increase religious tourism of its current 100,000 faith-based visitors annually
- *India*: Largest portion of visitors are religious pilgrims
- *Israel*: Tourism ministry looks to boost tourism from North America
- *Italy*: Religious tourism in Italy alone generates over $4.5 billion each year.
- *Jordan*: Promoting niche markets such as religious tourism is a large part of Jordan's overall tourism strategy
- *Scotland*: Projected to triple from religious tourism dollars of GBP 80-100 to GBP 300 million by 2014
- *Switzerland*: Seeking to highlight its religious sites and attract more visitors

PILGRIMAGE

In religion and spirituality, a pilgrimage is a long journey or search of great moral significance. Sometimes, it is a journey to a sacred place or shrine of importance to a person's beliefs and faith. Members of every major religion participate in pilgrimages. A person who makes such a journey is called a pilgrim. Buddhism offers four sites of pilgrimage: the Buddha's birthplace at Kapilavastu, the site where he attained Enlightenment Bodh Gaya, where he first preached at Benares, and where he achieved Parinirvana at Kusinagara.

Israel acts as a focal point for the pilgrimages of many religions, such as Judaism, Christianity, Islam and the Bahá'í Faith. In the kingdoms of Israel and Judah, the visitation of certain ancient cult-centres was repressed in the 7th century BC, when the worship was restricted to Jahweh at the temple in Jerusalem. In Syria, the shrine of Astarte at the headwater spring of the river Adonis survived until it was destroyed by order of Emperor Constantine in the 4th century AD. In mainland Greece, a stream of individuals made their way to Delphi or the oracle of Zeus at Dodona, and once every four years, at the period of the Olympic games, the temple of Zeus at Olympia formed the goal of swarms of pilgrims from every part of the Hellenic world.

When Alexander the Great reached Egypt, he put his whole vast enterprise on hold, while he made his way with a small band deep into the Libyan desert, to consult the oracle of Ammun. During the imperium of his Ptolemaic heirs, the shrine of Isis at Philae received many votive inscriptions from Greeks on behalf of their kindred far away at home. Although a pilgrimage is normally viewed in the context of religion, the personality cults cultivated by communist leaders ironically gave birth to pilgrimages of their own. Prior to the demise of the USSR in 1991, a visit to Lenin's Mausoleum in Red Square, Moscow can be said to have had all the characteristics exhibiting a pilgrimage—for Communists. This type of pilgrimage to a personality cult is still evident today on people who pay visits of homage to Mao Tse Tung, Kim Il Sung, and Ho Chi Minh.

BELONGINGS ON TRADE

Pilgrims contributed an important element to long-distance trade before the modern era, and brought prosperity to successful pilgrimage sites, an economic phenomenon unequalled until the tourist trade of the 20th century. Encouraging pilgrims was a motivation for assembling relics and for writing hagiographies of local saints, filled with inspiring accounts of miracle cures. Lourdes and other modern pilgrimage sites keep this spirit alive.

NEW PILGRIMAGE

Pilgrimages are still made throughout the world: modern-day pilgrimages include the Way of St. James, the Hajj, and the pilgrimage to Mount Kailash. In modern usage, the terms pilgrim and pilgrimage can also have a somewhat devalued meaning as they are often applied in a secular context. For example, fans of Elvis Presley may choose to visit his home, Graceland, in Memphis, Tennessee. Similarly one may refer to a cultural centre such as Venice as a "tourists' Mecca".

PILGRIMAGE CENTRES IN DIFFERENT TIMES AND CULTURES

Antiquity

Many ancient religions had holy sites, temples and groves, where pilgrimages were made.

- Baalbek Lebanon.
- Delphi, Greece. Oracle.
- Dodona, Epirus, Greece. Oracle.
- Ephesus Temple of Diana.
- Karnak, Egypt.
- Kurukshetra, India
- Thebes, Egypt.

Bahá'í Faith

A Bahá'í pilgrimage currently consists of visiting the holy places in Haifa, Akká, and Bahjí in Northwest Israel. Bahá'ís do not have access to other places designated as sites for pilgrimage. Bahá'u'lláh decreed pilgrimage in His Motherbook to two places: the House of Bahá'u'lláh in Baghdad, Iraq, and the House of the Báb in Shiraz, Iran. In two separate Tablets, known as Suriy-i-Hajj, He prescribed specific rites for each of these pilgrimages. It is obligatory to make the pilgrimage, "if one can afford it and is able to do so, and if no obstacle stands in one's way".

Bahá'ís are free to choose between the two Houses, as either has been deemed sufficient. And although women are not bound to perform pilgrimage, they are certainly not prohibited to do so.

Buddhism

Gautama Buddha spoke of the four sites most worthy of pilgrimage for his followers to visit:

- *Bodh Gaya*: Place of Enlightenment

- *Kusinara*: Where he attained mahaparinirvana.
- *Lumbini*: Birth place
- *Sarnath*: Where he delivered his first teaching

Other pilgrimage places in India and Nepal connected to the life of Gautama Buddha are: Savatthi, Pataliputta, Nalanda, Gaya, Vesali, Sankasia, Kapilavastu, Kosambi, Rajagaha, Varanasi.

Other famous places for buddhist pilgrimage in various countries include:

- *Cambodia*: Angkor Wat, Silver Pagoda.
- *China*: Yung-kang, Lung-men caves.
- *India*: Sanchi, Ellora, Ajanta.
- *Indonesia*: Borobudur.
- *Japan*: Kyoto, Nara.
- *Laos*: Luang Prabang.
- *Myanmar*: Bagan, Sagaing Hill.
- *Nepal*: Bodhnath, Swayambhunath.
- Sri Lanka: Polonnaruwa, Temple of the Tooth, Anuradhapura.
- *Thailand*: Sukhothai, Ayutthaya, Wat Phra Kaew, Wat Doi Suthep.
- *Tibet*: Lhasa, Mount Kailash, Lake Nam-tso.

Communism

- *China*: Peking, Mausoleum of Mao Tse Tung in Tiananmen Square.
- *Germany*: Trier, Birthplace of Karl Marx in Trier
- *USSR*: Moscow, Mausoleum of Lenin in Red Square.

Christianity

Pilgrimages were first made to sites connected with the birth, life, crucifixion and resurrection of Jesus. Surviving descriptions of Christian pilgrimages to the Holy Land date from the 4th century, when pilgrimage was encouraged by church fathers like Saint Jerome. Pilgrimages also began to be made to Rome and other sites associated with the Apostles, Saints and Christian martyrs, as well as to places where there have been apparitions of the Virgin Mary. The crusades to the holy land are also considered to be mass armed pilgrimages. The second largest single pilgrimage in the history of Christendom was to the Funeral of Pope John Paul II after his death on April 2, 2005. An estimated four million people travelled to Vatican City, in addition to the almost three million people already living in Rome, to see the body of Pope John Paul II lie in state. World Youth Day is a major Catholic Pilgrimage, specifically for people aged 16-35. It is held internationally every 2-3 years. In 2005, young Catholics visited Cologne, Germany. In 1995, the largest gathering of all time was to World Youth Day in Manila, Philippines, where four million people from all over the world attended.

The major Christian pilgrimages are to:

- *Constantinople*: Former capital of the Byzantine Empire and the see of one of the five ancient Patriarchates and spiritual see of the Eastern Orthodox Church. Hagia Sophia, former cathedral and burial place of many Ecumenical Patriarchs.
- *Jerusalem*: Site of the crucifixion and resurrection of Jesus.
- *Lourdes, France*: Apparition of the Virgin Mary. The second most visited Christian pilgrimage site after Rome.
- *Rome on roads such as the Via Francigena*: Site of the deaths of Saint Peter, Saint Paul and other early martyrs. Location of sacred relics of various saints, relics of the Passion, important churches and headquarters of the Catholic Church.
- Santiago de Compostela in Spain on the Way of St James. This famous medieval pilgrimage to the shrine of Saint James is still popular today.

Other important Christian pilgrimage sites include:

- Assisi, Italy, St. Francis of Assisi and St Clare, relics
- Avila, Spain, St Theresa of Avila, relics
- Bethlehem, in Israel, Birthplace of Jesus and King David.
- Canterbury Cathedral associated with Saint Thomas Becket.

- Cap-de-la-Madeleine, Quebec, Canada in honour of Our Lady of the Cape.
- Carey, Ohio to the Basilica and National Shrine of Our Lady of Consolation. Catholic pilgrims from the Middle East journey here to mark the Feast of the Assumption.
- Cathedral of Chartres, France.
- *Cologne, Germany*: Relics of the Three Magi.
- Conques, France
- *Croagh Patrick, Ireland*: Saint Patrick.
- *Czestochowa, Poland*: Black Madonna of Czêstochowa is housed pernamently in theJasna Góra Monastery
- *Fatima, Portugal*: Apparition of the Virgin Mary.
- Glastonbury, England. St Joseph of Arimathea.
- Goa, India. St. Francis Xavier
- Guadalupe, Spain
- Hill of Crosses, Lithuania
- House of the Virgin Mary, Turkey. Pope John-Paul II declared the Shrine of Virgin Mary as a pilgrimage place for Christians.
- *Issoudun, France*: Notre-Dame du Sacré-Coeur
- Kapel in 't Zand, Limburg
- Kevelaer, Germany
- Knock, Ireland
- Lakefield, Ontario, Canada
- Licheñ Stary, Sanctuary of Our Lady of Licheñ
- *Lisieux, France*: Saint Therese of Lisieux, burial place.
- *Lourdes, France*: Apparition of the Virgin Mary. Place of healing.
- *Mariazell, Austria*: Marian Shrine to Austria and Hungary
- *Meaugorje, Bosnia-Herzegovina*: Apparitions of the Virgin Mary at the present.
- *Miercurea Ciuc, Transylvania, Romania*: Whit Sunday gathering of Catholics.
- *Montserrat, Catalonia, Spain*: The Virgin of Montserrat is housed pernamently in the monastery of Santa María de Montserrat.

- *Mount Athos, Greece*: Orthodox monastic centre.
- *Mount Nebo, Jordan*: Traditional site of the death of Moses.
- Mount Sinai, Egypt, holy mountain to the ancient Hebrews, traditional site has been commemorated since time of Constantine
- Nazareth, Israel, hometown of Jesus
- Nidaros, Trondheim, Norway. Shrine of St. Olav. 4th most visited pilgrimage site in Middle Ages.
- Padua, Italy, St Anthony, relics
- Paris
- PemaiEion Kalvarija, Samogitia, Lithuania.
- Rosslyn Chapel, Scotland
- *Sacri Monti, Italy*: The Sacred Mountains of Piedmont and Lombardy.
- San Giovanni Rotondo, Italy, St Pio from Pietrelcina
- Sea of Galilee, Israel, site of Jesus' early ministry.
- Shrine of Our Lady of Guadalupe, Mexico City. Apparition of the Virgin Mary.
- St. Andrews, Scotland, it is said that Saint Andrew was given, by God, directions to the location of St Andrews
- St. Patrick's Purgatory, Donegal, Ireland
- St. Thomas Mount, India. Place where St. Thomas was martyred.
- Taize Community, France, modern monastery that actively encourages pilgrimages to it
- *Trondheim, Norway*: Nidaros Cathedral, shrine of St. Olav.
- *Turin, Italy*: Holy Shroud.
- Vailankanni, India. 16th-century Mary apparition site.
- Vierzehnheiligen, Germany.
- *Walsingham, England*: Virgin Mary apparition site.
- *Wittenberg, Germany*: Church of Martin Luther and centre of the Protestant Reformation.

Hinduism

Hindus are required to undertake pilgrimages during their lifetime.

Most Hindus who can afford to go on such journeys travel to numerous sites including those below:

- Allahabad
- Arunachala
- Ayodhya
- Benares
- Chidambaram
- Dakshineshwar
- Dharmasthala
- Dwarka
- Gaya
- Guruvayoor
- Hampi
- Haridwar
- Kalahasti
- Kanchipuram
- Kanyakumari
- Kateel
- Kollur
- Kumbakonam
- Kukke Subramanya
- Kunrakudy
- Madurai
- Mahabalipuram
- Marudamalai
- Mathura
- Mandher Devi temple in Mandhradevi
- Mayapur
- Mount Kailash
- Nashik
- Nathdwara
- Palani
- Pazhamudircholai
- Puri
- Pushkar
- Puttaparthi
- Rameswaram
- Rishikesh
- Sabarimala
- Shirdi
- Sikkal
- Sivagiri, Kerala
- Somnath
- Sringeri
- Srirangam
- Swamimalai
- Swamithope
- Talapady
- Tanjavur
- Thiruchendur
- Thiruparamkunram
- Thiruthani
- Tirupati
- Ujjain
- Udupi
- Malai Mandir
- Vaishno Devi
- Vayalur
- Viralimalai
- Virpur
- Vrindavan
- Badrinath
- Gangotri
- Kedarnath
- Yamunotri

The last four sites in the list together comprise the Chardham, or four holy pilgrimage destinations. It is believed that travelling to these places leads to moksha, the release from samsara. Vrindavan is most important place of pilgrimage for every Vaishnava, especially for the followers of Gaudiya Vaishnavism who regard Krishna as the original Personality of Godhead. Here one can attain love of God.

Islam

The pilgrimage to Mecca–the Hajj–is one of the Five Pillars of Islam. It should be attempted at least once in the lifetime of all able-bodied Muslims who can afford to do so. It is the most important of all Muslim Pilgrimages. Many Muslims also undergo ziyarat, which is a pilgrimage to sites associated with the prophet Muhammad, his companions, or other venerated figures in Islamic history, such as Shi'a imams or Sufi saints. Sites of pilgrimage include mosques, graves, battlefields, mountains, and caves. Local Pilgrimage traditions-those undertaken as ziarah visits to local graves, are also found throughout Muslim countries. In some countries, the grave sites of heroes have very strong ziyarah traditions as visiting the graves at auspicious times is a display of national and community identity. Some traditions within Islam have negative attitudes towards grave visiting. The third religiously sanctioned pilgrimage for Muslims is to the Al Quds mount in Jerusalem which hosts Al-Aqsa Mosque and the Dome of the Rock.

Judaism

Within Judaism, the Temple in Jerusalem was the centre of the Jewish religion, until its destruction in 70 AD, and all who were able were under obligation to visit and offer sacrifices known as the korbanot, particularly during the Jewish holidays in Jerusalem. Following the destruction of the Second Temple and the onset of the diaspora, the centrality of pilgrimage to Jerusalem in Judaism was discontinued. In its place came prayers and rituals hoping for a return to Zion and the accompanying restoration of regular pilgrimages. Until recent centuries, pilgrimage has been a fairly difficult and arduous adventure. But now, Jews from many countries make periodic pilgrimages to the holy sites of their religion. The western retaining wall of the original temple, known as the Wailing Wall, or Western Wall remains in the Old City of Jerusalem and this has been the most sacred site for religious Jews. Pilgrimage to this area was off-limits from 1948 to 1967, when East Jerusalem was controlled by Jordan. Some Reform and Conservative Jews who no longer consider themselves exiles, still enjoy visiting Israel even if it is not an official "pilgrimage."

ADVENTURE TOURISM

Adventure tourism is a type of niche tourism involving exploration or travel to remote areas, where the traveller should expect the unexpected. Adventure tourism is rapidly growing in popularity as tourists seek unusual holidays, different from the typical beach vacation. Adventure Tourism can take many forms with the increase in numbers of people with disabilities around the World and recent veterans from Wars have opened the doors to Adventure Travel for the Disabled. Albeit this may not be in exotic areas some tourism areas that have been developing include Australia, USA and Canada.

Whistler and Vancouver British Columbia, Canada have been taking the lead with the 2010 Paralympics coming up fast. Adapting to the needs of the Disabled to attract a $ 13 billion dollar a year industry in North America alone. The global Adventure Travel Trade Association, "adventure travel" may be any tourist activity including two of the following three components: a physical activity, a cultural exchange or interaction. Mountaineering expeditions, trekking, bungee jumping, rafting and rock climbing are frequently cited as an examples of adventure tourism.

MOUNTAINEERING

Mountaineering is the sport, hobby or profession of walking, hiking, trekking and climbing up mountains. It is also sometimes known as alpinism, particularly in Europe. While it began as an all-out attempt to reach the highest point of unclimbed mountains, it has branched into specializations addressing different aspects of mountains and may now be said to consist of three aspects: rock-craft, snow-craft and skiing, depending on whether the route chosen is over rock, snow or ice. All require great athletic and technical ability, and experience is also a very important part of the matter.

Snow

While certain compacted snow conditions allow mountaineers to progress on foot, typically some form of mechanical device is required to travel efficiently over snow and ice. Crampons 10-12 point spikes which are attached to a mountaineers boots, are used on hard snow and ice to provide additional traction and allow very steep ascents and descents. There a many different varieties, ranging from lightweight aluminum models intended for walking on glaciers to aggressive steel models intended for vertical and overhanging ice and rock.

Snowshoes can be used to walk through deep snow approaching the mountain or on lesser slopes up the mountain. Skis can be used almost everywhere snowshoes can and also in steeper, more alpine landscapes although it takes more practice to develop sufficiently strong skiing skills for difficult terrain. The practice of combining the techniques of alpine skiing and mountaineering to ascend and descend a mountain is a form of the sport by itself, called Ski Mountaineering. Ascending and descending a snow slope involves many different techniques of the feet and an ice axe which have been developed over the last hundred years, originating in Europe. The progression of footwork from the lowest angle slopes to the steepest terrain is first to splay the feet to a rising traverse, to kick stepping, to front pointing the crampons.

The progression of the ice axe technique from the lowest angle slopes to the steepest terrain is to use the ice axe first as a walking stick, then a stake, then to use the front pick as a dagger below the shoulders or above, and finally to swing the pick into the slope over the head. This also involves different designs of ice axe depending on the terrain to be covered, and even whether a mountaineer uses one or two ice axes.

Glaciers

When traveling over glaciers, crevasses pose a grave danger. These giant cracks in the ice are not always visible as snow can be blown and freeze over the top to make a snowbridge. At times snowbridges can be as thin as a few inches. Climbers use a system of ropes to protect themselves from such hazards. Basic gear for glacier travel includes crampons and ice axes. Teams of two to five climbers tie into a rope equally spaced. If a climber begins to fall the other members of the team perform a self-arrest to stop the fall. The other members of the team enact a crevasse rescue to pull the fallen climber from the crevasse.

Ice

Multiple methods are used to safely travel over ice. If the terrain is steep but not vertical, then protection in the form of pickets or ice screws can be driven into the snow or ice and attached to the rope by the lead climber. Each climber on the team must clip past the anchor, and the last climber picks up the picket. This allows for safety should the entire team be taken off their feet. This technique is known as Simul-climbing. If the terrain becomes vertical then standard ice climbing techniques are used.

Shelter

Climbers use a few different forms of shelter depending on the situation and conditions. Shelter is a very important aspect of safety for the climber as the weather in the mountains is very unpredictable. Tall mountains require many days of camping on the mountain.

Hut

The European alpine regions, in particular, have a network of mountain huts. Such huts exist at many different heights, including in the high mountains themselves–in extremely remote areas bivouac shelters may have been provided. The mountain huts are of varying size and quality but each is typically centred on a communal dining room and have dormitories equipped with mattresses, blankets or duvets, and pillows–guests are expected to bring and to use their own sleeping bag liner.

The facilities are usually rudimentary but, given their locations, huts offer vital shelter, make routes more widely accessible and offer good value. In Europe, all huts are staffed during the summer and some are staffed in the spring. Elsewhere, huts may also be open in the fall. Huts also may have a part that is always open, but unmanned, a so-called winter hut. When open and manned, the huts are generally run by full-time employees, but some are staffed on a voluntary basis by members of Alpine clubs. The manager of the hut, termed a guardian or warden in Europe, will usually also sell refreshments and meals–both to those visiting only for the day and to those staying overnight.

The offering is surprisingly wide–given that most supplies, often including fresh water, must be flown in by helicopter–and may include glucose-based snacks on which climbers and walkers wish to stock up, cakes and pastries made at the hut, a variety of hot and cold drinks, and high carbohydrate dinners in the evenings. Not all huts do offer a catered service, though, and visitors may need to provide for themselves. Some huts offer facilities for both, enabling visitors wishing to keep costs down to bring their own food and cooking equipment and to cater using the facilities provided. Booking for overnight stays at huts is deemed obligatory, and in many cases is essential as some popular huts–even with over 100 bed spaces-may well be full during good weather and at weekends. Once made, the cancellation of a reservation should be advised to the hut as a matter of courtesy–and, indeed, potentially of safety, as many huts keep a record of where climbers and walkers state they planned to walk to next. Most huts are contactable by telephone and most take credit cards as a means of payment for the service they provide.

Bivy

A bivy or bivouac is simply getting a sleeping bag and Bivouac sack and laying down to sleep. Many times small half sheltered areas like cracks in rocks or simply a trench dug in the snow are used to provide a basic means of shelter as well.

This technique is performed by most people only in cases of emergency, however in good weather this can be pleasant. Some climbers steadfastly committed to Alpine Style climbing plan on bivying in order to save the weight of a tent when snow conditions are not suitable for a snow cave.

Tent

Tents are the most common form of shelter used on the mountain. A four season tent is recommended for any camp above timberline in the mountains. Some climbers do not use tents at high altitudes unless the snow conditions do not allow for snow caving, although digging a snow cave is a time consuming and work intensive endeavor.

Sometimes walls of snow or rock can be built instead to shelter the tent from high winds and storms. One of the downsides to tenting is that high storm winds and snow loads can be unnerving and cause the tent to collapse, however modern mountaineering tents are usually tested for wind speeds up to 125 mph. Even so, constant flapping of the tent fabric can hinder sleep and raise doubts about the security of the shelter in windy conditions.

Snow Cave

Snow caves are another way for some climbers to shelter high on the mountain. Unlike tents snow caves are silent and actually warmer. A correctly made snow cave will hover around freezing, which relative to outside temperatures can be very warm.

They require carrying a snow shovel, which some may consider to be extra equipment, to build easily. They can be dug from a deep snowdrift, out of a slope, or anywhere there is at least four feet of snow. Another shelter that works well is a quinzee, which is excavated from a pile of snow that has been work hardened or sintered. Igloos are used by some climbers, but are deceptively difficult to build and require specific snow conditions.

Hazards

The craft of climbing has been developed to avoid three main types of danger: the danger of things falling on the climber, the danger of the climber falling and inclement weather. The things that may fall include rocks, ice, snow, other climbers or their gear; the mountaineer may fall from rocks, ice or snow, or into a crevasse. In all, there are eight chief dangers: falling rocks, falling ice, snow-avalanches, falls, the climber falling, falls from ice slopes, falls down snow slopes, falls into crevasses and dangers from weather. To select and follow a route using one's skills and experience to mitigate these dangers is to exercise the climber's craft.

Falling Rocks

Every rock mountain is slowly disintegrating due to erosion, the process being especially rapid above the snow-line. Rock faces are constantly swept by falling stones, which are generally possible to dodge. Falling rocks tend to form furrows in a mountain face, and these furrows have to be ascended with caution, their sides often being safe when the middle is stoneswept. Rocks fall more frequently on some days than on others, just as to the recent weather. Ice formed during the night may temporarily bind rocks to the face but warmth of the day or direct sun exposure may easily dislodge these rocks. Local experience is a valuable help on determining typical rockfall on such routes. The direction of the dip of rock strata often determines the degree of danger on a particular face; the character of the rock must also be considered. Where stones fall frequently debris will be found whilst on snow slopes falling stones cut furrows visible from a great distance. In planning an ascent of a new peak mountaineers must look for such traces. When falling stones get mixed in considerable quantity with slushy snow or water a mud avalanche is formed. It is vital to avoid camping in their possible line of fall.

Falling Ice

The places where ice may fall can always be determined beforehand. It falls in the broken parts of glaciers and from overhanging cornices formed on the crests of narrow ridges. Large icicles are often formed on steep rock faces, and these fall frequently in fine weather following cold and stormy days. They have to be avoided like falling stones. Seracs are slow in formation, and slow in arriving at a condition of unstable equilibrium.

They generally fall in or just after the hottest part of the day, and their debris seldom goes far. A skillful and experienced ice-man will usually devise a safe route through a most intricate ice-fall, but such places should be avoided in the afternoon of a hot day. Hanging glaciers often discharge themselves over steep rock-faces, the snout breaking off at intervals. Their track should be avoided.

Falls from Rocks

The skill of a rock climber is shown by one's choice of handhold and foothold, and his adhesion to those one has chosen. Much depends on a correct estimate of the firmness of the rock where weight is to be thrown upon it. Many loose rocks are quite firm enough to bear a person's weight, but experience is needed to know which can be trusted, and skill is required in transferring the weight to them without jerking. On rotten rocks the rope must be handled with special care, lest it should start loose stones on to the heads of those below. Similar care must be given to handholds and footholds, for the same reason.

When a horizontal traverse has to be made across very difficult rocks, a dangerous situation may arise unless at both ends of the traverse there be firm positions. Mutual assistance on hard rocks takes all manner of forms: two, or even three, people climbing on one another's shoulders, or using an ice axe propped up by others for a foothold. The great principle is that of co-operation, all the members of the party climbing with reference to the others, and not as independent units; each when moving must know what the climber in front and the one behind are doing. After bad weather steep rocks are often found covered with a veneer of ice, which may even render them inaccessible. Crampons are useful on such occasions.

Avalanches

The avalanche is the most underestimated danger in the mountains. People generally think that they will be able to recognize the hazards and survive being caught. The truth is a somewhat different story. Every year, 120-150 people die in small avalanches in the Alps alone. The vast majority are reasonably experienced male skiers aged 20-35 but also include ski instructors and guides. There is always a lot of pressure to risk a snow crossing. Turning back takes a lot of extra time and effort, supreme leadership, and most importantly there seldom is an avalanche to prove the right decision was made. Making the decision to turn around is especially hard if others are crossing the slope, but any next person could become the trigger.

The Slab Avalanche

This type of avalanche occurs when a plate of snow breaks loose and starts sliding down; these are the largest and most dangerous.

- Hard slab avalanche-formed by hard-packed snow in a cohesive slab. The slab will not break up easily as it slides down the hill, resulting in large blocks tumbling down the mountain.
- Soft slab avalanche-formed again by a cohesive layer of snow bonded together, the slab tends to break up more easily.

The Loose Snow Avalanche

This type of avalanche is triggered by a small amount of moving snow that accumulates into a big slide. Also known as a "wet slide or point release" avalanche. This type of avalanche is deceptively dangerous as it can still knock a climber or skier off their feet and bury them, or sweep them over a cliff into a terrain trap. Dangerous slides are most likely to occur on the same slopes preferred by many skiers: long and wide open, few trees or large rocks, 30 to 45 degrees of angle, large load of fresh snow, soon after a big storm, on a slope 'lee to the storm'. Solar radiation can trigger slides as well. These will typically be a point release or wet slough type of avalanche. The added weight of the wet slide can trigger a slab avalanche. Ninety per cent of reported victims are caught in avalanches triggered by themselves or others in their group. When going off-piste or traveling in alpine terrain, parties have a moral responsibility to always carry:

- Avalanche beacon
- Probe
- Shovel

Paradoxically, expert skiers who have avalanche training make up a large percentage of avalanche fatalities; perhaps because they are the ones more likely to ski in areas prone to avalanches, and certainly because most people do not practice enough with their equipment to be truly fast and efficient rescuers. Even with proper rescue equipment and training, there is a one-in-five chance of dying if caught in a significant avalanche, and only a 50/50 chance of being found alive if buried more than a few minutes. The best solution is to learn how to avoid risky conditions.

Ice Slopes

For travel on slopes consisting of ice or hard snow, crampons are a standard part of a mountaineer's equipment. While step-cutting can sometimes be used on snow slopes of moderate angle, this can be a slow and tiring process, which does not provide the higher security of crampons. However, in soft snow or powder, crampons are easily hampered by balling of snow which reduce their effectiveness. In either case, an ice axe not only assists with balance but provides the climber with the possibility of self-arrest in case of a slip or fall. On a true ice slope however, an ice axe is rarely able to effect a self-arrest. As an additional safety precaution on steep ice slopes, the climbing rope is attached to ice screws buried into the ice. True ice slopes are rare in Europe, though common in mountains located in the tropics, where newly-fallen snow quickly thaws on the surface and becomes sodden below, so that the next night's frost turns the whole mass into a sheet of semi-solid ice.

Snow Slopes

Snow slopes are very common, and usually easy to ascend. At the foot of a snow or ice slope is generally a big crevasse, called a bergschrund, where the final slope of the mountain rises from a snow-field or glacier. Such bergschrunds are generally too wide to be stepped across, and must be crossed by a snow bridge, which needs careful testing and a painstaking use of the rope. A steep snow slope in bad condition may be dangerous, as the whole body of snow may start as an avalanche. Such slopes are less dangerous if ascended directly than obliquely, for an oblique or horizontal track cuts them across and facilitates movement of the mass.

New snow lying on ice is especially dangerous. Experience is needed for deciding on the advisability of advancing over snow in doubtful condition. Snow on rocks is usually rotten unless it is thick; snow on snow is likely to be sound. A day or two of fine weather will usually bring new snow into sound condition. Snow cannot lie at a very steep angle, though it often deceives the eye as to its slope. Snow slopes seldom exceed 40°. Ice slopes may be much steeper. Snow slopes in early morning are usually hard and safe, but the same in the afternoon are quite soft and possibly dangerous; hence the advantage of an early start.

Crevasses

Crevasses are the slits or deep chasms formed in the substance of a glacier as it passes over an uneven bed. They may be open or hidden. In the lower part of a glacier the crevasses are open. Above the snow-line they are frequently hidden by arched-over accumulations of winter snow. The detection of hidden crevasses requires care and experience. After a fresh fall of snow they can only be detected by sounding with the pole of the ice axe, or by looking to right and left where the open extension of a partially hidden crevasse may be obvious. The safeguard against accident is the rope, and no one should ever cross a snow-covered glacier unless roped to one, or even better to two companions. Anyone venturing onto crevasses should be trained in crevasse rescue.

Weather

The primary dangers caused by bad weather centre around the changes it causes in snow and rock conditions, making movement suddenly much more arduous and hazardous than under normal circumstances. Whiteouts make it difficult to retrace a route while rain may prevent taking the easiest line only determined as such under dry conditions. In a storm the mountaineer who uses a compass for guidance has a great advantage over a merely empirical observer. In large snow-fields it is, of course, easier to go wrong than on rocks, but intelligence and experience are the best guides in safely navigating objective hazards. Summer thunderstorms may produce intense lightning.

If a climber happens to be standing on or near the summit, they risk being struck. There are many cases where people have been struck by lightning while climbing mountains. In most mountainous regions, local storms develop by late morning and early afternoon. Many climbers will get an "alpine start"; that is before or by first light so as to be on the way down when storms are intensifying in activity and lightning and other weather hazards are a distinct threat to safety.

Altitude

Rapid ascent can lead to altitude sickness. The best treatment is to descend immediately. The climber's motto at high altitude is "climb high, sleep low", referring to the regimen of climbing higher to acclimatize but returning to lower elevation to sleep. In the South American Andes, the chewing of coca leaves has been traditionally used to treat altitude sickness symptoms.

Common symptoms of altitude sickness include severe headache, sleep problems, nausea, lack of appetite, lethargy and body ache. Mountain sickness may progress to High Altitude Cerebral Edema and High Altitude Pulmonary Edema, both of which can be fatal within 24 hours.

In high mountains, atmospheric pressure is lower and this means that less oxygen is available to breathe. This is the underlying cause of altitude sickness. Everyone needs to acclimatize, even exceptional mountaineers that have been to high altitude before. Generally speaking, mountaineers start using bottled oxygen when they climb above 7,000 m. Exceptional mountaineers have climbed 8000-metre peaks without oxygen, almost always with a carefully planned programme of acclimatization. In 2005, researcher and mountaineer John Semple established that above-average ozone concentrations on the Tibetan plateau may pose an additional risk to climbers.

Locations

Mountaineering has become a popular sport throughout the world. In Europe the sport largely originated in the Alps, and is still immensely popular there. Other notable mountain ranges frequented by climbers include the Caucasus, the Pyrenees and the Tatra mountains. In North America climbers frequent the Rockies and Sierra Nevada of California, the Cascades of Washington and the high peaks of Alaska. There has been a long tradition of climbers going on expeditions to the Greater Ranges, a term generally used for the Andes and the high peaks of Asia including the Himalaya, Pamirs and Tien Shan. In the past this was often on exploratory trips or to make first ascents. With the advent of cheaper long-haul air travel mountaineering holidays in the Greater Ranges are now undertaken much more frequently and ascents of even Everest and Vinson Massif are offered as a "package holiday". Other popular mountaineering areas of more local interest include the Southern Alps of New Zealand, the Japanese Alps the Scottish Highlands and the mountains of Scandinavia.

HISTORY

- Though it is unknown whether his intention was to reach a summit, Ötzi ascended at least 3,000 m in the Alps about 5,300 years ago. His remains were found at that altitude, preserved in a glacier.
- The first recorded mountain ascent in the Common Era is Roman Emperor Hadrian's ascent of Etna to see the sun rise in 121.

- Peter III of Aragon climbed Canigou in the Pyrenees in the last quarter of the 13th century.
- The first ascent of the Popocatépetl was reported in 1289 by members of a local tribe
- Jean Buridan climbed Mont Ventoux around 1316.
- The Italian poet Petrarch wrote that on April 26, 1336 he, together with his brother and two servants, climbed to the top of Mont Ventoux. His account of the trip was composed later as a letter to his friend Dionigi di Borgo San Sepolcro.
- The Rochemelon in the Italian Alps was climbed in 1358.
- In the late 1400s and early 1500s ascents were made of numerous high peaks in the Andes, for religious purposes by the citizens of the Inca Empire and their subjects. They constructed platforms, houses and altars on many summits and carried out sacrifices, including human sacrifices. The highest peak they are known for certain to have climbed is Llullaillaco. They may also have ascended the highest peak in the Andes, Aconcagua as a sacrifice victim has been found at over 5,000 m on this peak.
- In 1492 the ascent of Mont Aiguille was made by order of Charles VIII of France. The Humanists of the 16th century adopted a new attitude towards mountains, but the disturbed state of Europe nipped in the bud the nascent mountaineering of the Zurich school.
- Leonardo da Vinci climbed to a snow-field in the neighbourhood of the Val Sesia and made scientific observations.
- In 1642 Darby Field made the first recorded ascent of Mount Washington, then known as Agiocochook, in New Hampshire.
- Konrad Gesner and Josias Simler of Zurich visited and described mountains, and made regular ascents. The use of ice axe and rope were locally invented at this time. No mountain expeditions of note are recorded in the 17th century.

- Richard Pococke and William Windham's historic visit to Chamonix was made in 1741, and set the trend for visiting glaciers.
- In 1744 the Titus was climbed, the first true ascent of a snow-mountain.
- The first attempt to ascend Mont Blanc was made in 1775 by a party of natives. In 1786 Dr Michel Paccard and Jacques Balmat gained the summit for the first time. Horace-Bénédict de Saussure, the initiator of the first ascent followed next year.
- The Norwegian mountain climber, Jens Esmark was the first person to ascend Snøhetta in 1798, part of the Dovrefjell range in Southern Norway. The same year he lead the first expedition to Bitihorn, a small mountain in the southernmost outskirts of Jotunheimen, Norway. In 1810 he was the first person to ascend Mount Gaustatoppen in Telemark, Norway.
- The Jungfrau was climbed in 1811, the Finsteraarhorn in 1812, and the Breithorn in 1813. Thereafter, tourists showed a tendency to climb, and the body of Alpine guides began to come into existence as a consequence.
- Citlaltépetl was first climbed in 1848 by F. Maynard and G. Reynolds.
- Systematic mountaineering, as a sport, is usually dated from Sir Alfred Wills's ascent of the Wetterhorn in 1854. The first ascent of Monte Rosa was made in 1855.
- The Alpine Club was founded in London in 1857, and was soon imitated in most European countries. Edward Whymper's ascent of the Matterhorn in 1865 marked the close of the main period of Alpine conquest–the Golden age of alpinism–during which the craft of climbing was invented and 'perfected', the body of professional guides formed and their traditions fixed.
- Passing to other ranges, the exploration of the Pyrenees was concurrent with that of the Alps. The Caucasus followed, mainly owing to the initiative of

D. W. Freshfield; it was first visited by exploring climbers in 1868, and most of its great peaks were climbed by 1888.

- The Edelweiss Club Salzburg was founded in Salzburg in 1881, and had 3 members make the First Ascent on 2 Eight-thousanders, Broad Peak and Dhaulagiri.
- Trained climbers turned their attention to the mountains of North America in 1888, when the Rev. W. S. Green made an expedition to the Selkirk Mountains. From that time exploration has gone on apace, and many English and American climbing parties have surveyed most of the highest peaks; Pikes Peak having been climbed by Mr. E. James and party in 1820, and Mt. Saint Elias by the Duke of the Abruzzi and party in 1897. The exploration of the highest Andes was begun in 1879-1880, when Whymper climbed Chimborazo and explored the mountains of Ecuador. The Cordillera between Chile and Argentina was visited by Dr. Gussfeldt in 1883, who ascended Maipo and attempted Aconcagua. That peak was first climbed by the Fitzgerald expedition in 1897.
- The Andes of Bolivia were first explored by Sir William Martin Conway in 1898. Chilean and Argentine expeditions revealed the structure of the southern Cordillera in the years 1885-1898. Conway visited the mountains of Tierra del Fuego.
- New Zealand's Southern Alps were first visited in 1882 by the Rev. W. S. Green, and shortly afterwards a New Zealand Alpine Club was founded, and by their activities the exploration of the range was pushed forward. In 1895, Major Edward Arthur Fitzgerald, made an important journey in this range. Tom Fyfe and party climbed Aoraki/Mount Cook on Christmas Day 1894, denying Fitzgerald the first ascent. Fitzgerald was en route from Britain with Swiss guide Matthias Zurbriggen to claim the peak.

So piqued at being beaten to the top of Mount Cook, he refused to climb it and concentrated on other peaks in the area. Later in the trip Zubriggen soloed Mount Cook up a ridge that now bears his name.

- The first mountains of the arctic region explored were those of Spitzbergen by Sir W. M. Conway's expeditions in 1896 and 1897.
- Of the high African peaks, Kilimanjaro was climbed in 1889 by Dr. Hans Meyer, Mt. Kenya in 1899 by Halford John Mackinder, and a peak of Ruwenzori by H. J. Moore in 1900.
- The Asiatic mountains were initially surveyed on orders of the British Empire. In 1892 Sir William Martin Conway explored the Karakoram Himalaya, and climbed a peak of 23,000 ft. In 1895 Albert F. Mummery died while attempting Nanga Parbat, while in 1899 D. W. Freshfield took an expedition to the snowy regions of Sikkim. In 1899, 1903, 1906 and 1908 Mrs Fannie Bullock Workman made ascents in the Himalayas, including one of the Nun Kun peaks. A number of Gurkha sepoys were trained as expert mountaineers by Major the Hon. C. G. Bruce, and a good deal of exploration was accomplished by them.
- The Rucksack Club was founded in Manchester, England in 1902.
- The American Alpine Club was founded in 1902.
- In 1902, the Eckenstein-Crowley Expedition, lead by mountaineer Oscar Eckenstein and occultist Aleister Crowley, was the first to attempt to scale Chogo Ri. They reached 22,000 feet before turning back due to weather and other mishaps.
- In 1905, Aleister Crowley led the first expedition to Kanchenjunga, the third highest mountain in the world. Four members of that party were killed in an avalanche. Some claims say they reached around 21,300 feet before turning back, however Crowley's autobiography claims they reached about 25,000 feet.
- The 1950s saw the first ascents of all the eight-

thousanders but two, starting with Annapurna in 1950 by Maurice Herzog and Louis Lachenal. The world's highest mountain, Mount Everest was first climbed on May 29, 1953 by Sir Edmund Hillary and Tenzing Norgay from the south side in Nepal. Just a few months later, Hermann Buhl made the first ascent of Nanga Parbat, a remarkable solo climb, the only eight-thousander to be solo'd on the first ascent. K2, the second highest peak in the world was first scaled in 1954. In 1964, the final eight-thousander to be climbed was Shishapangma, the lowest of all the 8,000 metre peaks.

BACKPACKING

Backpacking combines hiking and camping in a single trip. A backpacker hikes into the backcountry to spend one or more nights there, and carries supplies and equipment to satisfy sleeping and eating needs. A backpacker packs all of his or her gear into a backpack. This gear must include food, water, and shelter, or the means to obtain them, but very little else, and often in a more compact and simpler form than one would use for stationary camping. A backpacking trip must include at least one overnight stay in the wilderness. Many backpacking trips last just a weekend but long-distance expeditions may last weeks or months, sometimes aided by planned food and supply drops. Backpacking camps are more spartan than ordinary camps. In areas that experience a regular traffic of backpackers, a hike-in camp might have a fire ring and a small wooden bulletin board with a map and some warning or information signs. Many hike-in camps are no more than level patches of ground without scrub or underbrush. In very remote areas, established camps do not exist at all, and travellers must choose appropriate camps themselves. In some places, backpackers have access to lodging that are more substantial than a tent.

In the more remote parts of Great Britain, bothies exist to provide simple accommodation for backpackers. Another example is the High Sierra Camps in Yosemite National Park.

Mountain huts provide similar accommodation in other countries, so being a member of a mountain hut organization is advantageous to make use of their facilities.

On other trails there are somewhat more established shelters of a sort that offer a place for weary hikers to spend the night without needing to set up a tent. Most backpackers purposely try to avoid impacting on the land through which they travel. This includes following established trails as much as possible, not removing anything, and not leaving residue in the backcountry. The Leave No Trace movement offers a set of guidelines for low-impact backpacking.

Professional Backpacking

For some people, backpacking is a necessary and integral part of their job. In the military a framed backpack is referred to as a "rucksack" or simply a "ruck". Soldiers who serve in the militaries of most nation-states usually receive at least some rudimentary backpacking training while infantrymen are often trained to a more advanced backpacking skill level. They share many common attributes with amateur backpackers: being self-contained, use of land-navigation skills and actively minimizing their environmental foot-print.

Although there are also a few differences such as the need to carry an assault rifle, other weapons, ammunition and communication equipment as well as at times maintaining "noise and light discipline", which means remaining silent and in darkness to avoid detection. Other professional backpackers may be scientific and academic researchers, professional guides, photographers, park-rangers and "search and rescue" personnel.

Motivation

People are drawn to backpacking primarily for recreation, to explore places that they consider beautiful and fascinating, many of which cannot be accessed in any other way. A backpacker can travel deeper into remote areas, away from people and their effects, than a day-hiker can. However, backpacking presents more advantages besides distance of travel. Many weekend trips cover routes that could be hiked in a single day, but people choose to backpack them anyway, for the experience of staying overnight. These possibilities come with disadvantages.

The weight of a pack, laden with supplies and gear, forces backpackers to travel more slowly than day-hikers would, and it can become a nuisance and a distraction from enjoying the scenery. In addition, camp chores can easily consume several hours every day. Backpackers face many risks, including adverse weather, difficult terrain, treacherous river crossings, and hungry or unpredictable animals. They are subject to illnesses, which run the gamut from simple dehydration to heat exhaustion, hypothermia, altitude sickness, and physical injury. The remoteness of backpacking locations exacerbates any mishap. However, these hazards do not deter backpackers who are properly prepared. Some simply accept danger as a risk that they must endure if they want to backpack; for others, the potential dangers actually enhance the allure of the wilderness.

BUNGEE JUMPING

Bungee jumping is the sport that originated from New Zealand and was created by maverick daredevil A J Hackett, and his original jump from a bridge in Greenhithe, Auckland. The sport denotes jumping from a tall structure while connected to a large rubber cord. The tall structure is usually a fixed object, such as a building, bridge, or crane; but it is also possible to jump from a movable object, such as a hot-air-balloon or a helicopter, that has the ability to hover over one spot on the ground; fixed-wing aircraft are clearly unsuitable because they only stay aloft when moving rapidly forward.

The intense thrill comes as much from the free-falls as from the rebounds. When the person jumps, the cord stretches to absorb the energy of the fall, then the jumper flies upwards again as the cord snaps back. The jumper oscillates up and down until all the energy is used up. The word bungee first appeared around 1930 and was the name for rubber eraser.

The word bungy, as used by A J Hackett, is said to be "Kiwi slang for Elastic Strap".

Cloth-covered rubber cords with hooks on the ends have been available for decades under the generic name bungee cords. In the 1950s David Attenborough and a BBC film crew had brought back footage of the "land divers" of Pentecost Island in Vanuatu, young men who jumped from tall wooden platforms with vines tied to their ankles as a test of courage. This film inspired Chris Baker of Bristol, England to use elastic rope in a kind of urban vine jumping. The first modern bungee jump was made on 1 April 1979 from the 250ft Clifton Suspension Bridge in Bristol, and was made by four members of the Dangerous Sports Club. The jumpers, led by David Kirke, were arrested shortly after, but continued with jumps in the US from the Golden Gate and Royal Gorge bridges, spreading the concept worldwide.

By 1982 they were jumping from mobile cranes and hot air balloons, and putting on commercial displays. One of the first operators of a commercial bungee jumping concern enabling the general public to experience these leaps of faith was New Zealander, A J Hackett, who made his first jump from Auckland's Greenhithe Bridge in 1986. During the following years Hackett performed a number of jumps from bridges and other structures building public interest in the sport. Hackett remains one of the largest commercial operators, with concerns in several countries.

The worlds first permanent commercial bungee site was the Kawarau Bridge Bungy at Queenstown in the South Island of New Zealand. Despite the inherent danger of jumping from a great height, several million successful jumps have taken place since 1980. This is attributable to bungee operators rigorously conforming to standards and guidelines governing jumps, such as double checking calculations and fittings for every jump. As with any sport, injuries can still occur, but there have been few fatalities. A relatively common mistake in fatality cases is to use too long a cord.

The cord should be substantially shorter than the height of the jumping platform to allow it room to stretch. When the cord reaches its natural length the jumper either starts to slow down or keep accelerating. depending upon the speed of descent. One may not even start to slow until the cord has already stretched somewhat, because the cord's resistance to distortion is zero at the natural length, and increases only gradually after, taking some time to even equal the jumper's weight.

RAFTING

Rafting or whitewater rafting is a recreational activity utilizing a raft to navigate a river or other bodies of water. This is usually done on whitewater or different degrees of rough water, in order to thrill and excite the raft passengers. The development of this activity as a leisure sport has become popular since the mid 1970s. Rafting is one of the earliest means of transportation, used as a means for shipping people, hunting, and transferring food. In 1842, Lieutenant John Fremont of the U.S. Army first journalized his rafting expedition on the Platte River.

Horace H. Day designed the equipment he used in rafting. Day's rafts were constructed from four independent rubber cloth tubes and wrap-around floor. In 1960s, rafting was then recognized and paths like Grand Canyon were routed and whitewater rafting companies were established. In 1970s, rafting marked its major development as a leisure sport when it was then included in the Munich Olympic Games.

In 1980s, as rafting continued to gain its popularity, a lot of rivers were opened for rafting activities. Rivers in South America and Africa were just a few of them. In 1990s, rafting was included in major game events like the Barcelona Games in 1992, Atlanta Games in 1996, and the whitewater events of the Summer Olympic Games hosted by Ocoee River in Tennessee Valley.

In addition, the International Federation of Rafting was instituted in 1997 and in 1999 the first Official International Championship was held. Nowadays, river rafting is still gaining popularity among extreme water sports in order to thrill and excite the raft passengers.

ROCK CLIMBING

Rock climbing, broadly speaking, is the act of ascending steep rock formations. Normally, climbers use gear and safety equipment specifically designed for the purpose. Strength, endurance, and mental control are required to cope with tough, dangerous physical challenges, and knowledge of climbing techniques and the use of essential pieces of gear and equipment are crucial.

Although the practice of rock climbing was an important component of Victorian mountaineering in the Alps, it is generally thought that the sport of rock climbing began in the last quarter of the nineteenth century in various parts of Europe. Rock climbing evolved gradually from an alpine necessity to an athletic sport in its own right.

As rock climbing matured, grading systems were created in order to more accurately compare relative difficulties of climbs. Over the years, both climbing techniques, and the equipment climbers use to advance the sport, have evolved in a steady fashion.

ADVENTURE TOURISM IN INDIA

ANGLING IN INDIA

Today, in India, the sport of angling is combined with conservation. As per the existing Indian protection laws, the fish is allowed to be caught, but must be released within a stipulated time period. The average time taken to land a Mahseer is in ratio to its weight—5 minutes to 5 lbs. With just enough time to record its weight, and preserve your moment of glory with the prize catch of film, before the fish is revived-you have to be really quick or else it could just end up as one of those fishy stories of, "the great one that got away."

CAMEL SAFARI IN INDIA

Thar Desert Camel Safaris of India are now one of Asia's fastest selling adventure holidays. These include camel treks ranging from short rides around Jaisalmer to extensive trips that remind you of Lawrence of Arabia on his epic journey across the Sahara, Marco Polo, on the historic silk route, a medieval trader leading his caravan through the hostile spice route or a royal caravan serai heading for one of the medieval kingdoms of the Thar desert- without many of the hardships of course! They are a great way to see the desert and to enjoy a novel and adventurous holiday.

The Great Indian Desert may not have great expanses of sand dunes and incredible spaces of wilderness as large as those of the Sahara and Namibia, but more than makes up for it with some glorious citadels and extremely colourful and unspoilt villages. Its sand dunes are more easily accessible from airports and railway stations than those of many African countries.

CAMEL SAFARI CIRCUIT IN INDIA

The Camel Safari Circuit in India comprises of Jaisalmer, Jodhpur, and Bikaner, all in Rajasthan. They were the princely kingdoms in the desert belt of India Rajasthan. Each was comparable in size to many modern nations of Europe. All the former capitals prospered from trade with the camel caravans that traveled from West Asia and Europe to Mongolia, and were impressively fortified to protect these riches. The result was a wealth of palaces built for royalty, havelis or courtyard mansions built for merchants and nobility and intricately carved temples for the subjects.

Materials used were normally sandstone, which was easily available and provided a better medium to the silavats who specialized in making stone resemble lace. A camel safari is a great way to see the desert-visiting the villages, seeing wildlife, and riding across the open desert sands. Typical camel safaris organized around Jaisalmer take in the architectural ruins of Lodurva which was the former capital of the Bhatti Rajput desert kingdom before the founding of Jaisalmer, the Anasagar oasis, the sand dunes of Samm and the water source of Moolsagar where village women gather with pitchers at dusk. Night halts on basic safaris are at villages on the way or temporary bivouac camps in the desert scrub where camels are hobbled and let out to browse.

CAMEL SAFARI IN INDIA -TRAVEL KIT

The climate is extreme in the desert-afternoons may seem much hotter than the actual 26-30 degree temperature may suggest. Night temperatures may drop below zero on the dunes. It is essential to stock both woolen and cotton clothing. Shorts and skirts are comfortable wear for camel safaris but remember some of the off beat routes visit villages that have not seen many tourists and locals may look askance at ladies who do not wear ankle length clothing and men in shorts. Sun hats with large rims or cotton caps that can be dipped in water when it gets too hot around midday, are essential preferably with a balaclava or scarf for covering the neck and forehead.

At Jodhpur you can buy umbrellas that are quite convenient for camel safaris. Sunscreen cream, moisturizers and lip salve area must. A water bottle can be comfortably slung on the camel saddle and it is practical also to carry tangerines as even on a deluxe safari it may not be practical to dismount each time to drink from the carted water supply. Bottled mineral water is available at Jodhpur and Jaisalmer. Find out if the baggage is being transferred by camel cart or vehicle.

In case of the latter, a small handbag can carry the essentials you are likely to need on the way. If prone to sickness, carry suitable medication against the swaying gait of the camel. A torch, penknife an even cutlery will be required. Finally patience is an important piece of baggage on a camel safari as it takes time to get to grips with camel travel and to reach destinations that may be on your travel priorities.

MOUNTAINEERING IN INDIA

Mountaineering as a sport has a history as old as the history of the evolution of human race itself. Mountaineering started when the need was felt for people who could climb difficult heights and terrains to meet people across the border, to trade, or to conquer new territories. In the course of time, man developed new modes of transportation and communication and venturing out on these difficult routes were not needed. Nevertheless, what remained was his nature to take risks and getting pleasure in conquering something totally unknown and unexplored.

This inner urge to take up challenges has led man to do things that are quite daring. In India, mountaineering as a sport came with the Europeans in the 18th century. That was a time when entire Europe was experiencing a new phase. New regions were being explored, won, and native peoples were being made to become civilized. This zeal of adventurism found its ultimate fruition in the Himalayas-lofty, extremely difficult to conquer, and challenging enough to send a man back to his mother's womb. But, being men, these challenges were accepted and there began a tussle between men's ambitions and nature's reluctance.

New heights were conquered, new routes were discovered, many lives lost, but the mission was accomplished. Today, almost all the major peaks are conquered and even general people have started taking mountaineering as a serious hobby. For starters, India offers a wide spectrum of options for mountaineering as well as other related sports. Peaks and trekking routes are classified and maps are available for the interested travellers. Many institutes provide basic and advanced level courses in mountaineering and other related sports. All the equipment is locally available and other support resources can be found here.

PARAGLIDING IN INDIA

If you like Icarus ever wished to fly, as suggested, make your dream realise. The adventure of paragliding is something you just cannot miss. Soar over the hills, dip whenever you aspire to get a better view of the Earth, glide and sail, feel the freedom of the bird. The adventure of being at the altitude needs an attitude! No noise pollution, no smoke just plain fun. The thrill of have your own wings, the big wide sky with no traffic jams is a safe and easy aero adventure.

Paragliding is fun for the people who constantly would love to reach new heights. Be amongst the stars during the day and count the constellations at night! Live life happily in the lap of Mother Nature. The package offers training for the novice too. Come fly, with us. The paraglider, harness, helmets, radios and ankle boots are equipments required for the adventure. Besides the monsoon season, the sky is your road for the escapade, come on touch the sky.

ELEPHANT SAFARI

How about a safari atop an elephant? Jeeps and other mechanical means of transportation may distract the fellow animals in the jungle. The Elephant is the best possible option available to admire the beauty of nature. The wildlife adventure in India is incomplete if an Elephant safari is not include in the itinerary. Come and explore the wild terrain of the Corbett National Park on the most majestic animal of all. Even horse safaris do well with the tourists in India. The strong and sturdy animal has since long been galloping across the terrific terrain in India.

ROCK CLIMBING IN INDIA

It is not quite easy to define rock climbing, but it is not difficult too. Anyone who claims to be a rock climber has his own version of the game. Rock climbing for some is to challenge their spirits and explore new heights, to give a fillip to their unbounded imaginations; for others, it is a way telling the world that he/she has finally arrived. For many of the professional rock climbers, it is not a sport. Can you call a mission to moon a sport or pastime? If not, then why should rock climbing be called a sports is the argument. For them, rock climbing is an adventure of the greatest magnitude; it is a fight against self, against the elements, and the ultimate goal is to reach the summit and return back alive.

SCUBA DIVING IN INDIA

One of the greatest adventures in life can be to explore the totally unknown and unexplored world under sea. The joy of floating inside the sea like a fish where every creature is your friend and every new sight is a discovery can be immense. In addition, the sheer thrill of watching the rich flora and fauna of the sea in their natural habitat is unparalleled. The curiosity to know the underwater world of the sea is not a new phenomenon for human civilization. We have so many stories from the epic Ramayana describing the world beneath the sea when Hanuman was crossing the sea to reach Lanka.

The origin of many mythical characters and objects are related to the sea. There is a legend about Samudra Manthan that tells us that the sea was churned around a hill known as Meru with a snake around it. The gods pulled one end of the snake while the other end was pulled by the demons. Many amazing things came out of this exploration-an elephant called Airavata that became the property of Indra, a tree called Kalpavriksa that could grant anything, a cow known as Kamdhenu that gave milk everyday, the Goddess of wealth Lakshmi, the god of Ayurveda Dhanawantari, the Visha and Amrit. Scuba diving and snorkeling as sports came with the Europeans who saw the vast expanse of the Indian coastline. Besides, many Indians who experienced this unique adventure also brought with them a new and exciting option for their fellow countrymen.

Stretching many thousand kilometers, the Indian coastline spans the mighty waters of the Arabian Sea, the Indian Ocean and the Bay of Bengal. Dotted with the finest beaches, cliff promontories, mangroves, backwater, jewel-like island groups and marine life, there are wide diving possibilities. While there are many popular easily accessible sites, many more can be explored which are not at all known. The sight of the smashing waves creating foaming breakers on the coral reef, which enclose azure lagoons whose crystal clear waters wash the fine grained white sands of the palm dotted low islands, is one of the few marvels of God's creations left untouched by the encroaching hands of industrialization and progress. The underwater city is a unique and diverse collection of colourful and weirdly patterned sea animals. Corals take pride of place in these reef cities.

Rich in variety and colour, the thousands of types of corals range from tall sea fans to small hydroids, from languidly waving sea anemones to glassy jellyfish. Danger there is, but only enough to add to the sense of adventure and thrill. This fun is multiplied many times over as you don the scuba gear. This gear has been especially devised for the deep sea diver and gives an opportunity for thrill and adventure unparalleled and unimagined by ones who think of the sea as nothing but a large saltwater lake.

India is fast becoming the adventure tourism destination of the world; and scuba diving and snorkeling as well as other water sports are going to be an integral part of this. If you have not had adventure in India, you do not know what adventure is all about.

SKIING IN INDIA

The sheer joie de vivre inspired by one's first successful slide down a ski slope defies description. Once limited to a privileged few, the adrenalin-producing pastime of skiing has been brought within the range of the common man now. For the purist, there is unsullied, powdery snow. For the accomplished and ego-conscious, there are punishing runs. For wobbly beginners and confident intermediates, there are easy slopes and understanding instructors who soon inspire dreams of Olympic glory.

With a first run to buoy one under the belt, there follows a succession of blissful days. Each day brings a fresh challenge to conquer and relish when you are at any skiing resort. Mastering the twists and turns and jumps of skiing, completing a longer ski run, and achieving faster speed are all part of this process. Every winter in the Indian Himalayas the slopes are warmed by the excited cries and laughter of entrants being introduced to the joys of winter sports: the magic of the wind rushing past as you whiz down a slope of skis, or the sheer pleasure of gliding gracefully, artistically cutting figures of eight in the snow. Skiing, like any other high-altitude adventure sports in India, is a contribution of the Europeans. The summers in north India have always been unpleasant, more so for the Europeans who were mostly from the cold countries.

To save themselves from this oppressive heat, they went to the Himalayas, not too far from major centres in north India.

Many hill stations were established, the prominent among them being Shimla, Manali, Mussoorie, and Nainital. These places served not only as the home away from home for them but also as the centre where they could participate in recreational activities like skiing and trekking. Some of these places still have the best skiing slopes in the country. Affluent Indians started participating in this sport even before independence.

After independence, with the efforts of adventure sport bodies, local youths were encouraged to participate in this sport. They took to it enthusiastically and later helped in training hordes of tourists coming from other parts of the county and even abroad. Today, skiing is quite popular in the hill stations of North India and new facilities have added up to make it more popular among the masses.

TREKKING IN INDIA

Off late, trekking in India is becoming popular among the tourists all over the world. This might have been a new phenomenon for the travellers from abroad, for Indians, these mountains signify not only the natural beauty but also a source of spiritual guidance. Trekking has remained men's passion from the day he took his first step on the earth. He always ventured out of home and his natural surroundings to explore something new, a world that was unknown to him. It is astonishing to learn that the human race migrated from one continent to another when there were no means of communication, no helping hands, and most of them who left their home could never return back.

WHITE WATER RAFTING IN INDIA

If you want to get some kick, some change in life, or just to have some fun, river rafting can satisfy most of your desires. If you have the zeal, then go for the challenge and show others that you can do it. White-water rafting is not for fashionable thrill seekers, but for those who thrive on hair-soaking risks, which keep the adrenalin flowing overtime! The thrill of rushing down fast-flowing mountain streams a froth with huge waves, dashing against dangerous boulders and dizzy rapids, while you cling for dear life dependent on a fragile, inflatable rubber raft or dinghy. Be swept along a rushing river in a rubber raft, tumble over rapids, plunge over waterfalls and feel the icy spray splash on your face, as your raft races along a mountain river in India.

Experience the thrill of white water rafting in India along tumbling snow-fed Himalayan rivers in summer destinations in India. River rafting in India is an exhilarating experience that you can enjoy on your Indian Holiday. One of the best regions for river rafting in India is the stretch upto Rishikesh in Uttaranchal. White water rafting on Alaknanda, Bhagirathi and Ganga rivers is a popular adventure tourism activity in summer in India. For the more adventurous traveller, white water rafting tours in India can also be organized on the Indus River in Ladakh and Brahmaputra River in Arunachal Pradesh White water rafting in India on the Alaknanda River is the most easily accessible white water river rafting stretch from Delhi. We drive from Delhi to Rishikesh and further north to Devprayag, where the Alaknanda River and Bhagirati River combine to form the Ganges, a river considered holy by Hindus in India.

Further North is Rudraprayag, where the Alaknanda and Mandakini Rivers combine. The white water rafting Alaknanda tour, consists of an approximately 130 Km long stretch from Rudraprayag to Shivpuri near Rishikesh in Uttaranchal, India. You will be given training by experienced river rafting instructors and guides. You will travel in groups in rafts, with an instructor at all times. Life jackets and other essential safety equipment are provided. You can stay overnight in luxury tents, pitched on beaches alongside the river, as we halt each night.

You can also enjoy campfires and bonfire nights on river rafting tours in India. As you swoop and tumble over the rapids with exotic names such as 'Roller Coaster;' 'Crossfire' and 'The Wall' you will feel the excitement and heart-racing thrill of white water rafting in India, on adventure tours to India this summer, with Indian Holiday.

MEDICAL TOURISM

Medical tourism can be broadly defined as provision of 'cost effective' private medical care in collaboration with the tourism industry for patients needing surgical and other forms of specialized treatment. This process is being facilitated by the corporate sector involved in medical care as well as the tourism industry-both private and public. Medical tourism refers to traveling to other countries to obtain medical, dental, and surgical treatment. At the same time they could also tour, and fully experience the attractions of the countries they visit. Exorbitant costs of healthcare in industrialized nations, ease and affordability of international travel, favourable currency exchange rates in the global economy, rapidly improving technology and standards of care in many countries of the world, and most importantly proven safety of healthcare in select foreign nations have all led to the rise of medical tourism. Medical tourism is a term initially coined by travel agencies and the mass media to describe to the rapidly-growing practice of traveling to another country to obtain health care.

Such services typically include elective procedures as well as complex specialized surgeries such as joint replacement cardiac surgery, dental surgery, and cosmetic surgeries. The provider and customer use informal channels of communication-connection-contract, with less regulatory or legal oversight to assure quality and less formal recourse to reimbursement or redress, if needed. Leisure aspects typically associated with travel and tourism may be included on such medical travel trips. The concept of medical tourism is not a new one. The first recorded instance of medical tourism dates back thousands of years to when Greek pilgrims traveled from all over the Mediterranean to the small territory in the Saronic Gulf called Epidauria. This territory was the sanctuary of the healing god Asklepios. Epidauria became the original travel destination for medical tourism. Spa towns may be considered an early form of medical tourism.

DESCRIPTION

Factors that have led to the recent increase in popularity

of medical travel include the high cost of health care or wait times for procedures in industrialized nations, the ease and affordability of international travel, and improvements in technology and standards of care in many countries of the world. Medical tourists can come from anywhere in the world, including Europe, the UK, Middle East, Japan, U.S. and Canada. This is because of their large populations, comparatively high wealth, the high expense of health care or lack of health care options locally, and increasingly high expectations of their populations with respect to health care. A large draw to medical travel is convenience and speed. Countries that operate public health-care systems are often so taxed that it can take considerable time to get non-urgent medical care.

The time spent waiting for a procedure such as a hip replacement can be a year or more in Britain and Canada; however, in Singapore, Hong Kong, Thailand, Cuba, Colombia, Philippines or India, a patient could feasibly have an operation the day after their arrival. In Canada, the number of procedures in 2005 for which people were waiting was 782,936. Additionally, patients are finding that insurance either does not cover orthopedic surgery or imposes unreasonable restrictions on the choice of the facility, surgeon, or prosthetics to be used.

Medical tourism for knee/hip replacements has emerged as one of the more widely accepted procedures because of the lower cost and minimal difficulties associated with the traveling to/from the surgery. Colombia provides a knee replacement for about $5,000 USD, including all associated fees such as FDA approved prosthetics and hospital stay over expenses. However, many clinics quote prices that are not all inclusive and include only the surgeon fees associated with the procedure. Medical tourists may seek essential health care services such as cancer treatment and brain and transplant surgery as well as complementary or 'elective' services such as aesthetic treatments.

A research found in an object by a famous university: "the cost of surgery in Bolivia, Argentina, Cuba, India, Thailand,

Colombia, Philippines or South Africa can be one-tenth of what it is in the United States or Western Europe, and sometimes even less. A heart-valve replacement that would cost US$200,000 or more in the U.S., for example, goes for $10,000 in the Philippines and India—and that includes round-trip airfare and a brief vacation package. Similarly, a metal-free dental bridge worth $5,500 in the U.S. costs $500 in India or Bolivia and only $200 in the Philippines, a knee replacement in Thailand with six days of physical therapy costs about one-fifth of what it would in the States, and Lasik eye surgery worth $3,700 in the U.S. is available in many other countries for only $730.

Cosmetic surgery savings are even greater: A full facelift that would cost $20,000 in the U.S. runs about $3,000 in Cuba, $2,700 in the Philippines or $2,500 in South Africa or $ 2,300 in Bolivia."To understand the phenomenon of medical travel, we can compare the average costs of cosmetic surgeries between the industrialized nations and Latin America countries where medical tourism and cosmetic surgery tourism are becoming popular, such as Argentina, Bolivia, Brazil, Costa Rica, Colombia, Philippines, and Mexico.

Popular medical travel worldwide destinations include: Brunei, Cuba, Colombia,Hong Kong, Hungary, India, Israel, Jordan, Lithuania, Malaysia, The Philippines, Singapore, South Africa, Thailand, and recently, UAE and New Zealand. Popular cosmetic surgery travel destinations include: Argentina, Bolivia, Brazil, Colombia, Costa Rica, Cuba, Mexico and Turkey. In Europe Belgium, Poland and Slovakia are also breaking into the business. South Africa is taking the term "medical tourism" very literally by promoting their "medical safaris": Come to see African wildlife and get a facelift in the same trip. However, perceptions of medical tourism are not always positive.

In places like the U.S., where most have insurance and access to quality health care, medical tourism is viewed as risky. In some parts of the world, wider political issues can influence where medical tourists will choose to seek out health care; for example, in late 2006, some patients from the Middle

East were choosing to travel to Singapore or Hong Kong for health care rather than to the U.S. because of international tensions. While the tourism component might be a big draw for some Southeast Asia countries that focus on simple procedures, India is positioning itself the primary medical destination for the most complex medical procedures in the world.

India's commitment to this is demonstrated with a growing number of hospitals that are attaining the U.S. Joint Commission International accreditation to help to capture the US medical tourism market, while others looking beyond just the US market to potential clients from the United Kingdom, Europe and Australia may also look towards other international healthcare accreditation schemes for brand advantage. Singapore positions itself as a medical hub for health care services, medicine, biomedical research and pharmaceutical manufacturing converge. Singapore has made international news for many complex surgeries in specialties such as neurology, oncology, and organ transplants procedures.

Currently Singapore boasts the largest number of U.S. Joint Commission accredited hospitals in the region. In South America, countries such as Argentina, Bolivia, Brazil and Colombia lead on plastic surgery medical skills relying on the vast experience their surgeons have in treating the style-obsessed. It is estimated that 1 in 30 Argentineans have had plastic surgery procedures, making this population the most operated in the world after the U.S. and Mexico. In Bolivia and Colombia, plastic surgery has become quite common. The "Sociedad Boliviana de Cirugia Plastica y Reconstructiva", more that 70% of middle and upper class women in the country have had some form of plastic surgery. Colombia also provides advanced care in cardiovascular and transplant surgery.

Companies are beginning to offer global health care options that will enable North American and European patients to access world health care at a fraction of the cost of domestic care. Companies that focus on 'Medical Value Travel' typically provide experienced nurse case managers to assist patients with pre- and post-travel medical issues. They also help provide resources for follow-up care upon the patient's return. While these services will initially be of interest to the self-insured patient, several studies indicate that the rapid growth of Health Savings Accounts in the U.S. will also drive interest to health care in other countries.

INDIA

India is known in particular for heart surgery, hip resurfacing and other areas of advanced medicine. The government and private hospital groups are committed to the goal of making India a world leader in the industry. The industry's main appeal is low-cost treatment. Most estimates claim treatment costs in India start at around a tenth of the price of comparable treatment in America or Britain. Estimates of the value of medical tourism to India go as high as $2 billion a year by 2012. The Indian government is taking steps to address other infrastructure issues that can serve as a deterrant to the country's growth in medical tourism. The south Indian city of Chennai has been declared India's Health Capital, as it nets in 45% of health tourists from abroad and 30-40% of domestic health tourists.

CULTURAL TOURISM

'Cultural tourism' is the subset of tourism concerned with a country or region's culture, especially its arts. It generally focuses on traditional communities who have diverse customs, unique form of art and distinct social practices, which basically distinguishes it from other types/forms of culture. Cultural tourism includes tourism in urban areas, particularly historic or large cities and their cultural facilities such as museums and theatres. It can also include tourism in rural areas showcasing the traditions of indigenous cultural communities and their values and lifestyle. It is generally agreed that cultural tourists spend substantially more than standard tourists do. This form of tourism is also becoming generally more popular throughout Europe.

DEFINITION

By definition, the term destination refers broadly to any given area where tourism is a relatively important activity, like for instance having an economy significantly influenced by tourism revenues. However, it is complicated by the fact that a single, recognizable destination may include several cities, towns or municipalities, provinces, or other government entities-in island archipelago it may be the entire country.

LIVING CULTURAL AREAS

Due to globalization, technology and the onset of cultural tourism and ecotourism, the number of living cultural areas is continually declining. For an indigenous culture that has stayed largely separated from the surrounding majority, tourism can present both advantages and problems. On the positive side are the unique cultural practices and arts that attract the curiosity of tourists and provide opportunities for tourism and economic development. On the negative side is the issue of how to control tourism so that those same cultural amenities are not destroyed and the people do not feel violated.

Chiloé, Chile

Chiloé is Chile's largest island, located at the midway point between the capital, Santiago, and the country's extreme south at Tierra del Fuego. Chiloé is the site of the Chiloé Model Forest, member of the same network as the Calakmul and Eastern Ontario Model Forests. Having evolved for centuries isolated from mainland Chile, the "Chilotes" developed a strong, self-reliant culture, rich in folklore, mythology and tradition. This very identity is what constitutes the island's major attraction for domestic tourists in Chile and increasingly, for international tourists. As in the Calakmul case above, tourism to Chiloé is very strongly based on the island's cultural heritage, predominantly consisting of crafts markets, appreciation of cultural landscapes, museum exhibitions, seafood cuisine and architectural heritage.

However, the average tourist to the island will have little opportunity to see Chilotes involved in their living cultural activities, such as the elaborate preparation of the islands famous "curanto" meal, rich in shellfish, meat and potatoes, the management practices of their farm and forest lands, boat building and more. In order to overcome the cultural and organizational barriers that keep suppliers of living cultural heritage and tour operators apart, the Chiloé diocese of Ancud established a private foundation called "Fundación con Todos". Among other activities, the Foundation has played a key role in helping a number of Chilote households organize themselves into an "agrotourism" network.

The Foundation helped Chilote households make the preparation required to accommodate tourists and complemented this effort with a professional marketing campaign. These works were undertaken with the financial support of other agencies. Again, in cooperation with the EOMF and the Chiloé Model Forest, a cultural and natural heritage tour was organized to Argentina and Chile, including a three-day visit to Chiloé, permitting some of the Chilote households to host a group of cultural heritage tourists for the first time. The visits were very successful and should be the first of more to come, helping establish the credibility of Chiloé's agrotourism network among other tour operators.

Orrissa Tribes

Nestling on the eastern coast of India, Orissa is one of the most exquisite regions dominated by exotic sandy beaches, plenteous wild life, and holy temples famous for their architectural splendor and primitive lifestyle.

The charm of the city is still well- nigh chaste and unrevealed by the visitors, up to its full extent. The other lure of the city lies in its tribal population dotted with more than 62 tribal communities. The tribal communities of Orissa constitute about 23% of its total population. Orissa is inhabited by tribes like Saora or Sabar that had a respectable mentioning in the epic of Mahabharata. Mostly the Orissa tribes are high land habitats with opulent ethnic trait, cultures and customs dominated by varying languages. The culture conscious tribes are able to preserve their social customs and dignified values.

The most primitive tribes are Bondas, Gadabas, Koyas, Kondhas and Sauras.

The culture of tribal Orissa is affluent with their own folk songs and dances, their tattoos. Tribal culture of Orissa is well depicted in its modern city in form of poems, art and craft or music. The tribes have adapted the Hindu traditions and culture from centuries, which is mixed with their own culture giving a distinct zest to the entire racial. Songs and dances are the essence of the tribal culture of Orissa. The traditions and the ceremonies for wedding, birth and death all are represented by singing songs, rural dances along with feasts. The Tribal Folk Orissan tribes are strong, assiduous and simple hospitable tribes, normally like to be reserved and maintain distance from the people of other communities, as they are too shy. The major occupation of these tribes is agriculture and fishing and hunting.

Men usually wear loin attire and women rap long stretch of cloth around them. Women are adorned with ornaments like bangles, armlets, bracelets, necklaces, rings, hairpins etc usually made of silvers, aluminum, and brass. The practice of tattooing is prevalent among women folk. Girls above 5 years are found with tattoo mark on their faces and hands. Festival Celebration Numbers of deities are worshiped by the tribes for their happy life. Many festivals are also celebrated with much of enthusiasm and excitement. The ceremony rituals are observed through out the year in order to appease their deities and ascendant. The most significant festival of the year are the chaita parab and push parab- this day all able men of the village go on a hunting expedition. The tribes with their cultural dance, song and music all distinguish custom of their artistic life, which demarcate them from the other non tribal groups.

Orissa acquire every thing Orissa is a state, embellished with hilly terrain of the Eastern Ghats, where primitive tribes dwell and a beautiful stretch of the Indo-Aryans coast where modern life persists. A blend of 2 discrete civilization with contrast cultures, beautiful landscapes, beaches, rich wildlife, offers the best of India to its visitors. As the issue of globalization takes place to this modern time, the challenge of preserving the few remaining cultural community around the world is becoming hard. In a tribal based community, reaching economic advancement with minimal negative impacts is an essential objective to any destination planner. Since they are using the culture of the region as the main attraction, sustainable destination development of the area is vital for them to prevent the negative impacts because of tourism.

MANAGEMENT ISSUES

Certainly, the principle of "one size fits all" doesn't apply to destination planning. The needs, expectations, and anticipated benefits from tourism vary greatly from one destination to another. This is clearly exemplified as local communities living in regions with tourism potential develop a vision for what kind of tourism they want to facilitate, depending on issues and concerns they want to be settled or satisfied.

DESTINATION PLANNING RESOURCES

Culture: The Heart of Development Policy

It is important that the destination planner takes into account the diverse definition of culture as the term is subjective. Satisfying tourists' interests such as landscapes, seascapes, art, nature, traditions, ways of life and other products associated to them -which may be categorized cultural in the broadest sense of the word, is a prime consideration as it marks the initial phase of the development of a cultural destination.

The quality of service and destination, which doesn't solely depend on the cultural heritage but more importantly to the cultural environment, can further be developed by setting controls and policies which shall govern the community and its stakeholders. It is therefore safe to say that the planner should be on the ball with the varying meaning of culture itself as this fuels the formulation of development policies that shall entail efficient planning and monitored growth.

Local Community, Tourists, the Destination and Sustainable Tourism

While satisfying tourists' interests and demands may be a top priority, it is also imperative to ruminate the subsystems of the destination's. Development pressures should be anticipated and set to their minimum level so as to conserve the area's resources and prevent a saturation of the destination as to not abuse the product and the residents correspondingly. The plan should incorporate the locals to its gain by training and employing them and in the process encourage them to participate to the travel business. Keep in mind that the plan should make travellers not only aware about the destination but also concern on how to help it sustain its character while broadening their travelling experience.

SOURCES OF DATA

The core of a planner's job is to design an appropriate planning process and facilitate community decision. Ample information which is a crucial requirement is contributed through various technical researches and analyses.

Here are some of the helpful tools commonly used by planners to aid them:

- Key Informant Interviews
- Libraries, Internet, and Survey Research
- Census and Statistical Analysis
- Spatial Analysis with Geographical Information System and Global Positioning System technologies

KEY INSTITUTIONS

Participating structures are primarily led by the government's local authorities and the official tourism board or council, with the involvement of various NGOs, community and indigenous representatives, development organizations, and the academe.

Cultural and Ecotourism in the Mountainous Regions of Central Asia and in the Himalayas

Tourism is coming to the previously isolated but

spectacular mountainous regions of Central Asia, the Hindu Kush and the Himalayas. Closed for so many years to visitors from abroad, it now attracts a growing number of foreign tourists by its unique culture and splendid natural beauty. However, while this influx of tourists is bringing economic opportunities and employment to local populations, helping to promote these little-known regions of the world, it has also brought challenges along with it: to ensure that it is well-managed and that its benefits are shared by all. As a response to this concern, the Norwegian Government, as well as the UNESCO, organized an interdisciplinary project called the Development of Cultural and Eco-tourism in the Mountainous Regions of Central Asia and the Himalayas project.

It aims to establish links and promote cooperation between local communities, national and international NGOs, and tour agencies in order to heighten the role of the local community and involve them fully in the employment opportunities and income-generating activities that tourism can bring.

Project activities include training local tour guides, producing high-quality craft items and promoting home-stays and bed-and-breakfast type accommodation. As of now, the project is drawing on the expertise of international NGOs and tourism professionals in the seven participating countries, making a practical and positive contribution to alleviating poverty by helping local communities to draw the maximum benefit from their region's tourism potential, while protecting the environmental and cultural heritage of the region concerned.

ETHNIC TOURISM

Ethnic tourism is related to the more popularly known nature or eco-tourism. In nature tourism, people visit a region, usually in a third world country, in order to enjoy its natural beauty. Nature tourism can also imply social awareness because it "creates an understanding of cultural and natural history, while safeguarding the integrity of the ecosystem and producing economic benefits that encourage conservation".

Ethnic tourism is the addition of an indigenous or traditional group of people who live in this environment and interact and depend upon it. Visitors enjoy both the natural environment and the singular ethnic experience. Because of the ethnic groups' dependence on the environment, it is difficult to separate ethnic tourism from the landscape in which it occurs. Hence, nature and ethnic tourism are often interrelated and inseparable.

From the visitor's point of view, ethnic tourism is "travel motivated by the search for the firsthand, authentic and sometimes intimate contact with people whose ethnic and/or cultural background is different from the tourists". Ethnic tourists are also driven by the desire to see some of the "threatened" cultures which may soon disappear through assimilation into the nation's majority. The visitor's experience usually includes opportunities to see and photograph people in their traditional dress, observe their living conditions, and purchase local handicrafts.

Ethnic and nature tourism can help protect indigenous people and their environments by providing a sustainable alternative to subsistence agriculture and extractive activities such as timber harvesting. The added income and exposure can satisfy national goals of development while contributing to cultural pride and autonomy. Ethnic tourism can also have many negative consequences including commoditization of culture, social tension, and loss of cultural identity. In any case, tourism brings changes as groups gain or lose ownership, access, and use rights, and adjust to a new economic system. The varying controllers of tourism play a major role in the changes and effects wrought by tourism on the resident population.

National parks and similar protected areas are the most recognizable forms of nature and ethnic tourism. These large scale, federally controlled land management systems preserve the land which is often in danger of encroachment and extraction activities. Some national parks are designed to protect the environment and the indigenous group dependent on that environment such as Odzalla National Park in Congo, the Kalahari Reserves in Botswana, Manu Park in Peru, Gates of the Arctic Monument in Alaska, Kluane Park in the Yukon, Kakadu National Park in the Northern Territory in Australia, Varirata National Park in Papua New Guinea, and Honduras Rio Platano Biosphere Reserves. However, federal control of these lands often neglect the needs or input of the parks' residents.

For example, the nomadic Masai who migrate seasonally with their cattle through Amboseli and Serengeti National Parks in Kenya and Tanzania have increasingly come into conflict with park administrators who have placed priority on preserving large tracts of savanna woodlands and wildlife over that of the Masai's traditional sustainable lifestyle. Although most tourists come to see the wildlife, increasing numbers also want to view the Masai. This form of ethnic tourism brings few benefits for the Masai who have hardly any crafts and no control over tourism.

In other parks, like Sagarmatha National Park in Nepal, much of the resident population does benefit from tourism. The Sherpa have supplemented their herding lifestyle with jobs relating to tourism but have little control over tourist access. As the national government promotes Sagarmatha for tourism, the demand for material needs like wood for heat increases. As the environment is degraded due to deforestation, the Sherpa must compete with outsiders for their own resources. Hence, national parks sometimes hurt more than help the local populations who live in and around these protected areas. An alternative to national, people-exclusive projects is a project or approach to tourism that includes the resident population and recognizes the value of traditional techniques that can help manage the environment.

Outside assisted projects vary from obvious governmental or organizational influence and control to projects promoted as "grassroots" or "bottom-up" but which include outside influence in planning and implementation. "Local participation at all stages" is a phrase included in most project documents but not always strictly followed. Outside assistance can provide ideas and needed capital but can also produce many problems. One example is the Toraja of southern Sulawesi in Indonesia who receive federal assistance in planning, promotion, and infrastructure.

Although the Toraja have some control and earn most of the benefits, government interference has designated some areas over others as tourist destinations, so that competition and animosity between formerly cooperative communities has begun. Less obvious outside interference from the national majority has caused social problems among the Ladakhi of Northern India. Most tourism benefits go to the small percentage of hotel owners and to outside tour operators.

To help remedy this situation, the Swedish-backed Ledeg foundation has helped the Ladakhi develop souvenirs and promote native dancing which builds on their traditional background. It remains to be seen if Ledeg's involvement helps distribute benefits more uniformly or just allows another minority to profit over others. Outside involvement is not always apparent.

The Kuna of Panama have developed a rainforest reserve with the administrative and monetary help of multinational organizations including the Inter-American Foundation and the World Wildlife Fund. The Kuna benefit from selling their colourful weavings but have seen a decline in tourist visitation since the implementation of their project because it severed cooperative relations with individuals and groups who formerly helped to advertise, transport, and provide lodging for the visitors. One alternative to outside assistance is no assistance. This allows an approach to tourism to evolve from the existing social order and within the limits of the natural environment and culture. Of course, economic unfairness and social disruption can still occur. Indigenous-developed tourism has some clear advantages.

Tourism on Taquile island on Lake Titicaca is one example of indigenous-controlled tourism. In order to develop a tourist infrastructure, the Quechua-speaking residents of Taquile pooled together their money and energy. They bought a boat motor to speed tourist transport to the island and take turns lodging the guests. Without the influence or investment of outside groups or the government, the residents of Taquile have fostered tourism without many of the problems of outside-assisted tourism.

In Ecuador, the small community of Capirona near the Napo river wanted to avoid becoming a "tourist zoo" like many of the neighbouring villages. By designing and running their own tours and constructing a thatch guest hut as a community, Capirona residents have more control over tourist access and accommodation as well as the distribution of the resultant benefits. While there is cooperation with outside groups, the tourism project or approach is a community desire and not one imposed from the outside.

All of the examples, fit into three main categories of nature and ethnic tourism: national projects which generally exclude the resident population, smaller-scale projects that are implemented and/or assisted by outside groups, and approaches initiated by the indigenous people without outside assistance. Large national projects such as national parks and reserves are important to recognize as options. National parks in Mexico are nearly nonexistent; green dots connoting parks on tourist maps have more to do with politics than tangible reality.

4

Tourism and Economy

TOURISM: AN INDUSTRY

Tourism industry is the one that deals with the tourists as consumers, the money spent by them, and the resources rendering various goods and services which facilitate the composition of the tourism product. This industry has been named as a 'smokeless industry' because unlike other industries it is invisible and non-polluting. The tourism industry is an extraordinarily complex integration of many industries spread over many sectors.

Tourism is an umbrella industry containing a set of inter-related business participants. For example, industries like Transport, Accommodation, and Travel Companies, Recreation and Entertainment Institutions, Handicrafts business, etc and the provision of the many goods and services demanded by tourists. Interestingly, most of the component industries also get related to varied commercial and non-commercial activities over and above providing their services to the tourists.

Over the years, there has been a growing awareness of tourism as a human activity, an industry, and a catalyst for economic growth and development. Like any other industry the tourism industry draws resources from the economy, adds value and produces marketable products. The only difference here is that no tangible product is produced like in the case of a manufacturing industry. The product in this case is intangible and joint or composite in nature. The tourism industry impacts various auxiliary and ancillary industries as well. Tourism today is undergoing a rapid transformation towards a new industry having far-reaching implications for organizations in the travel and tourism industry in particular, and consequences of import for developing and developed countries in general, growing increasingly dependent on the tourist dollar. The forces driving the change in this industry are many.

In olden times people travelled mainly for commercial and religious reasons and leisure travel was for the rich. Today people travel for a variety of motivations, including business, leisure, religion, culture, visiting friends and relatives, education and health. The means of transportation have become varied and faster and as the transport becomes faster, new travellers emerge and people travel greater distances. Another important force driving the growth within the industry is the growth and expansion of the middle class and an increase in their disposable income. The travel industry is complex in nature and challenging to manage. This is for three main reasons- their process type, cost structure and market features.

In terms of process, most operations are a combination of customer processing operations, material processing operations and information processing operations. There is a mix of cost structures based around provision of service, food, accommodation, sightseeing, airfare etc. Forecasting and packaging are some key market features. Originally segmentation in the industry was based on social class however, currently many factors influence segmentation in the industry.

Now there are products that are specially marketed to specific groups of people or market segments based on lifestyle. Due to segmentation more choice is created for consumers and branding has emerged, major companies are developing brands that are easily recognizable, for example, Thomas Cook holidays, Star Cruises, etc. Tourists are now a sophisticated lot. They are demanding and constantly looking for new variations in the products and newer destinations. In addition, there is growing environmental awareness and travellers are increasingly prepared to shun over-commercialized and polluted destinations for newer and less popular ones. Parallel to all these changes in the market place, there is deregulation of the airline industry, an explosion of technology both for automated reservations and for travel management, and an increasing trend towards concentration of the industry reflected by the large numbers of mergers, takeovers and acquisition of the industry from 'old' to 'new' tourism.

New tourism is a transition from the existing to the tourism of the future typified by:

- Enhanced tourism experiences
- Flexible tourist products
- Management of the tourist industry
- Segmentation
- Thrust towards diagonally integrated organizations and

There are clear and apparent manifestations that the tourist industry is beginning to take on newer dimensions. The emerging new practice is the creation of a number of factors including the system of new information technologies in the tourism industry, deregulation of the airline industry, environmental pressures; technology compensation; changing consumer tastes, leisure time, work patterns and income distribution.

The economics of new tourism is quite different from the old. From system gains, segmented markets, designed and customised holidays the focus now is also on, profitability and competitiveness in tourism. The new tourists show greater care and have a concern for conservation of the natural environment. There has been a shift towards eco tourism, green tourism, rural tourism, farm tourism, sustainable tourism, etc. with perpetual opportunities of benefit from this new tourism. Competitive Strategies for success have to be employed today for survival.

There are new techniques and trends to be followed by the industry players. To gain competitive advantage, the players and participants of the industry will have to

- Be customer friendly,
- Be quality conscious,
- Innovate new and better products,
- Make meaningful value additions.

And for tourist destinations to be competitive, certain key principles need to be incorporated into the policy framework.

Some of these are:

- Be environmentally sensitive,
- Encourage private sector participation,
- Make tourism a leading sector,
- Strengthen the distribution channels in the market place.

Today tourism is sensitive to the environment as well as inhabitants of the region or area, tourism is sustainable, and tourism is capable of transforming tourism-dependent and vulnerable areas' economies into viable entities. Tourism is in a stage of revolutionary change and a new kind of tourism is emerging fast. New tourism promises flexibility, segmentation and diagonal integration. It is driven by information technologies and changing consumer requirements. Today this industry can produce an entire system of value addition and wealth generation.

The objective today is 'tourism should be planned in a manner that it benefits the community as a whole, has benefits for the locals, and optimizes the expectations of the tourists besides taking care of the environment.'

TOURISM IS A GROWTH INDUSTRY

In the 21st century the global economy will be driven by three major service industries–Technology, Telecommunications and Tourism. Travel and tourism will be one of the world's highest growth sectors in the current century. Tourism, just as to experts is expected to capture the global market and become the largest industry in the world. The statistics and projections point to an era of unprecedented growth of tourism around the world. From 70 million international tourist arrivals in the year 1960 the WTO has estimated that international tourism arrivals worldwide would be 1.5 billion by the year 2020. The latest report from the World Travel and Tourism Council "in the year 1999 Travel and Tourism generated about 3.5 trillion US dollars of GDP and almost 200 million jobs across the world economy: approximately.

World travel and tourism GDP is forecast to increase in real terms at 3% per annum in the decade 2000-2010. During the same period employment in travel and tourism is expected to grow at about 2.6% per annum."

World Travel and Tourism Council has summarized some of the highlights concerning worldwide travel and tourism industry as follows:

- The Travel and Tourism Industry contributed 11.7% towards world GDP in 1999;
- Travel and Tourism has emerged strongly from the South- Asian crisis with leisure tourism rising by 4.7% in 1999 and business travel by 4.4%;
- Tourism related spending by international visitors amount to 8% of world exports in 1999 with a further impact by export of Travel and Tourism related goods;
- Travel and Tourism related GDP is forecast to increase at 3% per annum in real terms;
- In the coming years, over 8% of all jobs worldwide will depend upon Travel and Tourism;
- Travel and Tourism will support the creation of over 5.5 million jobs per year over the next decade.

Thus, tourism today is a shining sector and a great economic force. Its status as a major economic activity has been recognized by almost all the nations of the world. During the 1960s there was emphasis on tourism as an earner of foreign exchange, a catalyst of development, and a security against the uncertain fluctuations of commodity prices. Today however, its impact is not only economic but social and cultural as well.

Cultural tourism is a fertile ground for exercising creative talents, fostering special kinds of relations between visitor and the host populations. It enables the tourist to form a view of his present world and a global concept of the historic past.

Thus, tourism has wider implications encompassing not only economic benefits but also social and cultural benefits as well.

TOURISM AND DEVELOPMENT

Development can be viewed from various dimensions, however, for the purpose of this current session, we use the following definition of economic development: Economic development is a process of economic transition that involves the structural transformation of an economy and a growth of the real output of an economy over a period of time. It is a long run concept. Structural transformation is achieved through modernization and industrialization and is measured in terms of the relative contribution to gross domestic product of agriculture, industry and service sectors. The potential of tourism to contribute to development is widely recognized in the industrialized countries, with tourism playing an increasingly important role and receiving government support. Tourism along with some other activities like financial services and tele-communications is a major component of economic strategies. Tourism has become a favoured means of addressing the socio- economic problems facing rural areas on one end, while enhancing development of urban areas on the other.

TOURISM AND NATIONAL DEVELOPMENT

Tourism emerged as a global phenomenon in the 1960s and the potential for tourism to generate economic development was widely promoted by national governments. They appreciated that tourism generated foreign exchange earnings, created employment and brought economic benefits to regions with limited options for alternative economic development. National tourism authorities were created to promote tourism and to maximize international arrivals. However, an awareness of the negative environmental, social and some other impacts also increased. The importance of economic benefits at the local level, environmental and social sustainability was also widely accepted. It was observed that tourism presents excellent opportunities for developing entrepreneurship, for staff training and progression and for the development of transferable skills. Tourism development focuses on national and regional master planning. It also focuses on international promotion, attracting inward investment. The primary concern has been with maximizing foreign exchange earnings. These earnings enable the government to finance debt and also to finance some investment in technology and other imports for economic development.

NO TRADE BARRIERS TO TOURISM

Unlike many other forms of international trade, tourism does not suffer from the imposition of trade barriers, such as quotas or tariffs. Mostly, destination countries have free and equal access to the international tourism market. This position has become strengthened by the inclusion of tourism in the General Agreement on Trade in Services, which became operational in January 1995.

REDISTRIBUTION OF WEALTH

Both internationally and domestically, tourism is seen as an effective means of transferring income, wealth and investment from richer, developed countries or regions to less developed, poorer areas. This redistribution occurs as a result of both tourist expenditures in destination areas and also of investment by the richer, tourist generating countries in tourist facilities. Thus it appears as if, the developed countries support the economic growth and development of less developed countries.

TOURISM AND POVERTY REDUCTION

Tourism can contribute to development and the reduction of poverty in a number of ways. Economic benefits are generally the most important element, but there can be social, environmental and cultural benefits and costs as well. Tourism contributes to poverty reduction by providing employment and various livelihood opportunities. This additional income helps the poor by increasing the range of economic opportunities available to them. Tourism also contributes to poverty alleviation through direct taxation of tourism generated income. Taxes can be used to alleviate poverty through education, health and infrastructure development. Some tourism facilities also improve the recreational and leisure opportunities available for the poor themselves at the local level. Tourism is not very different from other productive sectors but it has four potential advantages for pro-poor economic growth:

- It has higher linkage with other local businesses because customers come to the destination;
- It is relatively labour intensive and employs a large proportion of women workers;
- It has high potential in poor countries and areas with few other competitive exports;
- Tourism products can be built on natural resources and culture, which might sometimes be the only assets that people have.

The contribution of tourism to the local economy is also important to note. It has five kinds of positive economic impacts on livelihood, any or all of which can form part of a poverty reduction strategy:

- Collective income which may include profits from a community run enterprise, land rent, dividends from joint ventures. These incomes can provide significant development capital and provide finance for corngrinding mills, a clinic, teachers housing and school books
- Dividends and profits arising from locally owned firms and business units
- Earnings from selling goods and service or casual labour
- Infrastructure gains, for example, roads, water pipes, electricity and communications.
- Wages from formal employment

At this point it must also be mentioned that there are some disadvantages of tourism as well. For example, leakages and volatility of revenue. These are also common to other economic sectors. However, tourism may involve greater trade-offs with local livelihoods through more competition for natural resources, particularly in coastal areas.

STRATEGY FOR DEVELOPING COUNTRIES

Tourism plays a very important role in the economies of many countries. Earnings from tourism-related activities contribute a considerable portion to their GDPs. Tourism is now being viewed as a significant tool and an important strategy in achieving economic growth in these countries. The WTO is convinced that tourism has considerable potential for growth in many developing countries and Less Developed Countries where it is a significant economic sector and promising high growth rate; and that it has advantages when compared with other economic sectors. This case can be summarized as follows: Comparative Advantages of Tourism as a Development Strategy for Developing Countries.

- Access to international markets is a serious problem for developing countries particularly in traditional sectors like food, agriculture and textiles where they confront tariff and non-tariff barriers. This is not the case for the tourism sector, where barriers would involve visa restrictions and related taxes only. The example of Cuba is instructive in this regard. Whilst Cuba has struggled to find export markets for its sugar and tobacco, it has been much more successful in maintaining a dynamic tourism industry.
- In many developing countries, for example South Africa, China, Philippines and India, domestic tourism is growing rapidly and like international tourism brings relatively wealthy consumers to areas where they constitute an important local market. Domestic tourism can be accessed by people with lower budgets and is often equally valuable to the economy.
- Most export industries depend on financial, productive and human capital. The tourism industry not only depends on these, but also on natural capital

and culture, which are sometimes the only assets owned by the poor.

- Tourism has particular potential in many countries with few other competitive exports.
- Tourism is a much more diverse industry than many others and can build upon a wide resource base. This diversity results in wider participation of the informal sector, for example a farming household produces and sells local handicrafts.
- Tourism is consumed at the point of production. This results in great opportunities for individuals and micro-enterprises, in urban or marginal rural areas, to sell additional products or services to the potential consumers.
- Tourism is often reported to be more labour intensive than other productive sectors. Data from six countries with satellite tourism accounts does indicate that it is more labour intensive than nonagricultural activities, particularly manufacturing, although less labour intensive than agriculture.
- Tourism provides various employment opportunities especially to women as compared to some of the other sectors.

Perceived Disadvantages of Tourism as a Development Strategy:

- Foreign private interests drive tourism and it is difficult to maximize local economic benefits due to the high level of foreign ownership, which means that there are high levels of leakages and few local linkages. But that might not be the case many times.
- Many small enterprises and individual traders sustain themselves around hotels and other tourism facilities and these small companies are not foreign owned. There is often confusion about levels of foreign ownership as local ownership is often masked by franchise agreements and management contracts. WTO is studying this issue in collaboration with UNCTAD as part of its poverty elimination research.
- Tourism can impose substantial non-economic costs

on the poor. For example, loss of access to resources, displacement from agricultural land, social and cultural disruption and exploitation.

- Many forms of development bring with them disadvantages that need to be managed. The economic and non-economic negative impact needs to be determined and the issues addressed. It is for this reason that the WTO supports a holistic livelihood approach to assessing the impact of tourism-positive and negative–on the poor. Issues like environmental management and planning at local level need to be addressed through the good governance agenda.
- Tourism is a vulnerable industry. It reacts immediately to factors like changes in economic conditions in the originating markets, levels of economic activity in tourism in the destination markets. Thereby affecting international visitor arrivals. It is also very vulnerable to civil unrest, crime, political instability and natural disasters in destination countries.
- It has been observed that the volatility of export markets for tourism is not significantly greater than other commodities. Many times tourism has the advantage noted that it is not subject to tariff or other non-tariff barriers and that the destination has some control over civil unrest, crime and political instability
- Tourism requires highly sophisticated marketing. International tourism marketing is expensive, although there are more efficient and less costly forms of marketing available today. Many government agencies at the national level, tie ups of domestic hotels and resorts with international participants, word of mouth publicity, target marketing are some of the methods used.

Tourism in many developing countries and many LDCs has been growing strongly in recent years and there are strong reasons to think that these trends will continue. Many developing countries have comparative advantages in tourism where tourism constitutes one of their better opportunities for development. The disadvantages, which are often identified in relation to international tourism in developing countries, are few when tourism is compared with other sectors of the economy. WTO believes that tourism is considered alongside other industries as a development option and that where tourism presents the best opportunity for local economic development and antipoverty strategies, development banks, bilateral and multilateral development agencies should back it with determination.

LINKAGES AND LEAKAGES

The term leakage in used to refer to the amount spent on importing goods and services to meet the needs of tourists. Leakages take place across national boundaries that can have impact on the balance of payments of the countries. It results from the economic exchange between the two countries. It also occurs when the local economy is unable to provide reliable, continuous, supplies on the basis of competitive prices of the required product or service and of a consistent quality to meet the market demand.

From a tourism and poverty perspective it is generally more productive to focus on the other side of the coin-linkages. When the local economic linkages are weak, the revenue received from tourism in the local economic area leaks out. In order to reduce such leakages, it becomes necessary to deliver consistently at an appropriate quality and at competitive prices, at the same time, engaging the local suppliers who use local capital and resources.

LEAKAGES

From the perspectives of local economic development and poverty reduction, we are not concerned how much a tourist spends outside the country, but how much he is not spending in the local economy, which means, limiting the benefit to local communities and the poor among them.

Leakages, which have negative impact on the development of local tourism, are:

- Advertising and marketing efforts abroad
- Impact skills, expatriate labour
- Imported commodities, goods and services
- Imported technology and capital goods
- Increased oil imports
- Repatriation of profits
- Transporting tourists to the destination country

However developing local sources of supply, encouraging local ownership and enhancing linkages to the local economy can improve this. The last two of these can create more jobs and opportunities for small and medium enterprises at the same time.

LINKAGES

There are many ways in which local communities can be benefitted by these propositions. The best way is to increase the extent of linkages between formal tourism sector and the local economy. By formal tourism sector we mean hotels, restaurants, lodges, and tour and transport agencies. To the extent linkages to the local economy can be increased, the extent of leakages will be reduced.

The increased integration can further develop strong linkages between tourism and other economic sectors. Not only do agriculture, fisheries, manufacturing, construction and domestic industries get integrated, the auxiliary and ancillary industries are also strengthened.

This in turn provides additional revenue and jobs, which reduces the import content and foreign exchange leakages from the tourism industry. Government and development agencies should create local linkages as part of their overall tourism development strategy in the planning, construction and operational phases.

There are three sets of factors, which are important in enhancing the extent of local linkages:

- The creation of employment at all skill levels and particularly where there is existing capacity.

- The Anti-poverty tourism development strategies have suggested 'new attractions'. The tour operators at the ground level should integrate these. The critical areas include creating mutually beneficial business linkages between the formal and informal sectors. Small and emerging entrepreneurs are often neglected. Local government should ensure that microenterprises and emerging entrepreneurs are promoted while taking local tourism marketing initiatives. Visitor attractions, parks, cultural sites and hotels should be encouraged to provide information about local products and services provided by the poor.
- There is need to understand tourist expectations thoroughly. Also, small enterprises to meet the credit needs and marketing needs are also required. Small enterprises sometimes face difficulties in meeting the requirements of health and safety, licensing and other regulatory requirements. There is a need to systematically educate and train the poor in such a way that they are able to integrate themselves with the growing requirements relating to regulations.

The local market should be geared up to deliver qualitatively reliable and competitive goods and services to tourists. The local business community should be actively involved in the process through partnership approaches. This requires continuous efforts, which is possible through long-term partnership to benefit from linkages. Once planning commission concessions are being granted, private sector companies can be asked to make the development of such linkages part of their bid.

Tourism can help in diversifying other sectors of the local economy and can create new ones, offering additional community livelihood opportunities. Local economic benefits and ownership are likely to be greater, if local communities participate in diversified business activities. Now with the growing awareness governments are adopting policies, to encourage and facilitate participation by the local communities. The participation by the poor in the development of tourism projects may result in increasing employment and growth of complementary products. These benefits can further be maximized through partnerships at the destination level. There is a tremendous possibility of bringing about sustainable development for the local economy if Hotels and tour operators work together with local communities, local government and NGOs.

This can help in reducing poverty and can provide a richer experience to domestic and international tourists. Such partnerships will benefit both the host communities and the tourism industry. This will also help them earn more tourism dollars, euros or pounds without any leakages. This can further be utilized for community development. Through affirmative policies, enterprises can contribute significantly to economic development, in both their constructional and operational phases. Some practical strategies for developing local economic linkages.

Market Access and Enclave Tourism

There is practically no link between local people and tourism market. Tourists are not accessible to the local community when they are within their hotels, coaches, and safari vehicles or inside sites and attractions such as museums. These are all enclave forms of tourism. The local community people who wish to sell their products to tourists don't have access to them. They end up hawking and touting at entry points.

The problem is still more difficult in case of Cruise ship passengers and tourist on "all inclusive" hotel or resort packages where local entrepreneurs hardly interact with them. Access to the market plays major role in involving entrepreneurs in the tourism industry. This is particularly true in the case of the informal sector; where the return on local skills and services is often maximized and where the scale of capital investments is low. There is a need to keep this aspect in mind at the time of tourism planning, as access to tourists for the informal sector is often neglected. Some tourists prefer all-inclusive packages, as they do not always feel safe in a new destination and are happier in a protected environment. They feel protected from the poverty and hassle from beggars, touts and hawkers in some destinations. But there is a way to solve this problem. This requires partnership approach between Hotel and informal traders.

This allows informal traders to provide such an environment where tourists feel secure in moving beyond the enclave and to approach "hassle-free" crafts markets. Local guides can also help in establishing contact between tourists and traders by rotation for which they may have agreement among themselves.

This also requires observing certain code of conduct by the local traders and guide. There should be a design to link the informal sector with formal sector so that poor members of community can be helped and tourist market becomes accessible to them. This can help them gain the economic benefit from it. There are a number of strategies that can be used to enhance overall economic benefits and can further reduce poverty.

Growth and Selection

Attracting more of the most appropriate market Segments It has been observed that the tourism sector in the poorest countries is generally highly dependent on international markets, as they do not have significant domestic markets. However, it has also been noted earlier that a significant number of developing countries have strong domestic tourism sectors as well as significant outbound tourists. It becomes imperative that the domestic market should always be considered first by the poorest countries, but in order to maximize foreign exchange revenues, the primary focus continues to be on international arrivals.

There is a challenge to attract larger numbers of those international and domestic tourists who are most likely to benefit the poor, those predisposed to visit local markets and to seek first hand experiences of nature, culture and daily life which are most likely to be provided by poor people. It is worth mentioning the importance of intra-regional tourism in this regard; WTO reported intra-regional tourism as growing in most regions of the world. It is significant that 40% of Africa's tourism comes from neighbouring African countries. This opportunity can be grabbed by opening up the roads and improving the modes of transport between countries in Africa, which would greatly enhance the movement of people and contribute in reducing poverty. Intra-regional tourism is especially valuable for pro-poor tourism and local economic development.

This is because of the fact that there is greater likelihood of shared cultural values and familiarity with social systems between the people of neighbouring countries. There is no doubt that there is a case for attracting more visitors in order to increase the economic impact. At the same time we must understand that this strategy will only assist in poverty reduction if the additional tourists can be encouraged to spend in ways that benefit the poor and if it results in overall sustainability.

The World Bank's World Development Report recognized that economic growth does not necessarily result in swift poverty reduction. This requires an explicitly pro-poor strategy. This means that there should be constant growth, which favours poor in a disproportionate way.

Some of the key components of broad-based growth which assist in benefiting the poor include:

- Government commitment and responsiveness to the needs of the poor
- The expansion of employment opportunities for the poor
- Improved productivity for the poor,
- Improved access for the poor to credit, knowledge and infrastructure,
- Investment in the human capital of the poor.

Increasing Tourists' Length of Stay

The economic returns can be increased with the same number of tourist arrivals if efforts can be made to extend their stay for a longer period. This results in the development of the product by increasing the numbers of bed nights and the expenditure of tourists on boarding and lodging.

There will be a poverty reduction impact, if the additional bed nights can create extra employment or create greater opportunities for the poor to sell goods and services to the tourists or to the tourism industry.

Increasing Visitor Expenditure

Now-a-days there is a market trend towards more experiential holidays. Tourists want to learn more about the countries they are visiting: the people, their cultures, traditions, cuisine, etc. It is much more than mere holidaymaking. The trend is towards more active holidays, greater personal involvement and active participation instead of passive relaxation. This again has potential for the diversification and enrichment of the tourism product. There is scope to develop more activities and attractions, with increased demand for interpreters and services of guides and transport necessary for their enjoyment. This increases both expenditure and length of stay. Making more extensive use of natural and cultural heritage, at the same time carefully managing the tourism impacts so as to ensue the conservation of resources, can make an important contribution both to economic development and conservation. This leads to growth in "Special interest tourists" who tend to spend more money on and during their holidays and to stay longer, whether those interests are based on natural, archaeological, historical or cultural heritage, or based on adventure and physical challenge.

Developing Complementary Products

Providing a greater variety and richness of attractions and activities at destination can increase tourists' expenditure. This will increase the propensity of travellers to visit various attractions at the destination and may extend their length of stay and increase their expenditure. This translates into creating more promising opportunities for the development of complementary products that enable the poor to engage in the industry and to profit from it. The growth in established industry results in stimulating interest in the development of complementary products: tourism services and goods.

This complements the core tourism facilities of transport, excursions and accommodation. The list of complementary effects goes on increasing. These complementary tourism products often provide experiences that are not provided by the tour operators but which enrich their product. Hoteliers and tour operators can encourage local people to develop tourism products and services and to support them in doing so with training and marketing. This will increase the attractiveness of the destination and increase tourist expenditure in the local economy and will also develop the complementary products.

Local communities can often engage in the provision of complementary products because it requires less capital investment and is therefore less risky. Tourism is often best considered as an additional diversification option for the poor, rather than a substitute for their core means of livelihood. As an additional source of income it can play an important part in improving living standards and raising people above the poverty threshold. The poor can maximize their returns by choosing forms of participation, which complement their existing livelihood strategies. It also helps them earn from their cultural and social assets.

Tourists are interested in the "everyday lives" of local communities and there are a host of smallenterprise opportunities for local people. Local guides and cyclerickshaw driver/guides in India's Keoladeo National Park, and guides and charter-boat operators in Indonesia's Komodo National Park are examples of local people diversifying their livelihood strategies. The boat operators also earn their living from fishing and many of the cycle-rickshaw drivers work in town when the tourist season is low.

Spreading the Benefits of Tourism Geographically

Tourism destinations are geographically diverse in nature. There are different geographical sites like beaches, mountains and urban attractions and holidaymakers can be encouraged to travel further, beyond established destinations, which can enhance and diversify their experience of particular environmental, cultural or natural heritage attractions. Heritage Trails and other similar products have been developed to extend length of stay and to spread the advantages of tourism development to new areas and communities.

They can be used as initiatives, which may benefit the poor. National Parks, cultural sites and World heritage sites are often the major attractions, the primary "tourism magnets" in significant parts of the developing world and they often attract people to marginal rural areas. It can be argued that natural and cultural heritage sites as the major attractions should be taking a wider view of their potential to contribute to tourism development and the well-being of local communities. These areas otherwise are of no interest to tourists.

Changing the way in which tourism is organized in and around attractions can increase the economic development impact. For example, at Kamodo National Park in Indonesia, non-local carriers and package tour operators take away a big slice of tourism trip expenditure, *i.e.*, about 85%, which could have otherwise gone to local economy. Estimates for average local expenditure at Komodo per visitor demonstrate the importance of minimizing enclave tourism.

Cruise ship tourists spent on average US $0, 03 in the local economy, package tourists spent US $52.5 and independent travellers US $97.4. The Parks and other major tourism attractions in rural areas can be developed to assist the development of small-scale, locally owned attractions and tourism services. Nature-based tourism and cultural heritage tourism in rural areas can provide significant local markets and economic development opportunities. It contributes to integrated rural development and offers local employment and supplementary income-generating opportunities for poor people. The development of tourism in such areas can significantly improve incomes for local communities and the poor. For this these flagship attractions can be planned and managed so as to maximize the opportunities for local economic development and poverty reduction.

Infrastructure and Planning Gain

The development of infrastructure and tourism development are interrelated. Tourism can contribute to overall socio-economic development through the provision of roads, telephones, and electricity, piped and treated water supplies, waste disposal and recycling and sewage treatment. Roads developed for tourism provide opportunities for trade and new roads opened to improve trade also bring tourism opportunities if they open access to tourism resources. New economic corridor development projects often create tourism development opportunities for local communities in addition to improving trade linkages.

These facilities enhance opportunities for other forms of local economic development, but more could be done at the local and national level to maximize those benefits, particularly when new projects are licensed. It is possible to maximize the planning gains through appropriate policies by government and tourism planners. The right policy in the right direction will encourage local economic development and benefit the poor.

Local Management of Tourism and Partnerships

Local communities and the poor amongst them are more likely to benefit from planning gain where they are involved in discussions and decisions about tourism developments. Benefits can be maximized where the complementarities between different forms of tourism development and their livelihood strategies are given due consideration. Appropriate planning structures can facilitate effective community participation in the tourism development process and provide a mechanism for capturing planning gain through infrastructure, employment and economic linkages. A planning process should define carrying capacity and set limits of acceptable change.

This will influence local communities' active participation in tourism development and help in achieving anti-poverty goals. It is through participation by these local community people whose traditional and local knowledge can be utilized for empowering them. This will also help in maintaining the environmental, social and cultural integrity of destinations.

Small and Medium Enterprises Development

The increased interest in local tourism experience results in increased opportunities for the development of new locally owned enterprises. This helps in providing competitive and complementary goods and services. This trend is found in developed country destinations. This can be supported by government policy and SME development strategies. The tourism industry offers viable opportunities for the development of a wide range of SME's. Even in the developed countries they contribute to the largest part of local tourism supply.

In Europe small and medium-sized firms meet 70% of tourist accommodation demand. Some estimates for the developing world put the comparable figure as high as 85% In well-established developing country destinations, like Goa, increasing numbers of international tourists are staying in locally owned accommodation. SME's are very important in the provision of restaurants and bars, handicrafts, the supply of furnishings and other consumables to hotels, the provision of transport, local tour operating, guiding and attractions. All this requires access to capital resources and training in business management for SME's. This requirement is critical in the field of marketing. Providing information, advice and mentoring to small and micro enterprises and emerging entrepreneurs can make a significant contribution to their success.

Reducing Seasonality

Seasonality in tourist arrivals is the major cause of seasonal and casual unemployment. There are a number of strategies that can be employed to extend the tourism season. During festivals arranging melas generates curiosity and helps the development of special interest products. Other strategies include developing places for seminars and conventions, and such pricing policies, which specially address senior citizens who have more flexibility to travel in the low season.

These strategies have an overall impact on the local economy. Strategies that reduce seasonality and successfully attract tourists in significant numbers for a larger part of the year, benefit the hotels and tour operators, their employees and those in the destination who earn all or part of their livelihood by direct or indirect sales to tourists or the tourism industry. Those who benefit from this are most often poor.

EMPLOYMENT LINKAGES

The employment impact of tourism is felt by both direct employment in tourism enterprises and indirect employment in those enterprises and micro-enterprises that supply raw material, goods and services to the tourism industry. The demand of direct employment in tourism is dependent upon the scale and level of tourism development and the extent of tourists' engagement in the local economy and with SME's. This helps in maximizing the employment of locals and nationals in tourism, including managerial grades.

Income is also held within the local and national economies and reduces wage and salary leakages. When wages and salaries are remitted or spent outside the local boundaries, it amounts to leakages from the local economy. However, the success of the tourism enterprise will depend upon the delivery of the appropriate level of service, and in this global industry maintaining high levels of training is an important consideration in the economic sustainability of businesses. One of the ways in which the industry can contribute to poverty reduction is by committing to recruit more local poor people and imparting appropriate training and staff development programmes with the belief that those commitments can be met. Tourism can contribute to poverty alleviation through the creation of employment. Certain changes in existing employment practices can bring desirable developments. Pro-poor employment strategies can be pursued, for example prioritizing the employment of women and youth. Tourism is a relatively labour intensive industry providing direct employment in hotels and tour companies, and indirect employment in taxis, bars, restaurants and other indirect service suppliers, where a proportion of employee time serves the tourism industry and tourists.

Tourism can create jobs, which benefit the poor where specific measures are taken to recruit and train workers from amongst the poor. Where tourism enterprises make these efforts, proper estimates should be made; records should be maintained of its effects on employment to determine to what extent local people, and particularly the poor, benefit and to ensure that their efforts are acknowledged. Beyond the hotels, particular efforts should be made to train and employ local guides, artists, performers and craft workers who are able to interpret their heritage and in the process empower youth and women who have considerable control over it. Entrepreneurship development programmes for tourism SME's do complement these efforts.

These programmes typically include developing business opportunity awareness, business planning including project feasibility analysis and training in management skills. Provision of business advisors and mentoring services may be strengthened for emerging entrepreneurs over several years. Many countries already have small business development and credit programmes and tourism SME development can sometimes be attached to these existing programmes.

MOVING BEYOND "TRICKLEDOWN" EFFECT

It has long been established that tourism development projects, if successful, would attract foreign investment, contribute foreign exchange earnings to the national accounts and generate economic development. Through the process of trickledown, the magnitude of benefits would be amplified. Local communities would benefit through employment and local economic development generated by the additional spending and the new entrepreneurial opportunities which this would create. It must be understood that tourism operations need to be profitable in a competitive world market if they are to survive. There are a number of things, which can benefit the local economy in tourist destinations.

The benefits can arise in the following ways:

- Building and complementing existing livelihood strategies through employment and small enterprise development
- Controlling negative social impacts
- Ensuring the maintenance of natural and cultural assets
- Evaluating tourism projects for their contribution to local economic development not just for their national revenue generation and the increase in international arrivals
- Facilitating local community access to the tourism market
- Maximizing the linkages into the local economy and minimizing leakages

ECONOMIC IMPACT OF TOURISM

EARNER OF FOREIGN EXCHANGE

Tourism has major economic significance for a country. The receipts from international tourism are a valuable source of earning for all countries, particularly, the developing. Visitor-spending generates income for both public and private sectors, besides affecting wages and employment opportunities.

Although tourism is sensitive to the level of economic activity in the tourist-generating countries, it provides more fixed earnings than primary products. The income from tourism has increased at a higher rate than primary products. The income from tourism has tended to increase at a higher rate than merchandise export in a number of countries especially in countries having a low industrial base. Now there is practically an assured channel for financial flows from the developed countries to the developing countries raising the latter's export earnings and rate of economic growth. Tourism, therefore, provides a very important source of income for a number of countries, both developed and developing. The figures from World Tourism Organization indicate that, among the world's top 40 tourism earners about 18 were developing countries including India, in the year 1995. Regarding the number of visitor arrivals, in some countries there were more visitor arrivals than the population.

France with a population of 57 million received 74.5 million visitors in the year 2000. Similarly Spain with a population of 37 million received 48.5 million visitors during the same year. Several island countries, like the Caribbean Islands, depend greatly on tourist income resulting from visitor arrivals. These earnings form a major part of the gross domestic product. Even developed countries like Canada which derived over 13 per cent of its gross domestic product from international visitors in the year 1999, rely heavily on income from tourism.

Tourism forms a very important source of foreign exchange, for several countries. Although the quantum contributed in foreign currency per visitor varies from destination to destination, the importance of receipts from tourism in the balance of payment accounts and of tourist activities in the national revenue has become considerable for a number of countries. The major economic benefit in promoting the tourism industry is in the form of earning foreign exchange.

Income from these foreign-exchange earnings adds to the national income and, as an invisible export, may offset a loss of the visible trading account and be of critical importance in the overall financial reckoning. This is truer in the case of developing countries particularly the small countries, which depend heavily upon primary products such as a few basic cash crops where tourism often offers a more reliable form of income. In the case of some European countries, namely Spain, Portugal, Austria, France and Greece, the invisible earnings from tourism are of a major significance and have a very strong positive effect on the balance of payments. Tourism is therefore a very useful means of earning the much-needed foreign currency.

It is almost without a rival as an earning source for many developed as well as developing countries. These earnings assume a great significance in the balance of payment position of many countries. The balance of payments shows the relationship between a country's total payments to all other countries and its total receipts from them. In other words, it may be defined as a statement of income and expenditure on international account.

Payments and receipts on international account are of three kinds:

- The visible balance of trade relating to the import and export of goods
- Invisible items
- Capital transfers.

The receipts from foreign tourism form an 'invisible export', just like other invisibles which come from transportation and shipping, banking and insurance, income on investments, etc. Because most countries at times have serious problems with their international payments, much attention comes to be focused on tourism because of its potentially important contribution to, and also effect upon, the balance of payments. The receipts from international tourism, however, are not always net. Sometimes expenditures are involved which must be set against them.

Net foreign exchange receipts from tourism are reduced principally by the import cost of goods and services used by visitors, foreign exchange costs of capital investment in tourist amenities and promotion and publicity expenditure abroad. Peters, "Certain imports associated with tourist expenditures must be deduced... the importation of material and equipment for constructing hotels and other amenities, and necessary supplies to run them; foreign currency costs of imports for consumption by international tourists; remittances of interests and profits on overseas investment in tourism enterprises, mainly hotel construction; foreign currency costs of conducting a tourism development programme, including marketing expenditure overseas". Reliance on imports to meet the tourist's needs does not, in any way deny developing countries the opportunity of earning foreign exchange in supplying such goods and services. Imports are, to a large extent, essential to the operation of the tourist sector as to that of other sectors. The important question is whether the value added domestically on an item or service in is maximized? Maximization of import substitution without due regard to the effect on overall tourism receipts may be counter-productive.

Also, differences in the pattern and level of reliance on imported goods and services, capital equipment and manpower are very wide, depending upon the level of development of a country. In some cases, this reliance is simply due to a lack of resources that transform into items which are to be sold by the industry. In others, the industry has not yet drawn on such supply potential, for which it may be an important stimulus. There is a general need for careful programmes of positive import substitution.

MULTIPLIER EFFECT

The discussion in earlier paragraphs clearly indicates that earnings from tourism occupy an important place in the national income of any country. Without taking into account receipts from domestic tourism, international tourism receipts alone contribute to a great extent. The flow of money generated by tourist spending multiplies as it passes through various parts of the economy.

In addition to an important source of income, tourism provides a number of other economic benefits, which vary in importance from one country to another; depending upon the nature and scale of tourism. The benefits from infrastructure investments, justified primarily for tourism such as airports, roads, water supply and other public utilities, may be widely shared by the other sectors of the economy. This enables us to understand how tourism impacts development in the economy. Tourist facilities such as hotels, restaurants, museums, clubs, sports complexes, public transport, and national parks are also used by domestic tourists and visitors, businessmen and residents, but still a significant portion of the costs are sometimes borne by international tourists. Tourists also contribute to tax revenue both directly through sales tax and indirectly through property, profits and income taxes.

Tourism provides employment, develops infrastructural facilities and may also help regional development. Each of these economic aspects can be dealt with separately, but they are all closely related and are many times considered together. Let us first look at the income aspect of tourism. Income from tourism cannot be easily measured with accuracy and precision. This is because of the multiplier effect. The flow of money generated by tourist spending multiplies as it passes through various parts of the economy through the operation of the multiplier effect. The multiplier is an income concept. The Concept: The 'multiplier' measures the impact of extra expenditure introduced into an economy by a person. It is, therefore, concerned with the marginal rather than average changes.

In the case of tourism, this extra expenditure in a particular area can take the following forms:

- Spending on goods and services by tourists visiting the areas
- Investment of external sources in tourism infrastructure or services;
- Government spending
- Exports of goods stimulated by tourism

The expenditure can be analysed as follows:

- *Direct Expenditure*: In the case of tourism, this expenditure is made by tourists on goods and services in hotels and other supplementary accommodation units, restaurants, other tourist facilities like buses, taxis coaches, railways, domestic airlines, and for tourism-generated exports, or by tourism related investment in the area.
- *Indirect Expenditure*: This covers a sum total of inter-business transactions which result from the direct

expenditure, such as purchase of goods by hoteliers from local suppliers and purchases by local suppliers from wholesalers.

- *Included Expenditure*: This is the increased consumer spending resulting from the additional personal income generated by the direct expenditure, *e.g.*, hotel workers using their wages for the purchase of goods and services. Indirect and induced expenditure together are called secondary expenditure.

There are several different concepts of the multiplier. Most multipliers in common use incorporate the general principle of the Keynesian model.

The four types of multipliers are intrinsically linked as follows:

- *Sales Multiplier*: This measures the extra business turnover created by an extra unit of tourist expenditure. Output Multiplier: This is similar to the sales multiplier but it also takes into account inventory changes, such as the increase in stock levels by hotels, restaurants and shops because of increased trading activity.
- *Income Multiplier*: This measures the income generated by an extra unit of tourist expenditure. The problem arises over the definition of income. Many researchers define income as disposable income accruing to households within the area, which is available to them to spend. However, although salaries paid to overseas residents are often excluded, a proportion of these salaries may be spent in the local area and should therefore be included.

  Income Multipliers can be expressed in two ways:

  - The ratio method which expresses the direct and indirect incomes generated per unit of direct income;
  - Normal method, which expresses total income generated in the study area per unit increase in final demand created within a particular sector.

Ratio multipliers indicate the internal linkages which exist between various sectors of the economy, but do not relate income generated to extra sales. Hence, on their own, ratio multipliers are valueless as a planning tool. Employment Multiplier:

The employment multiplier can be expressed in one of the two ways:

- As a ratio of the combination of direct and secondary employment generated per additional unit of tourist expenditure;
- Direct employment created by tourism per unit of tourist expenditure. Multipliers can be further categorized by the geographical area which is covered by the research, such as local community, a region within a country or the country as a whole.

The multiplier mechanism has also been applied to tourism and, in particular, to tourist expenditure. The nature of the tourism multiplier and its effect may be described in the example: "The money paid by a tourist in paying his hotel bill will be used by the management of the hotel to provide for the costs which the hotel had incurred in meeting the demands of the visitor, *e.g.*, such goods and services as food, drink, furnishing, laundering, electricity, and entertainment. The recipients, in turn, use the money they have thus received to meet their financial commitments and so on.

Therefore, tourist expenditure not only supports the tourist industry directly but also helps indirectly to support many other industries which supply goods and services to the tourist industry. In this way money spent by tourists is actually used several times and spreads into various sectors of the economy. In sum, the money paid by the tourist, after a long series of transfers over a given period of time, passes through all sectors of the national economy, stimulating each in turn throughout the process".

On each occasion when the money changes hands, it provides 'new' income and these continuing series of exchanges of the money spent by the tourists form what economists term the multiplier effect. The more often the conversion occurs, the greater its beneficial effect on the economy of the recipient country.

However, this transfer of money is not absolute as there are 'leakages' which occur. Such leakages may occur as a result of importing foreign goods, paying interest on foreign investments, etc.

The following are some examples of such leakages:

- Payment for goods and services produced outside, and imported into, the area;
- remittance of incomes outside the area, for example, by foreign workers;
- indirect and direct taxation where the tax proceeds are not re-spent in the area;
- savings out of income received by workers in the area.

Any leakages of these kinds will reduce the stream of expenditure which, in consequence, will limit and reduce the multiplier effect. Income generated by foreign tourist expenditure in countries possessing more advanced economies, which generally are more self-sufficient and less in need of foreign imports which are less self-sufficient and need to support their tourist industries by substantial import. If the developing countries are desirous of gaining maximum economic benefits from tourism, they should strictly control the imported items for tourist consumption and keep foreign investment expenditure at a reasonable level. If the leakages are not controlled then the benefits arising from tourism will be greatly reduced or even cancelled.

The most important leakage would arise from expenditure on import of agricultural products like food and drink. In a primary macro-economic approach to the prospects opened up by tourism establishment in a developing country, it is regarded as advantageous that a good portion of tourist consumption should consist of food products. It is estimated that the major part of these products can be found in those countries, whose economic structure is largely agricultural in character. In this sense tourist consumption, derived from international flow, can offer an assured outlet to a production which is already active within the domestic economy, without raising problems connected with export of such products and could thus be substituted for imported foodstuffs and a significant saving effected thereafter. The host country derives maximum economic benefits from the tourism industry as these savings help in increasing the benefits from the tourism multiplier. This aspect of the question is all the more important as the multiplier effect maintains its efficacy and effectiveness as long as no importation takes place. It follows that if the national economy is to derive the maximum benefit from the impact of international and national tourism, there is an elementary obligation to find all those products needed for tourist consumption. The dynamics of agricultural production in recent years confirms the ability of developing countries to produce the major part of their agricultural products required for tourist consumption without resorting to massive imports. The tourist economy of any country, if it is to remain healthy, must rely upon local agricultural production and this condition seems today to be on its way to realization in most of the developing countries.

Multiplier of Tourism Income

To sum up, Multipliers are a means of estimating how much extra income is produced in an economy as a result of initial spending or after cash is injected. Every time the money changes hands it provides new income and the continuing series of conversion of money spent by the tourists form the multiplier effect. The more often the conversion occurs, the greater its beneficial effect on the economy of the recipient country.

GROWTH OF INFRASTRUCTURE

A significant benefit of tourism is development and improvement of infrastructure. The benefits from infrastructure investments, justified primarily for tourism–airports, roads, water supply and other public utilities–may be widely shared by the other sectors of the economy. In addition to development of new infrastructure, the improvements in the existing infrastructure which are undertaken in order to attract tourists are also of great importance. These improvements may benefit the resident population by providing them with amenities which they desire. Furthermore, the provision of infrastructure may provide the basis or serve as an encouragement for greater economic diversification. A variety of secondary industries may be promoted which may not directly serve the needs of tourism.

Therefore, it is evident that tourist expenditure is responsible for stimulating other economic activities. One of the characteristics of under development is that of deficiencies in the basic infrastructures, which lie at the root of a series of problems related to the development of tourism. Development of infrastructure requires a certain size of investment. Tourism provides the size of demand which justifies the development of infrastructure. On the basis of this minimum demand for such facilities and for such social capital, the size of such infrastructural services evolves. Construction of primary infrastructures represents the foundation of any future economic growth, even though they are not directly productive. The tourism industry shows the elementary need for basic infrastructure.

It has today the important benefit of being able to profit from the existing infrastructures and thus to make a decisive contribution to the growth of the national economy. The international and national tourist traffic, moreover, represents a reward for the capital invested and can now contribute to the financial efforts required for maintenance. The satisfactory degree of development achieved in this specific sector now permits major tourist progress, while also giving further proof of the complementary character of tourism in relation to other economic sectors. Creation of basic infrastructures for tourist usage will also be of service to the other sectors of the economy such as industry and agriculture. This results in better equilibrium of general economic growth.

TOURISM AND TAXATION

Tourism also results in tax revenues both at national and local levels. Taxes can provide the financial resources for the development of infrastructure, enhancing and maintenance of some types of attractions and other public facilities and services, tourism marketing and training required for developing tourism, as well as to help finance poverty alleviation programmes by governments both at local and national levels.

In addition, tourism-related tax revenues help finance general community improvements and services used by all residents. WTO's 1998 report on tourism taxation emphasizes that taxation policies in a country must be carefully evaluated in an integrated manner to ensure that tourism-related taxes are giving the necessary substantial revenues. However, taxes should not be so high for the country's international competitive position to be counter productive and produce a loss of tourist traffic.

The aim should be to strike a balance between, a level of taxation that maintains a competitive position for the country and reasonable profits for the industry, and, receiving adequate revenues to support investment in and maintenance of the tourism sector, and to contribute towards general community welfare.

BALANCED REGIONAL DEVELOPMENT

Another important domestic effect relates to the regional aspects of tourist expenditure. Such expenditure is of special significance in marginal areas, which are relatively isolated, economically underdeveloped, and have unemployment problems. The United Nations Conference on International Travel and Tourism held in Rome in 1963 stated that tourism was important not only as a source of earning foreign exchange, but also as a factor determining the location of industry and in the development of underdeveloped regions. It further stated that in some cases the development of tourism may be the only means of promoting the economic advancement of less-developed areas lacking in other resources. In fact underdeveloped regions of the country usually greatly benefit from tourism development. Many of the economically backward regions contain areas of high scenic beauty and of cultural attractions. These areas, if developed for use by tourists, can bring in a lot of prosperity to the local people.

Tourism development in these regions accordingly becomes a significant factor in redressing regional imbalances in employment and income. Tourist expenditure at a particular tourist area helps the development of the many areas around it. Many countries both developed as well as developing have realised this aspect of tourism development and are contemplating developing tourist facilities in underdeveloped regions with a view to bringing prosperity there. Khajuraho in India, which is now an internationally famous tourist spot, is an example of one such region.

To show, Khajuraho, a remote and unknown small village about forty years ago, is now on the world tourist map which attracts thousands of tourists, both domestic as well as international. Today, Indian Airlines flies a jet plane between the capital city of New Delhi and Khajuraho and seats are not easy to come by.

Thousands of tourists visit the place by air, rail and road transport every month to see the architectural beauty of temples and erotic sculptures whose creators were the Chandela kings, who ruled in North India from the 9th to the 13th centuries. Today 22 glorious temples remind us of the classic Indian architecture and culture of those times and represent the finest expression of the art of medieval India. The area around Khajuraho is well developed and full of life. The place has provided employment to hundreds of local people in hotels and shops.

There is a thriving clay-model industry devoted to making replicas of the famous temple sculptures and a number of shops dealing with items of presentation, handlooms and handicrafts, have created jobs for many. Tourists love to purchase various souvenirs to take home.

Thus local people are recipients of additional income which has increased the prosperity of the region. Subsequently areas around Khajuraho have also prospered and reaped the benefits from the tourist multiplier. There is no dearth of areas which could, after they are developed for tourism, become great assets to the region in particular and to the country as a whole. The French government has created a series of new resorts particularly to bring prosperity to the areas which traditionally have been underdeveloped. The Italian government is likewise attempting to develop tourism in Southern Italy in order to help redress the economic imbalances which have long existed between the northern and the southern parts of Italy. Tourism is to be regarded not as an area of peripheral investment whose benefits will help in creating employment opportunities and in the regeneration of backward regions. In India a similar approach needs to be adopted to develop areas with great tourism potential.

GENERATION OF EMPLOYMENT

Employment is an important economic effect of tourism. The problems of unemployment and under-employment are more active in the developing countries. Tourism can be looked upon in this light as a major industry which employs manpower on a large scale.

The problems which the industrialized countries face in recruiting manpower for the tourists industry confirm that, in any productive process consisting of services, human labour remains the basic need. If a comparison is to be drawn with the productive sector none of the technological progress achieved has succeeded in rendering the human factor less indispensable than in this sector, and this is true to an absolutely indisputable extent.

The high social impact of the tourist industry is well known, for it has repercussions in every other national economic sector through the multiplier effect, which is particularly marked in those services that are complementary to the tourist accommodation industry. The tourist industry is a highly labour-intensive service industry and hence is a valuable source of employment. It employs a large number of people and provides a wide range of jobs which extend from the unskilled to the highly specialized. In addition to those involved in management there are a large number of specialist personnel required to work as accountants, housekeepers, waiters, cooks and entertainers, who in turn need a large number of semi-skilled workers such as porters, chambermaids, kitchen staff, gardeners, etc. Tourism is also responsible for creating employment outside the industry in its more narrowly defined sense and in this respect those who supply goods and services to those directly involved in tourism are beneficiaries from tourism.

Such indirect employment includes, those involved in the furnishing and equipment industries, souvenir industries and farming and food supply. Construction industry is another very big source of employment. The basic infrastructures-roads, airports, water supply and other public utilities and also construction of hotels and other accommodation units create jobs for thousands of workers, both unskilled and skilled. In many of the developing countries, where chronic unemployment often exists, the promotion of tourism can be a great encouragement to economic development and, especially, employment.

However at this point it is, necessary to consider the seasonal nature of the tourism industry. Where general diversification alternatives are scarce, a combination of heavy dependence on tourism and highly marked seasonality calls for measures to develop off -season traffic. Employment multiplier: This multiplier is similar to the Income Multiplier except that in this case a multiplier impact on employment is observed.

Employment Multiplier can be expressed in the following two ways:

- As a ratio of the combination of direct employment. At the destination, the jobs are directly created in the industry there.
- As a ratio of secondary employment generated per additional unit of tourist expenditure to direct employment. The workers and their families require their own goods and services giving rise to further indirectly created employment in shops, schools, health care institutions, etc.

OTHER DIMENSIONS

The World Tourism conference which was held at Manila, Philippines in October 1980, considered the nature of tourism phenomenon in all its aspects. The role tourism is bound to play in a dynamic and vastly changing world was also identified. Convened by the World Tourism Organization the conference also considered the responsibility of various states for the development and enhancement as more than a purely economic activity of nations and peoples.

The significance of tourism was discussed in during the conference. The participants in the World Tourism Conference attached particular importance to its effects on the developing countries. It stated its conviction "that the world tourism can contribute to the establishment of a new international economic order that will help to eliminate the widening economic gap between developed and developing countries and ensure the steady acceleration of economic and social development and progress in particular of the developing countries."

5

Tourist Transportation

AIR TRANSPORTATION IN INDIA

Air transportation in India is under the purview of the Department of Civil Aviation, a part of the India's Ministry of Civil Aviation and Tourism. In 1995 the Indian government owned two airlines and one helicopter service, and private companies owned six airlines. The government-owned airlines dominated India's air transportation in the mid-1990s. Air India is the international carrier; it carried more than 2.2 million passengers in FY 1992. Indian Airlines is the major domestic carrier and also runs international flights to nearby countries.

It carried 9.8 million passengers in FY 1989, when it had a load factor of more than 80 per cent in its fifty-nine airplanes. Analysts, however, attributed this high load factor to a shortage of capacity rather than efficiency of operation. A major expansion was planned for the 1990s, but an airplane crash in 1990 and a pilots' strike in 1991 damaged the airline, which carried only 7.8 million passengers in FY 1992. Two other accidents in 1993, plus several hijackings, put constraints on the growth of both airlines.

A third government-owned airline, Vayudoot, was also a domestic carrier in the early 1990s. It provided feeder service between smaller cities and the larger places served by Air India and Indian Airlines. By 1994 Indian Airlines had taken over Vayudoot. Another publicly owned company, Pawan Hans, runs helicopter service, mostly to offshore locations and other areas that cannot be served by fixed-wing aircraft. In 1995

India's six private airlines accounted for more than 10 per cent of domestic air traffic. Both the number of carriers and their market share are expected to rise in the mid-1990s. The four major private airlines are East West Airlines, Jagsons Airlines, Continental Aviation, and Damania Airways. In addition to the Indian-owned airlines, many foreign airlines provide international service.

In 1995 forty-two airlines operated air services to, from, and through India. In the mid-1990s, India had 288 usable airports. Of these, 208 had permanent-surface runways and two had runways of more than 3,659 meters, fifty-nine had runways of between 2,400 and 3,659 meters, and ninety-two had runways between 1,200 and 2,439 meters. There are major international airports at Bombay, Delhi, Calcutta, Madras, and Thiruvananthapuram under the management of the International Airport Authority of India.

International service also operates from Marmagao, Bangalore, and Hyderabad. A consortium of Indian and British companies signed a memorandum of understanding with the state government of Maharashtra in June 1995 to build a new international airport for Bombay, across the harbor from the main city and to be linked by a cross-harbor roadway. Major regional airports are located at Ahmadabad, Allahabad, Pune, Srinagar, Chandigarh, Kochi, and Nagpur.

AVIATION POLICIES IN INDIA

REGULATORY FRAMEWORK

- In the context of a multiplicity of airlines, airport operators and the possibility of oligopolistic practices, there is need for an autonomous regulatory authority which could work as a watchdog, as well as a facilitator for the sector, prescribe and enforce minimum standards for all agencies, settle disputes with regard to abuse of monopoly and ensure level playing field for all agencies. Therefore, a statutory autonomous Civil Aviation Authority will be constituted. The basic objectives of setting up of the

Authority will be to ensure aviation safety, security and effective regulation of air transport in the country in the liberalised environment.

- *The functions of the CAA will be as under*:
  - Ensure level playing field for all agencies and
  - Ensure that there are no unfair trade practices and market dominance through encouragement of entry and fostering of competition in accordance with Competition Policy of the Government;
  - Ensure that these agencies and personnel continuously fulfil the standards;
  - Issue license to these agencies and personnel;
  - Regulate tariff;
  - Set the standards for various agencies and personnel of civil aviation sector;
  - Study and analyse the trends in international and domestic civil aviation, project likely future scenario and publish periodical reports.
  - Take appropriate preventive/corrective/punitive action against the agencies and personnel for violations of set standards;
- The agencies include airport, airport-operators, passenger aircraft operators, cargo aircraft operators, helicopters, private aircraft operators, flying clubs, aero-sports clubs, security agency, training institute, air-travel operators or any other agency having role in civil aviation sector.
  - The personnel include pilots, flight engineers, navigators, cabin crew, flight despatchers, aircraft maintenance engineers/technicians, air traffic controllers and personnel engaged in the maintenance of communication, navigation, surveillance/air traffic management systems and other ground aids.
- A comprehensive Indian Aviation Law will be framed to replace the existing Acts relating to aviation and security which will be in tune with the

present day civil aviation scenario, and would also put the proposed CAA in place.

- Civil Aviation Authority will also be required to make available information regarding passenger and cargo traffic including regular analysis in an appropriate consolidated format on a commercial basis.
- Civil Aviation Authority will be required to publish Annual Report on the Air Safety and Security Environment in the country.
- Civil Aviation Authority will conduct safety and security audit including flight inspections of the concerned agencies to ensure that they are meeting the prescribed standards.

PERSONAL SECTOR PARTICIPATION

- Private sector participation will be a major thrust area in the civil aviation sector for promoting investment, improving quality and efficiency and increasing competition.
- Competitive regulatory framework with minimal controls will be created to encourage entry and operation of private airlines/airports.
- Private sector investment in the construction/ upgradations/operation of new as well as existing airports including cargo related infrastructure will be encouraged.
- Rationalization of various charges and price of ATF/ AVGas will be undertaken to render operation of smaller aircraft viable so as to encourage major investment in feeder and regional air services by the private sector.
- Training Institutes for pilots, flight engineers, maintenance personnel, air-traffic controller, security will be encouraged in private sector.
- Private sector investment in non-aeronautical activities like shopping complex, golf course, entertainment park, aero-sports etc. near airports will be encouraged to increase revenue, improve viability

of airports and to promote tourism. CAA will ensure that this is not at the cost of primary aeronautical functions, and is consistent with the security requirements.

- Government will gradually reduce its equity in PSUs in the sector.
- Government will encourage employee participation through issue of shares and ESOP.

AIRPORT ROAD AND RAIL NETWORK

- The Government will aim at ensuring adequate world class airport infrastructure capacity in accordance with demand, ensuring maximum utilization of available capacities and efficiently managing the airport infrastructure by increasing involvement of private sector.
- Greenfield airport will be permitted by the Government where
  - The existing airport is unable to meet the projected requirement of traffic or
  - A new focal point of traffic emerges with sufficient viability and
  - The new location is normally not within an aerial distance of 150 kilometers of an existing airport
- Encouragement will be given to development/ construction in private sector of small airstrips/ helipads/heliports, which are smaller and cheaper to construct. These will be particularly suitable in remote hilly or island areas, large business, city centres, factory locations and at other important nodal points. This will also facilitate increase in small aircraft operations
- Private sector participation
  - Private sector will be free to undertake
    a. Construction and operation of new airports/ airstrips/helipads/heliports including cargo complexes, express cargo terminals, cargo satellite cities and cargo handling facilities

b. Upgradation and operation of existing airports/airstrips/helipads/heliports in consultation with the existing operator including cargo complexes, Express cargo terminals, cargo satellite cities and cargo handling facilities

- Foreign equity participation will be permitted up to 74% with automatic approval and 100% with special permission of government
- Private sector participation will include participation of state government, urban local bodies, private companies, individuals and joint ventures on Build-Own-Operate basis or any other pattern of ownership and management depending on the circumstances.
- Restructuring of major airports of Airports Authority of India will be undertaken through long-term lease to private investors for efficient management, improvement of standards of services/facilities and attracting private investment
- At privately managed airports, air traffic control and aviation security will continue to be provided by the Airports Authority of India and customs and immigration facilities by respective Government departments.
- The equipment needed for any service would normally be provided by the agency responsible for the service and an equitable system would be established for sharing of revenue between different agencies. Keeping in view their respective investments and responsibilities.

• All airports/airstrips/helipads/heliports used for scheduled air-transport services will be licensed by Civil Aviation Authority.
• Airport/airstrip/heliport/helipad operators will follow ICAO guidelines for levying airport/airstrip/heliport/helipad charges based on cost recovery principle. The

CAA would put in a place a regulatory mechanism to prevent abuse of monopolistic nature of such infrastructure.

- An objective and well-defined transparent mechanism for allocation of slots at airports will be ensued at all times.
- CAA will ensure fair play between different airport/airstrip/heliport/helipad operators and user agencies so that no airport/airstrip/heliport/helipad operator is accused of discriminating against any particular airline or any other user. Similarly, Government will ensure that no airport-operator is discriminated against with regard to allotment as point of call, if there is demand for air services from such airport.
- More international gateways shall be provided. It would be ensured that there is at least one international airport in every region of the country in order to give a boost to trade and tourism and adequate capacity in all the routes.
- Major thrust will be given for increasing the share of commercial revenue from non-aeronautical sources by giving total freedom to airport/airstrip/heliport/helipad operators in the matter of raising non-aeronautical revenue
- New Ground Handling regulations with following broad particulars envisage:
  - At airports managed by AAI, new private investors have been allowed by AAI to undertake ground handling besides national carriers and self-handling by carriers which will increase competition resulting in improvement in services and reduction in costs.
  - At private airports, at least limited competition will be mandatory.
- A rationalized dynamic system for airport charges for AAI airports will be introduced for
  - Optimum utilization of airport by using peak and off-peak time charges,

- Increasing revenue of airport operators
- Promoting airports in far-flung regions by having varying airport charges from airport to airport depending upon the facilities available at the airport.
- Promoting use of small aircraft

- A new Directorate of Lands shall be established in AAI and land use guidelines will be formulated for utilizing vacant land.
  - Vacant land at airports will be evaluated for construction of aviation related activities.
  - For optimal exploitation of airport land for civil aviation purposes, private-sector/State Government participation would be welcome.
  - Land at such airports where there is no likelihood of future use for civil aviation purposes will be utilized for other commercial purposes like gold courses, tennis, etc. either by AAI itself or in joint venture.
  - Effective steps will be taken for removing encroachments from AAI land and if necessary, comprehensive rehabilitation package will be formulated.
- Cargo handling
  - Infrastructure like satellite freight cities with multi-modal transport, cargo terminals, cold storage centres, automatic storage and retrieval systems, mechanized transport of cargo, dedicated express cargo terminals with airside and city side openings, computerization and automation etc. will be set up on priority basis.
  - Private sector participation in cargo handling will be encouraged.
  - Efficient Electronic Data Interchange systems will be developed and linked amongst all stakeholders in the trade.
  - Air cargo complexes and dedicated express cargo terminals will be integral part of all major airports.

- Operation of airports would be in accordance with the provisions relating to prevention of air, water and noise pollution.
- Guidelines for naming of airports will be formulated to ensure that the airports are named after the cities they are situated in as per international norms.
- Air Traffic services
  - Air Traffic controllers will be licensed by CAA.
  - AAI will continue to provide Air Traffic Services over the Indian air Space as per standards set by CAA in accordance with ICAO norms.
  - Approach and aerodrome control services may be provided by licensed ATCs engaged by the airport operators
  - New satellite based CNS/ATM systems will be introduced as per ICAO's Regional Plan
  - India to have a significant say in the provision of new satellite based CNS/ATM services in Asia-pacific/SAARC regional airspace
  - Fresh Air traffic Services and Controlling procedures will be evolved for helicopters and small aircraft to exploit their inherent advantages and to reduce the cost of their operations and efficient use of airspace without compromising safety. This will also give boost to Flying Clubs.
  - Efforts will be made for Civil-Military co-ordination for
    a. Greater sharing of civil and military airspace for unidirectional air-corridors and straightening of air-routes to save fuel and time,
    b. Uniform air-traffic procedures,
    c. Additional slots for civilian flights at military airports,
    d. Sharing of revenues at civil enclaves

DOMESTIC PASSENGER AND CARGO AIR TRANSPORT

- ATF will be taken out from administered price

mechanism for petroleum prices. The price of ATF for domestic airline will, therefore, be governed by market and customs duty. Airlines will also be permitted import of ATF.

- Capacity induction will be regulated with a view to ensuring safety, security and preventing unhealthy levels of capacity.
- Flying clubs, Aerosports like hang-gliding, ballooning, heli-skiing, para-jumping etc. will be promoted by encouraging private investment and formulating liberalized guidelines in consultation with users. This will include rationalized Avgas prices and liberalized air space control.
- Foreign equity up to 25% and Non-Resident Indian investment up to 100% will be permitted for domestic passenger transport services. However, participation from foreign airlines either directly or indirectly will not be permitted. Substantive ownership and effective control by Indians will be a pre-requisite.
- Government and CAA will ensure that there is no discrimination between different passenger and cargo air-operators.
- Helicopter operations will be given a new boost by a total change in outlook. At present, fixed wing norms with minor changes are broadly applied to rotary wing aircraft. Fresh guidelines will be formulated in consultation with user industry from the point of view of rotary wing aircraft. Fresh Air Traffic Services and controlling procedures, which exploit the inherent advantages of helicopter without compromising safety, will be evolved. This will also reduce the cost of operations of helicopters and efficient use of airspace. Encouragement will be given to use of helicopters in the areas of heli-tourism, adventure sports, mountaineering/trekking, point-to-point heli-services to bypass traffic congestion on the road, connecting remote areas and islands in Northeast, Andaman and Nicobar and Lakshdweep,

religious places, sky crane for construction/laying of transmission lines etc.

- It is necessary that both airline operations as well as airport infrastructure be treated as mutually dependent and complementary and given similar concessions to promote a balanced growth of the sector. Therefore, airline operations and acquisition of aircraft should be given the status of "infrastructure ".
- Permission to start scheduled passenger and cargo air transport service would be given by government on demonstration of competency, minimum capital requirement and viability of the company to provide a safe and reliable service. CAA may also fix a minimum number of aircraft for scheduled operators permit.
- Private sector participation in providing domestic passengers and cargo air transport services will be encouraged.
- Special consideration will also be given to Private operators and Corporate operators by way of rationalized Avgas prices, encouragement for construction of smaller airstrips/helipad et. in private sector.
- The government will encourage provision of safe passenger and cargo air transport services to every region of the country at economic prices.
- There will be freedom to operate non-revenue and passenger charter and cargo flights to any foreign destinations. Indian passport holders will also be allowed to travel on these flights.
- Wet leasing of foreign registered aircraft by operators will be permitted only in special circumstances like grounding of aircraft, augmentation of capacity for short term, to meet the capacity requirements for handling natural calamities, etc.

PROMOTION OF COMMON AVIATION AND PETITE AIRCRAFT OPERATION

- Single engine aircraft of seating capacity upto 10 seats

can be permitted for passenger charter and cargo flights. Such operations shall be in accordance with the single engine operation guidelines and over land areas having no hilly terrain or other obstructions.

- There is a need to change the traditional concept of airport development, ownership and operations in view of the economics of small aircraft/charters operations. Participation of state Government, urban local bodies, airline/aircraft operators, other private investors will be encouraged in development, upgradation and management of small airports/ airstrips. These airports will be distinct from traditional airport and will be bare-bone type with no frills. Such airports need not be mandatorily manned and onus of ensuring security and safety of operations will rest on the aircraft operator in conjunction with the local administration/bodies, etc. This will encourage the operation of small aircraft/ air taxis, as operators themselves or in collaboration with State Government/Urban local bodies/residents of a specific locality, factory, nearby factories, tourist operators will be able to manage such airports/ airstrip flexibly and efficiency at reduced cost. This will boost passenger transport and tourism
- There is need to open up the country and tap the latent demand for air services in many parts of the country currently not on the air map. However, the traffic profile in these areas does not permit viable operations of jet. Even smaller aircraft operations are not viable because of the high cost of operation and high break-even factor.
- Therefore, Aviation Turbine Fuel for turbo prop aircraft operations will be provided at par with price for international air services, with a cap of 4% on sales tax. Operation of smaller aircraft/charters will be further encouraged through rationalization of airport charges, Inland Air Travel Tax and Avgas prices. For the North-East region, IATT has been fully

exempted on all routes. Government will consider extending similar facilities to other category II areas.

- While Route-Dispersal Guidelines do help in providing air services in the remote and inaccessible areas, further measures are required to encourage widespread air-connectivity. Passenger and cargo air transport services to many regions will not be possible unless operation of small aircraft is made economically viable either on stand alone basis or in conjunction with major trunk routes.

WORLDWIDE AIR TRANSPORT

- Air India and Indian Airlines would be guaranteed the use of traffic rights actually being utilised by them for five years following privatisation.
- Efforts will be made by national carriers to join global alliances in their own commercial interest and in the interest of travelling passengers through code-sharing, exchange of frequent- flier programmes etc.
- Government will also establish, in the long run, an objective and well-defined mechanism for sharing of international traffic rights amongst all airlines in a transparent manner.
- Government will ensure that there will be no discrimination between different airport operators in allotting capacity to foreign carriers as per bilateral agreements if demand exists.
- Government will ensure that traffic rights are utilized to the maximum extent possible through direct operations, creation of virtual equipment by way of joint flights, code sharing arrangements etc. by the two national carriers *i.e.* Air India and Indian Airlines. Other domestic carriers who fulfill the minimum criteria for designation as Indian carrier to operate international passenger flights will also be permitted to meet this objective. Initially, they may be permitted to fly to neighbouring countries against unutilised rights subject to right of first refusal by

national carriers. The requirement of substantial ownership and effective control of the airlines by Indians would continue to be operative.

- Liberal bilateral rights will be given for promoting international operations to less developed regions of the country as well as to ill-connected far away countries to promote trade and tourism in those regions.
- The Government will aim at ensuring adequate capacity to fully meet the requirement of international trade and tourism.
- There will be freedom to international tourist Charter operation to different custom airports.
- There will be no restriction on international cargo flights. However, they will not be allowed to carry domestic cargo on their flights within the country.
- Tourist charters from domestic airports to foreign destinations will also be permitted subject to safeguards for scheduled operations.

TOURISM AND TRADE PROMOTION

- Tourism and trade sectors are closely linked to civil aviation sector. Therefore it is important that airport infrastructure and air services are planned keeping in view the requirement and promotion of these sectors. Multi-modal approach will be used for planning to ensure better connectivity.
- A thrust for international tourism in India will be given by
  - Providing freedom to International Tourist Charters to all airports linking places of tourist interest
  - Declaring additional airports as international airports resulting in easy connectivity and better services,
  - Upgradation of airports at places of Tourist interest like Buddhist circuit, sanctuaries, beach resorts etc.

  - Encouraging private sector participation in building tourist infrastructure near airports like transport services from airports to nearby cities, golf courses, amusement park, business centres, duty free shopping complexes of international class, aviation recreation activities, adventure aviation, hang-gliding, microlight aircraft, parachuting etc
  - Efforts will be made to issue visa on arrival at the airport in larger number of cases.
  - Improvement in passenger facilitation and sensitisation of personnel of immigration, customs, security and AAI at airport to make them more courteous and passenger friendly.
- For promotion to trade and industries, following steps will be undertaken:
  - Abolition of On-Board Courier Scheme to facilitate courier trade
  - Introduction of "Known Shipper "scheme for reducing dwell time in exports by doing away with "cooling off" requirement
  - Introduction of Electronic Data Interchange interlinking trade agencies, customs, immigration for faster efficient trade transactions
  - Private sector participation in cargo handling for increasing competition and improved services.

FUNCTIONING OF INDIAN CARRIERS

MAIN AIRLINES IN INDIA

There has been a revolution in air travel in India in the last decade. Ever since the government launched its open sky policy and allowed private players to enter the arena there has been a sea change in the airline industry in India. Air travel has become cheaper and more affordable and the number of people traveling by air has gone up drastically. Consequently, Indian Airports too have changed for the better. Airports in India have become more swanky and passenger friendly. Here is some useful information on airlines and airports in India.

SOME WELL-KNOWN DOMESTIC AIRLINES

Air Deccan

Air Deccan is India's first low-cost airline. It is a part of Deccan Aviation Private Limited, India's largest private heli-charter company. Air Deccan was established in 2003 and started operations in August that year with regular scheduled flights from Bangalore to Mangalore and Hubli. Captain G R Gopinath, is the Managing Director of Air Deccan and is one of the founders of Air Deccan. The other founder is Captain KJ Samuel. Air Deccan has grown rapidly since it first started air operations in 2003. It has revolutionized air travel in India and has brought air travel with in the reach of common man. Air Deccan was the first airline in India to link second rung cities like Hubli, Madurai and Visakhapatnam to metros like Bangalore and Chennai. The airline went public in May 2006.

The proceeds from the IPO will be used to set up a training centre in Bangalore and a maintenance facility in Chennai. Presently, Air Deccan covers 57 destinations in India, which is more than any other airline in India. The Air Deccan fleet consists of 31 aircrafts. These include 13 Airbus A320-200, 5 ATR 42-320, 9 ATR 42-500, and 5 ATR 72-212A. Air Deccan has massive expansion plans. The company has acquired 30 Airbus A320s, which are to be deployed starting in 2007.

Air India

Air India is India's national Airline. Air India's history can be traced to October 15, 1932. On this day J.R.D. Tata, the father of Civil Aviation in India and founder of Air India, took off from Drigh Road Airport, Karachi, in a tiny, light single-engine de Havilland Puss Moth on his flight to Mumbai via Ahmedabad. Air India was earlier known as Tata Airlines. At the time of its commencement, Tata Airlines consisted of one Puss Moth, one Leopard Moth, one palm-thatched shed, one whole time pilot, one part-time engineer, and two apprentice-mechanics.

Tata Airlines was converted into a Public Company under the name of Air India in August 1946. On March 8, 1948, Air

India International Limited was formed to start Air India's international operations. On June 8, 1948, Air India started its international services with a weekly flight from Mumbai to London via Cairo and Geneva with a Lockheed Constellation aircraft. In early 1950s due to deteriorating financial condition of various airlines, the Government decided to nationalize air transport.

On August 1, 1953 two autonomous corporations were created. Indian Airlines was formed with the merger of eight domestic airlines to operate domestic services, while Air India International was established to operate the overseas services. The word 'International' was dropped in 1962. With effect from March 1, 1994, the airline has been functioning as Air India Limited. Air India's worldwide network today covers 44 destinations by operating services with its own aircraft and through code-shared flights.

Important destinations covered by Air India are Bangkok, Hongkong, Jakarta, Kuala Lumpur, Osaka, Singapore, Tokyo, Seoul, Dar-es-Salam, Nairobi, Frankfurt, London, Paris, Birmingham, Abu Dhabi, Al Ain, Bahrain, Dammam, Doha, Dubai, Jeddah, Muscat, Riyadh, Kuwait, Los Angeles, Chicago, Newark, New York, and Toronto. Air India's fleet consists of 38 aircrafts. These include 12 Boeing 747-400, 1 Boeing 747-400 COMBI, 2 Boeing 747-300 COMBI, 19 Airbus 310-300, and 4 Boeing 777-200.

Air Sahara

Air Sahara is one of India's leading private airlines. It is part of the multi-crore Sahara India Pariwar. Air Sahara was established on September 20, 1991 and began operations on December 3, 1993 with a fleet of two Boeing 737-200 aircrafts. It was then known as Sahara Airlines. Sahara Airlines was rebranded as Air Sahara on October 2, 2000. On March 22, 2004 Air Sahara became an international carrier with the start of flights from Chennai to Colombo.

Presently, Air Sahara connects to 24 domestic and 4 international destinations with 134 daily direct flights and offer 13900 seats per day. Domestic destinations include important cities like Delhi, Bangalore, Mumbai, Kolkata, Lucknow, Hyderabad, Pune, Chennai along with regional destinations like Ahmedabad, Gorakhpur, Allahabad, Bhubaneshwar and Ranchi. International destinations covered by Air Sahara are Colombo, Kathmandu, Singapore, and Chicago. Four more international destinations: Kuala Lumpur, Bangkok, Hongkong and London are proposed to be covered soon.

Air Sahara currently has a fleet of 27 aircrafts. These include 1 Boeing 767, 5 Boeing 737-800, 8 Boeing 737-700, 4 Boeing 737-400, 2 Boeing 737-300, and 7 CRJ -200. Air Sahara also provides chartered helicopter services from Delhi and Mumbai. Its fleet of helicopters include 3 ECUREUILS AS-355-NM2, and 1 DAUPHIN AS-365-NM2.

Indian Airlines

Indian Airlines, India's premier airline, has now been renamed as Indian. But Indian Airlines had establish itself as such a strong brand name that majority of people are still not aware that its name has been changed to Indian. Indian Airlines is fully owned by the Government of India and came into came into being with the enactment of the Air Corporations Act 1953. Indian Airlines began its operation on 1st August 1953 and was entrusted with the responsibility of providing air transportation within the country as well as to the neighbouring countries.

Indian Airlines came into existence after nationalization of eight private airlines. At the time of nationalization, Indian Airlines inherited a fleet of 99 aircraft consisting of various types of aircrafts. With nationalization Indian Airlines started modernization in Indian civil aviation industry. Year 1964 heralded the beginning of the jet era in Indian Airlines when the Caravelle aircraft was inducted into the fleet. Continuous upgradation in its fleet has been going on ever since. Presently, Indian Airlines, together with its fully owned subsidiary Alliance Air, has a fleet of 70 aircraft. Another 43 new aircrafts are expected to be inducted in Indian Airlines by November 2006. Indian Airlines transport network spans from Kuwait in the west to Singapore in the east and covers 76 destinations.

The Indian Airlines international network covers Kuwait, Oman, UAE, Qatar and Bahrain in West Asia; Thailand, Singapore, Malaysia and Myanmar in South East Asia and Pakistan, Afghanistan, Nepal, Bangladesh, Sri Lanka and Maldives in the South Asia sub-continent.

Jet Airways

Jet Airways is India's premier private airlines. Naresh Goyal is currently the chairman of Jet Airways. Jet Airways operates over 320 flights daily to 43 destinations in India and currently controls about 40% of India's aviation market. Jet Airways was the first private airline of India to fly to international destinations.

It operates daily international flights to Colombo, Kathmandu, Singapore, Kuala Lumpur and London. Jet Airways has won a number of awards in recognition of standards of its service and has also received the ISO 9001:2000 certification for its In-flight Services. Jet Airways was established on 3 May 1991 with a fleet of 4 Boeing 737-300 aircraft, with 24 daily flights serving 12 destinations. Jet Airways presently operates 55 aircrafts and is now a public limited company.

Its fleet of 55 aircrafts include 3 Airbus 340-300E, 4 Boeing 737-800, 1 Airbus 330-200, 1 Boeing 737-700, 18 Boeing 737-800, 8 ATR 72-500, 2 Boeing 737-900, 12 Boeing 737-700, and 6 Boeing 737-400. Jet Airways was recently involved in a controversy. On January 19, 2006 Jet Airways announced its decision to buy fellow airlines Air Sahara for $500 million in an all-cash deal. The deal was touted as the biggest in India's aviation history. But the deal fell midway and now the two parties are involved in a fierce court battle.

Kingfisher Airline

Kingfisher Airline is a private airline based in Bangalore, India. The airline is owned by Vijay Mallya of United Beverages Group. Kingfisher Airlines started its operations on May 9, 2005 with a fleet of 4 Airbus A320 aircrafts. The airline currently operates on domestic routes. The destinations covered by Kingfisher Airlines are Bangalore, Mumbai, Delhi, Goa, Chennai, Hyderabad, Ahmedabad, Cochin, Guwahati, Kolkata, Pune, Agartala, Dibrugarh, Mangalore and Jaipur. In a short span of time Kingfisher Airline has carved a niche for itself.

The airline offers several unique services to its customers. These include: personal valet at the airport to assist in baggage handling and boarding, exclusive lounges with private space, accompanied with refreshments and music at the airport, audio and video on-demand, with extra-wide personalised screens in the aircraft, sleeperette seats with extendable footrests, and three-course gourmet cuisine.

Kingfisher Airlines currently operates with a brand new fleet of 8 Airbus A320 aircraft, 3 Airbus A319-100 aircraft and 4 ATR-72 aircraft.

It was the first airline in India to operate with all new aircrafts. Kingfisher Airlines is also the first Indian airline to order the Airbus A380. It placed orders for 5 A380s, 5 A350-800 aircrafts and 5 Airbus A330-200 aircrafts in a deal valued at over $3 billion on June 15, 2005. Delivery of the A330s is due to start in late 2007, followed by the A380s in 2010 and the A350s in 2012.

AIR CORPORATIONS BILL, 1994

BILL

To provide for the transfer and vesting of the undertakings of Indian Airlines and Air India respectively to and in the companies formed and registered as Indian Airlines Limited and Air India Limited and for matters connected therewith or incidental thereto and also to repeal the Air Corporations Act, 1953.

Be it enacted by Parliament in the Forty-fifth Year of the Republic of India as follows:

Short Title and Commencement:

- This Act may be called the Air Corporations Act, 1994.
- It shall be deemed to have come into force on the 29th day of January, 1994.

Definitions: In this Act, unless the context otherwise requires,

- "Appointed day" mean such date as the Central Government may, by notification in the Official Gazette, appoint under section 3;
- "Company" means "Indian Airlines Limited" or "Air India Limited" formed and registered under the Companies Act, 1956;
- "Corporations" means "Indian Airlines" and "Air India" established under section 3 of the Air Corporations Act, 1953 and "corporation" means either of the corporations.

Undertakings of Corporations to Vest in Companies

On such date as the Central Government may, by notification in the Official Gazette, appoint, there shall be transferred to, and vest in,

- Indian Airlines Limited, the undertaking of Indian Airlines; and
- Air India Limited, the undertaking of Air India.

General Effect of Vesting of Undertakings in the Companies

- All contracts and working arrangements subsisting immediately before the appointed day and affecting a corporation shall, in so far as they relate to the undertaking of that corporation, cease to have effect or to be enforceable against that corporation and shall be of as full force and effect against or in favour of the company in which the undertaking has vested by virtue of this Act and enforceable as fully and effectually as if, instead of the corporation, the company had been named therein or had been a party thereto.
- Any proceeding or cause of action pending or existing immediately before the appointed day be or against a corporation in relation to its undertaking may, as from that day, be continued and enforced by or against the company in which it has vested by

virtue of this Act, as it might have been enforced by or against that corporation if this Act had not been passed, and shall cease to be enforceable by or against that corporation.

- The undertaking of a corporation which is transferred to, and which vests in, a company under section 3 shall be deemed to include all assets, rights, powers, authorities and privileges and all properties, movable and immovable, real or personal, corporeal or incorporeal, in possession or reservation, present or contingent, of whatever nature and wheresoever situate, including lands, works, workshops, aircraft, cash balances, capital reserves, reserve funds, investments, tenancies, leases and book debts and all other rights and interests arising out of such property as were immediately before the appointed day in the ownership, possession or power of that corporation in relation to its undertakings, whether within or outside India, all books of account and documents relating thereto and shall also be deemed to include all borrowings, liabilities and obligations of whatever kind then subsisting of that corporation in relation to its undertaking.

Licenses, to be Deemed to have been Granted to Companies

With effect from the appointed day, all licenses, permits, quotas and exemptions granted to a corporation in connection with the affairs and business of that corporation under any law for the time being in force, shall be deemed to have been granted to the company in which the undertaking of that corporation has vested.

Tax Exemption or Benefit to Continue to have Effect:

- Where any exemption from, or any assessment with respect to, any tax has been granted or made or any benefit by way of set off or carry forward, as the case may be, of any unabsorbed depreciation or investment allowance or other allowance or loss has been extended or is available to a corporation under the income-tax Act, 1961, such exemption, assessment or benefit shall continue to have effect in relation to the company in which the undertaking of that corporation has vested.

- Where any payment made by a corporation is exempt from deduction of the tax at source under any provision of the Income-tax Act, 1961, the exemption from tax will continue to be available as if the provisions of the said Act made applicable to the corporation were operative in relation to the company in which the undertaking of that corporation has been vested.
- The transfer and vesting of the undertaking or any part thereof in terms of section 3 shall not be construed as a transfer within the meaning of the Income-tax Act, 1961 for the purposes of capital gains.

Guarantee to be Operative

Any guarantee given for or in favour of a corporation with respect to any loan or lease finance shall continue to be operative in relation to the company in which the undertaking of that corporation has vested by virtue of this Act.

Provisions in Respect of Officers and Other Employees of Corporations:

- Every officer or other employee of a corporation serving in its employment immediately before the appointed day shall, in so far as such officer or other employee is employed in connection with the undertaking which has vested in a company by virtue of this Act become, as from the appointed day an officer or other employee, as the case may be, of the company in which the undertaking has vested and shall hold his office or service therein by the same tenure, at the same remuneration, upon the same terms and conditions, with the same obligations and with the same rights and privileges as to leave, passage, insurance, superannuation scheme, provident fund, other funds, retirement, pension, gratuity and other benefits as he would have held under that corporation if its undertaking had not vested in the company and shall continue to do so as an officer or other employee, as the case may be, of the company or until the expiry of a period of six months from the appointed day if such officer of other employee opts not to be the officer or other employee of the company, within such period.

- Notwithstanding anything contained in the Industrial Disputes Act, 1947 or in any other law for the time being in force, the transfer of the services of any officer or other employee of a corporation to a company shall not entitles such offer or other employee to any compensation under this Act or under any other law for the time being in force and no such claim shall be entertained by any court, tribunal or other authority.
- Notwithstanding anything contained in this Act or in the Companies Act, 1956 or in any other law for the time being in force or in the regulations of a corporation, no Director of the Board, Chairman, Manageing Director or any other person entitled to manage the whole or a substantial part of the business and affairs of that corporation shall be entitled to any compensation against that corporation or against the company, as the case may be, for the loss of office or for the premature termination of any contract of management entered into by him with that corporation.
- Tax exemption granted to Provident Fund or Pilots Group Insurance and Superannuation Scheme would continue to be applied to the company.
- The officers and other employees who have retired before the appointed day from the service of a corporation and are entitled to any benefits, rights or privileges shall be entitled to receive the same benefits, rights or privileges from the company in which the undertaking of that corporation has vested.

- The trusts of the Provident Fund or Pilots Group Insurance and Superannuation Scheme of the corporation and any other bodies created for the welfare of officers or employees would continue to discharge their functions in the company as was being done hitherto in the corporation.
- Where an officer or other employee of a corporation opts under sub-section not to be in the employment or service of the company in which the undertaking of that corporation has vested, such officer or other employee shall be deemed to have resigned.

Power of Central Government to Provide Instructions

The Central Government may give to a company directions as to the exercise and performance by that company of its functions, and that company shall be bound to give effect to any such directions.

Power to Remove Difficulties:

- Every order made under sub-section shall be laid before each House of Parliament.
- If any difficulty arises in giving effect to the provision of this Act, the Central Government may, by order published in the Official Gazette, not inconsistent with the provisions of this Act, remove the difficulty:
- Provided that no such order shall be made after the expiry of a period of two years from the coming into force of this Act.

Repeal of Act 27 of 1953 and Cases of Corporations:

- On the appointed day, the Air Corporations Act, 1953 shall stand repealed.
- The corporations shall, with the repeal of the Air Corporations Act, 1953, cease to exist.

Repeal and Saving:

- Notwithstanding such repeal of the Air Corporations Ordinance, 1994, anything done or any action taken under the said Ordinance shall be deemed to have been done or taken under the corresponding provisions of this Act.

- The Air Corporations Ordinance, 1994 is hereby repealed.

RAIL TRANSPORT

Rail transport is the transport of passengers and goods by means of wheeled vehicles specially designed to run along railways or railroads. Rail transport is part of the logistics chain, which facilitates the international trading and economic growth in most countries. A typical railway/railroad track consists of two parallel rails, normally made of steel, secured to cross-beams, termed sleepers or 'ties'. The sleepers maintain a constant distance between the two rails; a measurement known as the 'gauge' of the track. To maintain the alignment of the track, it is either laid on a bed of ballast or else secured to a solid concrete foundation, and the whole is referred to as Permanent way.

Railway rolling stock, which is fitted with metal wheels, moves with low frictional resistance when compared to road vehicles; on the other hand locomotives and power cars normally rely solely for traction on the point of contact of the wheel with the rail whence they obtain adhesion *i.e.* the part of the transmitted axle load that makes the wheel "adhere" to the smooth rail. Whilst this is usually sufficient under normal dry rail conditions, adhesion can be reduced or even lost through the presence of unwanted material on the rail surface, such as grease, ice or dead leaves.

GENERAL

Rail transport is an energy-efficient and capital-intensive means of mechanized land transport and is a component of logistics. Rails, which along with various engineered components, are part of the permanent way. They provide very smooth and hard surfaces on which the wheels of the train may roll with a minimum of friction. As an example, a typical modern wagon can hold up to 125 tons of freight on two four-wheel bogies/trucks. The contact area between each wheel and the rail is tiny, a strip no more than a few millimetres wide, and hence suffers very little friction.

Furthermore, the track distributes the weight of the train evenly, allowing significantly greater loads per axle/wheel than in road transport, leading to less wear and tear on the permanent way. This can save energy compared with other forms of transportation, such as road transport which depends on the friction between rubber and road. Trains also have a small frontal area in relation to the load they are carrying, which cuts down on forward air resistance and thus energy usage, although does not necessarily account for the effect of side winds. In all, under the right circumstances, a train needs 50-70% less energy to transport a given tonnage of freight than does road transport.

Due to these various benefits, rail transport is a major form of public transport in many countries. In Asia, for example, many millions use trains as regular transport in India, China, South Korea and Japan. It is also widespread in European countries. By comparison, intercity rail transport in the United States is relatively scarce outside the Northeast Corridor, although a number of major U.S. cities have heavily-used, local rail-based passenger transport systems or light rail or commuter rail operations.

The vehicles traveling on the rails are arranged in a series of individual powered or unpowered vehicles linked together, called a train; this can include the locomotive where present. A locomotive is a powered vehicle used to haul a train of unpowered vehicles; calling a locomotive a "train" is a common popular misnomer.

A string of unpowered vehicles without the locomotive is also termed a train; in the U.S.A. individual unpowered vehicles are known as cars and are divided just as to the role: for a passenger-carrying vehicle the term carriage is used, whilst a freight-carrying vehicle is known as a freight car; in Britain, a freight car would be called a wagon. An individual powered passenger vehicle is known as a railcar or a power car; when one or more as these are coupled to one or more unpowered trailer cars as an inseparable unit, this is called a railcar set; several sets coupled together make up a multiple unit.

Collectively, rail vehicles of all types are known as rolling stock. As a result, rail transport is a major form of public transport in many countries. In Asia, for example, many millions use trains as regular transport in India, China, South Korea and Japan. It is also widespread in European countries. By comparison, intercity rail transport in the United States is relatively scarce outside the Northeast Corridor, although a number of major U.S. cities have heavily-used, local rail-based passenger transport systems or light rail or commuter rail operations.

HISTORY

The earliest evidence of a railway found thus far was the 6 kilometers Diolkos wagonway, which transported boats across the Corinth isthmus in Greece during the 6th century BC. Trucks pushed by slaves ran in grooves in limestone, which provided the track element, preventing the wagons from leaving the intended route. The Diolkos ran for over 1300 years, until 900 AD. The first horse-drawn wagonways also appeared in ancient Greece, with others to be found on Malta and various parts of the Roman Empire, using cut-stone tracks. Railways began re-appearing in Europe after a hiatus following the collapse of the Roman Empire from around 1550, usually operating with wooden track.

The first railways in Great Britain were constructed in the early 17th century, mainly for transporting coal from mines to canal wharfs where it could be transferred to a boat for onward shipment. Early examples of this can be found in Broseley in Shropshire, where wooden rails and flanged wheels were utilised, as on a modern railway. However, the rails were liable to wear out under the pressure, and had to be replaced. In 1768, the Coalbrookdale Iron Works laid cast iron plates on top of the wooden rails, providing a more durable load-bearing surface.

From the late 18th century, iron rails began to appear, with the British civil engineer William Jessop designing smooth iron edge rails, which were to be used in conjunction with flanged iron wheels. Jessop used this innovation on a route between

Loughborough and Nanpantan, Leicestershire in 1789. In 1803, Jessop opened the Surrey Iron Railway in south London, arguably the world's first horse-drawn public railway. The first locomotive to haul a train of wagons on rails was designed by Cornish engineer Richard Trevithick, and was trialled in 1804 on a plateway at Merthyr Tydfil, South Wales. Although the locomotive successfully hauled the train, the rail design was not a success, partly because its weight broke a number of the brittle cast-iron plates.

Despite this setback, another area of South Wales pioneered rail operations, when, in 1806, a horse-drawn railway was built between Swansea and Mumbles: the Swansea-Mumbles railway started carrying fare-paying passengers in 1807–the first in the world to do so. In 1811, John Blenkinsop designed the first successful and practical railway locomotive. He patented a system of moving coals by a rack railway worked by a steam locomotive, and a line was built connecting the Middleton Colliery to Leeds.

The locomotive was built by Matthew Murray of Fenton, Murray and Wood. The Middleton Railway was the first railway to successfully use steam locomotives on a commercial basis. It was also the first railway in Great Britain to be built under the terms laid out in an Act of Parliament. Blenkinsop's engine had double-acting cylinders and, unlike the Trevithick pattern, no flywheel. Due to previous experience of broken rails, the locomotive was made very light and this brought concerns about insufficient adhesion, so instead of driving the wheels directly, the cylinders drove a cogwheel through spur gears, the cogwheel providing traction by engaging with a rack cast into the side of the rail. The Stockton and Darlington Railway opened in northern England in 1825 to be followed five years later by the Liverpool and Manchester Railway, considered to be the world's first "Inter City" line. The rail gauge was used for the early wagonways, and had been adopted for the Stockton and Darlington Railway.

The 4 ft 8½ in width became known as the international "standard gauge", used by about sixty per cent of the world's railways. The Liverpool and Manchester Railway, on the other hand, proved the viability of rail transport when, after organising the Rainhill Trials of 1829, Stephenson's Rocket successfully hauled a load of 13 tons at an average speed of 12 miles per hour. The company took the step of working its trains from its opening entirely by steam traction. Railways then soon spread throughout the United Kingdom and the world, and became the dominant means of land transport for nearly a century, until the invention of aircraft and automobiles, which prompted a gradual decline in railways. The first railroad in the United States may have been a gravity railroad in Lewiston, New York in 1764. The 1810 Leiper Railroad in Pennsylvania was intended as the first permanent railroad, and the 1826 Granite Railway in Massachusetts was the first commercial railroad to evolve through continuous operations into a common carrier. The Baltimore and Ohio, opened in 1830, was the first to evolve into a major system. In 1867, the first elevated railroad was built in New York.

In 1869, the symbolically important transcontinental railroad was completed in the United States with the driving of a golden spike at Promontory, Utah. The development of the railroad in the United States helped reduce transportation time and cost, which allowed migration towards the west. Railroads increased the accessibility of goods to consumers, thus allowing individuals and capital to flow westward. The use of overhead wires conducting electricity, invented by Granville T. Woods in 1888, amongst several other improvements, led to the development of electrified railways, the first of which in the United States was operated at Coney Island from 1892. Richmond, Virginia had the first successful electrically-powered trolley system in the United States. Designed by electric power pioneer Frank J. Sprague, the trolley system opened its first line in January, 1888. Richmond's hills, long a transportation obstacle, were considered an ideal proving ground.

The new technology soon replaced horse-powered streetcars. Diesel and electric trains and locomotives replaced steam in many countries in the decades after World War II. In the USSR the phenomenon of children's railways was developed since the 1930s. Fully operated by children, they were extracurricular educational institutions, where teenagers learnt railway professions. A lot of them are functioning in post-Soviet states and Eastern European countries.

Many countries since the 1960s have adopted high-speed railways. On April 3, 2007, the French TGV set a new train speed record. The train, with a modified engine and wheels, reached 574.8 km/h. The record attempt took place on the new LGV Est line between Paris and Strasbourg using a specially equipped TGV Duplex train. The overhead lines had also been modified for the attempt to carry 31,000 V rather than the line's normal 25,000 V. On 24 August 2005, the Qingzang railway became the highest railway line in the world, when track was laid through the Tanggula Mountain Pass at 5,072 meters above sea level in the Tanggula Mountains, Tibet.

OPERATIONS

A railway can be broken down into two major components. Basically these are the items which "move", the rolling stock, that is the locomotives, passenger carrying vehicles, freight carrying vehicles and those which are "fixed", usually referred to as its infrastructure. This category includes the permanent way and buildings.

SIGNALLING

Railway signalling is a system used to control railway traffic safely, essentially to prevent trains from colliding. Being guided by fixed rails, trains are uniquely susceptible to collision; furthermore, trains cannot stop quickly, and frequently operate at speeds that do not enable them to stop within sighting distance of the driver. Most forms of train control involve movement authority being passed from those responsible for each part of a rail network to the train crew. The set of rules and the physical equipment used to accomplish this determine what is known as the method of working, method of operation or safeworking. Not all these methods require the use of physical signals and some systems are specific to single track railways.

RIGHT OF WAY

Railway tracks are laid upon land owned or leased by the railway. Owing to the requirements for large radius turns and modest grades, rails will often be laid in circuitous routes. Public carrier railways are typically granted limited rights of eminent domain.

In many cases in the 19th century railways were given additional incentives in the form of grants of public land. Route length and grade requirements can be reduced by the use of alternating earthen cut and fill, bridges, and tunnels, all of which can greatly increase the capital expenditures required to develop a right of way, while significantly reducing operating costs and allowing higher speeds on longer radius curves. In densely urbanized areas such as Manhattan, railways are sometimes laid out in tunnels to minimize the effects on existing properties.

SAFETY AND RAILWAY DISASTERS

Trains can travel at very high speed; however, they are heavy, are unable to deviate from the track and require a great distance to stop. Although rail transport is considered one of the safest forms of travel, there are many possibilities for accidents to take place. These can vary from the minor derailment, a head-on collision with another train coming the opposite way and collision with an automobile at a level crossing/grade crossing. Level crossing collisions are relatively common in the United States where there are several thousand each year killing about 500 people-although the comparable figures in the United Kingdom are 30 and 12. The most important safety measures are railway signalling and gates at level/grade crossings.

Train whistles warn others of the presence of a train, while trackside signals maintain the distances between trains. In the United Kingdom, vandalism or negligence is thought responsible for about half of rail accidents. Railway lines are zoned or divided into blocks guarded by combinations of block signals, operating rules, and automatic-control devices so that one train, at most, may be in a block at any time.

Such traffic control is done in a similar way to air traffic control. Compared with road travel, railways remain relatively safe. Annual death rates on roads are over 40,000 in the United States and about 3,000 in the United Kingdom, compared with 1,000 rail-related fatalities in the United States and under 20 in the UK.

TRACK

A typical railway/railroad track consists of two parallel steel rails, generally anchored perpendicular to beams, termed sleepers or ties, of timber, concrete, or steel to maintain a consistent distance apart, or gauge. The rails and perpendicular beams are usually then placed on a foundation made of concrete or compressed earth and gravel in a bed of ballast to prevent the track from buckling as the ground settles over time beneath and under the weight of the vehicles passing above. The vehicles travelling on the rails are arranged in a train; a series of individual powered or unpowered vehicles linked together, displaying markers.

These vehicles move with much less friction than do vehicles riding on rubber tires on a paved road, and the locomotive that pulls the train tends to use energy far more efficiently as a result. Trackage, consisting of sleepers/ties and rails, may be prefabricated or assembled in place. Rails may be composed of segments welded or bolted, and may be of a length comparable to that of a railcar or two or may be many hundreds of feet long. The surface of the ballast is sloped around curves to reduce side forces. This reduces the forces tending to displace the track, reduces the tendency to overturn at high speed, and makes for a more comfortable ride for standing cattle and standing or seated passengers in trains. This will be optimal at only one particular speed, however.

TRACK COMPONENTS

Railways are highly complex feats of engineering, with many hours of planning and forethought required for a successful outcome. The first component of a railway is the route, which is planned to provide the least resistance in terms of gradient and engineering works. As such, the trackbed is heavily engineered to provide, where possible, a level surface. As such, embankments are constructed to support the track, in order to provide a compromise in terms of the route's average elevation.

With this in mind, sundry structures such as bridges and viaducts are constructed in an attempt to maintain the railway's elevation, and gradients are kept within manageable constraints. Where such items are not always justified, such as in hilly terrain, where routes may require long detours to avoid such features, a cutting or tunnel is dug or bored through the obstacle. Once the sundry engineering works are completed, a bed of stone is laid over the compacted trackbed to ensure drainage around the ties and even distribution of pressure over a wider area, locking the track-work in place. This crushed stone is firmly tamped to prevent further settling and to lock the stones.

Minor watercourses are led through pipes before the grade is raised. The base of the trackage consists of treated wood or concrete "ties", also known as "sleepers". These ensure the proper distance between the rails and anchor the rail structure to the roadbed through the use of Plates. These are attached to the top of the ties in order to provide a secure housing for the rails. After placement of the rail atop the plate, spikes are driven through holes in the plate and into the tie where they are held by friction.

The top of the spike has a head that clamps the rail. Alternatively, lag bolts may be used to retain the clamps; this is preferred since screws do not tend to loosen. The spaces between and surrounding the ties are filled with additional ballast to stabilize the rail assembly against movement.

POINTS

Points or switches, technically known as turnouts, are the means of directing a train onto a diverging part of track, for example, a siding, a branch line, or a parallel running line. Laid similar to normal track, a point typically consists of a frog, check rails and two switch rails. The switch rails may be moved left or right, under the control of the signalling system, to determine which path the train will follow.

MAINTENANCE

Spikes in wooden ties can loosen over time, whilst split and rotten ties may be individually replaced with a concrete substitute. Should the rails settle owing to soil subsidence they may be lifted by specialized machinery and additional ballast tamped down to form a level elevation. Periodically, ballast must be removed and replaced with clean ballast to ensure adequate drainage, especially if wooden ties are used. Culverts and other passages for water must be kept clear lest water is impounded by the trackbed, causing landslips. Where trackbeds are placed along rivers, additional protection is usually placed to prevent erosion during times of high water, whilst Bridges are another important item requiring inspection and maintenance.

EURO RAIL

The European rail network, or Eurail as most Americans refer to it, is a complex web of rail lines serving over 30,000 European cities. North Americans are best to associate Europe's rail network with our Interstate road system. Virtually every city is serviced somehow. Over 80,000 train departures a day make traveling from city to city fast, comfortable and care free. Today, its meaning couldn't be more appropriate. Upgrades in services, trains and tracks leaves little chance of boredom en route, but it's still leisurely enough to relax and absorb the changing scenery. From hills, farms, and snowcapped mountains to castles peaking through the forest, rail travellers need only worry whether to stop by the dining car for lunch, chat with fellow passengers, or simply enjoy the view.

Of course there's always time to catch up on some needed rest. Packaged group tours offer an inexpensive option for many travellers, but they offer little free time or deviation from the itinerary. Traveling Europe on your own by rail gives you the opportunity to see what you like, when you like. You also have the opportunity to mingle with Europeans who are sharing the train ride with you, which is part of the reason to go to Europe.

Trains offer romance and aura that cannot be found in any other method of transportation. Just the mention of the Orient Express conjures visions of exquisite dining, intrigue and mystery. While many of the original famous trains have been upgraded by modern high-speed international trains, the thrill is still there. Traveling Europe by train is unique, enjoyable and memorable.

AMTRAK

The National Railroad Passenger Corporation, doing business as Amtrak, is a quasi-governmental corporation that was organized on May 1, 1971, to provide intercity passenger train service in the United States. "Amtrak" is a portmanteau of the words "American" and "track". All of Amtrak's preferred stock is owned by the Federal government. The members of its board of directors are appointed by the President of the United States and are subject to confirmation by the United States Senate.

Common stock was issued in 1971 to railroads that contributed capital and equipment; its current holders consider it worthless but declined a 2002 buy-out offer by Amtrak. Amtrak employs nearly 19,000 people. It operates passenger service on 21,000 miles of track primarily owned by other railroads connecting 500 destinations in 46 states. Some routes serve Canada. In fiscal year 2006, Amtrak served 24.3 million passengers, a company record. The estimates for fiscal year 2007, Amtrak has served over the 25 million passenger mark, a 6% increase from last year.

PASSENGER RAIL SERVICE BEFORE AMTRAK

The history of Amtrak begins with the decline of privately-operated passenger rail. From the middle 19th century until approximately 1920, if a person traveled from one city to another in the United States, the trip almost certainly was by rail. By 1910, close to 100% of intercity passenger trips were made by railroad. All of those services were provided by private, for-profit organizations. Approximately 65,000 railroad passenger cars were in operation in 1929. For a long time after 1920, passenger rail's popularity plateaued and there were a series of pullbacks and tentative recoveries. Rail passenger revenues declined dramatically between 1920 and 1934, but in the mid-1930s, railroads reignited the popular imagination with service improvements and introductions of new, diesel-powered streamliners, such as the gleaming silver Pioneer Zephyr and Flying Yankee.

Even with the improvements, on a relative basis, ridership continued to erode and by 1940 railroads held a far less dominant 67% share of all passenger-miles in the United States. World War II broke the malaise. During the war, troop movements and restrictions on use of automobile fuel generated a sixfold increase in passenger traffic from the low point of the Depression. After the war, railroads rejuvenated overworked and neglected fleets with a multitude of fast and often luxurious streamliners—epitomized by the Super Chief and California Zephyr—which inspired the last major resurgence in passenger rail travel.

In 1948, Santa Fe CEO Fred G. Gurley reported a "complete reversal of our passenger traffic picture", with 1947 revenues exceeding those of 1936 by 220%.Inspired by America's leadership, European and Japanese railroads also launched their own streamlined, high-speed rail services. The postwar resurgence was short-lived. In 1946, there remained 45% fewer passenger trains than in 1929, and the pace of decline quickened despite railroad optimism. Passengers disappeared, and so did the trains. Between 1946 and 1964, the annual number of passengers declined from 770 to 298 million.

The number of U.S. commuter trains declined by more than 80%, from greater than 2,500 in 1954 to fewer than 500 in 1969. Few trains generated profits; most produced losses. Broad-based passenger rail deficits appeared as early as 1948 and by the mid-1950s railroads claimed aggregate annual losses on passenger services of more than $700 million. By 1965, only 10,000 rail passenger cars were in operation, 85% fewer than in 1929. Passenger service was provided on only 75,000 miles of track, a stark decline.

Passenger rail service in the United States showed the signs of underinvestment. Rail facilities suffered from decrepit equipment, cavernous and nearly empty stations in dangerous urban centres, and management that seemed intent on driving away the few remaining customers. The 1960s also saw the end of railway post office revenues, which had helped some of the remaining trains break even despite the dearth of passengers.

CAUSES OF DECLINE OF PASSENGER RAIL

The causes of the decline of passenger rail were complex. The industry was hobbled by government regulation and labour inflexibility, which undermined passenger rail just as the industry faced an explosion of competition from massively subsidized automobile and airplane transportation. All this marked the path to oblivion.

Rail interests were structured to sell access to elaborate, efficient, roads at a profit; they could not compete for passengers with parallel turnpikes, air strips, and highways in the sky. The competing modes were in many ways convenient and faster. They fostered independence. But most importantly, as the costs of running a passenger railroad rose, highways in particular were cheaper, as they were built with public funds and without a profit motive. The decline was a failure of a business model as much as the failure of a technology.

GOVERNMENT REGULATION AND LABOUR ISSUES

Passenger rail's vibrancy first was interrupted by government intervention brought about by the Interstate Commerce Commission. Just after the turn of the 20th century, populist rate-setting schema and a WWI wartime nationalization of the rail industry erased ample railroad profits, reversed growth of the rail system, and contributed to massive underinvestment from approximately 1910 to 1921.

Meanwhile, labour costs advanced, and with them passenger fares, which discouraged passenger traffic just as automobiles gained a foothold. Later the ICC intervened in other ways, also to the detriment of passenger rail.

In 1947, the ICC ruled that passenger trains could not exceed 79 mph without special in-cab signaling systems; the systems were derided as unnecessary and prohibitively expensive, and after issuance of the regulation, plans to develop intercity high-speed rail services were shelved. In 1958, the ICC was authorized to allow or reject modifications and eliminations of passenger routes. Many routes at that time required beneficial pruning, but the ICC delayed action by an average of eight months and when it did authorize modifications, the ICC insisted that unsuccessful routes be merged with profitable ones. Thus, fast, popular rail service was transformed into slow, unpopular service. The ICC was even more critical of corporate mergers. Many combinations, which railroads sought to compete, were delayed for years and even decades, such as the merger of the New York Central Railroad and Pennsylvania Railroad, into what eventually became Penn Central, and the Delaware, Lackawanna and Western Railroad and Erie Railroad into the Erie Lackawanna Railroad. By the time the ICC approved the mergers in the 1960s, disinvestments by the federal government, years of deteriorating equipment and station facilities and the flight of passengers to the air and car had taken their toll and the mergers were unsuccessful. At the same time, government insisted that railroads carry a substantial tax burden. A World War II-era excise tax of 15% on passenger rail travel survived until 1962.

Local governments, far from providing needed support to passenger rail, viewed rail infrastructure as a ready source for property tax revenues. In one extreme example, in 1959 the Great Northern Railroad, which owned about a third of one per cent of the land in Lincoln County, Montana, was assessed more than 91% of all school taxes in the county. Railroads also were saddled with antiquated work rules and an inflexible relationship with labour unions. Work policies did not adapt to technological change. Average train speeds doubled from 1919 to 1959, but unions resisted efforts to modify their existing 100 to 150 mile work days. As a result, railroaders' work days were roughly cut in half, from 5 to 7½ hours in 1919, down to 2½ to 3¾ hours in 1959. Labour rules also perpetuated positions that had been obviated by technology. Between 1947 and 1957, passenger railroad financial efficiency dropped by 42% per mile.

SUBSIDIZED COMPETITION

While passenger rail faced internal and governmental pressures, new challenges appeared that undermined the dominance of passenger rail: highways and commercial aviation. The passenger rail industry wilted as government backed these upstarts with billions of dollars in construction. Beginning roughly in the WWI era, cars became more attainable to most Americans.

Soon, government actively began to support with public funds a non-profit network of roads not subject to property taxation that rivaled and then surpassed the for-profit network that the railroads had built in previous generations with corporate capital. The Federal Highway Act funded the Interstates, local governments built compatible networks of local roads, and all told between 1921 and 1955 governmental entities financed more than $93 billion worth of pavement, construction, and maintenance. In turn, more Americans embraced the flexibility, convenience and privacy of personal transportation by automobile over public transit alternatives. Intercity bus services also saw declines.

In the 1950s, a second and more formidable threat appeared: affordable commercial aviation. Government at many levels supported aviation. Governmental entities spawned sprawling urban and suburban airports, and funded construction of massive highways to provide access to the airports.

RAIL PASSENGER SERVICE ACT

In 1967, the National Association of Railroad Passengers

was formed to lobby for government funding to assure the continuation of passenger trains. Its lobbying efforts were hampered by the opposition of the Democratic Party to any sort of subsidies to the privately-owned railroads, and Republican Party opposition to the nationalization of the railroad industry.

The proponents were aided by the fact that few in the federal government wanted to be held responsible for the seemingly-inevitable extinction of the passenger train, which most regarded as tantamount to political suicide. The urgency of the need to solve the passenger train problem was heightened by the bankruptcy filing of the Penn Central, the dominant railroad in the Northeastern United States, on June 21, 1970. Under the Rail Passenger Service Act of 1970, Congress created the National Railroad Passenger Corporation to subsidize and oversee the operation of intercity passenger trains.

The Act provided that:

- Any railroad operating intercity passenger service could contract with the NRPC, thereby joining the national system.
- Participating railroads bought into the NRPC using a formula based on their recent intercity passenger losses. The purchase price could be satisfied either by cash or rolling stock; in exchange, the railroads received NRPC common stock.
- Any participating railroad was freed of the obligation to operate intercity passenger service after May 1, 1971, except for those services chosen by the Department of Transportation as part of a "basic system" of service and paid for by NRPC using its federal funds.
- Railroads that chose not to join the NRPC system were required to continue operating their existing passenger service until 1975 and thenceforth had to pursue the customary Interstate Commerce Commission approval process for any discontinuance or alteration to the service.

For some time, there was a veto threat from President Richard M. Nixon. The veto never materialized and the act was signed into law on October 30, 1970. The original working brand name for NRPC was Railpax, but shortly before the company started operating it was changed to Amtrak.

The Nixon administration and many Washington insiders viewed the NRPC as a politically expedient way for the President and Congress to give passenger trains the one "last hurrah" demanded by the public. Cynics expected Amtrak to quietly disappear as public interest waned. Proponents also hoped that government intervention would be short-lived, but their view was that Amtrak would soon support itself. Neither view has yet proved correct. Popular support has allowed Amtrak to continue in operation longer than critics imagined while financial results have made infeasible a return to private operation.

EARLY DAYS

Amtrak began operations May 1, 1971. The corporation was molded from the passenger rail operations of 20 out of 26 major railroads in operation at the time. The railroads made contributions of rolling stock, equipment, and capital. In return, they received approval to discontinue their own passenger services, and at least some acquired common stock in Amtrak. Notably, Amtrak received no railroad track or right-of-way at its inception. Railroads that shed passenger operations were expected to host Amtrak trains on their tracks, for a fee.

There was a period of adjustment. All of Amtrak's routes were continuations of prior service, although Amtrak immediately pruned about half of the existing passenger rail network. Out of the 364 trains that were operated previously, Amtrak only continued 182. On the trains that were continued, to the extent possible, schedules were retained with only minor changes from the Official Guide of the Railways. Former names largely were continued.

Several major corridors initially became freight-only, including New York Central Railroad's Water Level Route across New York and Ohio and Grand Trunk Western Railroad's Chicago to Detroit service, although service soon returned to the Water Level Route with introduction of the Lake Shore.

Reduced passenger train schedules created headaches. A 19-hour layover became necessary for eastbound travel on the James Whitcomb Riley between Chicago and Newport News. Amtrak also inherited problems dealing with station facilities, most notably stations with deferred maintenance, and redundant facilities resulting from competing companies that served the same areas.

On the day it started Amtrak was given the huge responsibility of rerouting passenger trains from the then seven existing train terminals in Chicago into just one, Union Station. In New York Amtrak had to pay to maintain Penn Station and Grand Central Terminal due to lack of track connections to bring trains from upstate New York into Penn Station, a problem that was not rectified until the building of the Empire Connection in 1991.

In many cases Amtrak had to abandon service into the huge old Union Stations such as ones in Cincinnati, Saint Paul, Buffalo, Detroit, Kansas City, and Saint Louis and route trains into smaller Amtrak-built facilities down the line. On the other hand, merged operations also presented efficiencies such as the combination of three West Coast trains into the Coast Starlight, running from San Diego to Seattle. The Northeast Corridor received an Inland Route via Springfield, Massachusetts, thanks to support from New York, Connecticut and Massachusetts.

The North Coast Hiawatha was implemented as a second Pacific Northwest route. The Milwaukee to St. Louis Abraham Lincoln and Prairie State routes also commenced. The first all-new Amtrak route, not counting the Coast Starlight, was the Montrealer/Washingtonian. That route was inaugurated September 29, 1972, along Boston and Maine Railroad and Canadian National Railway track that had last seen passenger service in 1966. Amtrak soon had the opportunity to acquire railway.

Following the bankruptcy declaration of several northeastern railroads in the early 1970s, including the Penn Central which owned and operated the Northeast Corridor, Congress passed the Railroad Revitalization and Regulatory Reform Act of 1976. A large part of the act was directed to the creation of a Conrail, but in addition the law enabled transfer to Amtrak of the vital Northeast Corridor railway from Boston, Massachusetts to Washington, DC. That trackage became Amtrak's crown jewel. In subsequent years, various short route segments not needed for freight operations were transferred to Amtrak.

Nevertheless, in general, Amtrak remained dependent on freight railroads for access to most of its routes. Amtrak fell far short of achieving financial independence in its first decade, but it did find modest success rebuilding ridership. Outside factors discouraged competing modes of transportation, such as fuel shortages which increased costs of automobile and airline travel, and airline strikes which disrupted airline operations. Intensive investments in Amtrak's track, equipment and information resources also made Amtrak more relevant to America's transportation needs. Amtrak's ridership increased from 16.6 million in 1972 to 21 million in 1981.

POLITICAL INFLUENCES

Unlike many large businesses, subsequent to its formation Amtrak has had only one active investor: the United States government. Like most investors, the Federal government has demanded a degree of accountability. Determination of congressional funding and selection of Amtrak's leadership have been infused with political considerations. Funding levels and capital support have varied over time. Political pressures extend to Amtrak's very route structure.

As with any federally supported activity, the more states and congressional districts served, the more political support in Congress. Some members of Amtrak's board and executive leadership have had little or no experience with railroads. Conversely, Amtrak also has benefited from the interest of highly motivated and politically-oriented public servants. For example, in 1982, former U.S. Secretary of the Navy and retired Southern Railway head W. Graham Claytor, Jr., brought his naval and railroad experience to the job. Claytor had served briefly as an acting U.S. Secretary of Transportation in the cabinet of President Jimmy Carter in 1979, and came out of retirement to lead Amtrak after the disastrous financial results during the Carter administration.

He was recruited and strongly supported by John H. Riley, an attorney who was the highly skilled head of the Federal Railroad Administration under the Reagan Administration from 1983-1989. Secretary of Transportation Elizabeth Dole also tacitly supported Amtrak. Claytor seemed to enjoy a good relationship with the Congress for his 11 years in the position. Of course, politics aside, that may have also been because he was perceived to have done a good job in reducing costs and living within a smaller appropriation, albeit through extensive use of short-term debt.

MODERN HISTORY

Ridership stagnated at roughly 20 million passengers per year amid uncertain government aid from 1981 to about 2000. Ridership increased in the 2000s after implementation of capital improvements in the Northeast Corridor and rises in automobile fuel costs. Since 2002, Amtrak has had four consecutive years of record ridership. During fiscal year 2006, Amtrak reported more than 24.3 million passengers, its highest total to date. Amtrak, an average of more than 67,000 passengers ride on up to 300 Amtrak trains per day. In the 1990s, Claytor was succeeded at Amtrak's helm by career public servants who inherited the goal of operational self-sufficiency.

First, Thomas Downs was assumed the leadership. Downs had overseen the Union Station project, which experienced substantial delays and cost overruns. Downs inherited monumental financial goals and departed after guiding Amtrak narrowly through a cash crunch. George Warrington succeeded Downs in January, 1998. Warrington previously led Amtrak's Northeast Corridor Business Unit. Warrington's sought to meet the requirements of a legislatively-imposed glide-path to self-sufficiency, excluding railroad retirement tax act payments. Passengers became "guests" and there were expansions into express freight work, but the financial plans failed. Amtrak's inroads in express freight delivery created additional friction with competing freight operators, including the trucking industry.

Warrington also had the burden of delays in implementation of the new Acela Express high-speed trainsets, which promised to be a strong source of income and favourable publicity along the Northeast Corridor between Boston and Washington DC. Under Warrington, Amtrak could not add sufficient express revenue or cut sufficient other services to break even. David L. Gunn was selected as president in April 2002.

By that time, self-sufficiency was falling out of favour as a realistic goal. Gunn had a strong reputation as a straightforward and experienced manager. He was not one to shy away from conflict with others. Years earlier, Gunn's refusal to "do politics" put him at odds with the WMATA board, which included representatives from the District of Columbia and suburban jurisdictions in Maryland and Virginia.

Gunn was an accomplished public servant and railroad person and his successes before Amtrak earned him a great deal of credibility, despite a sometimes-rough relationship with politicians and labour unions. Gunn was polite but direct in response to congressional criticism. In a departure from his predecessors' promises to make Amtrak self-sufficient in the short term, the Gunn administration took the stance that no form of passenger transportation in the United States is self-sufficient as the economy is currently structured, and that Amtrak should not be judged by different standards than other transport modes.

Highways, airports, and air traffic control all require large government expenditures to build and operate, coming from The Highway Trust Fund and Aviation Trust Fund paid for by user fees, highway fuel and road taxes and in the case of

The General Fund by people who own cars and do not. These expenditures are indirect subsidies unlike Amtrak's which fall under the watchful scrutiny of Congress when budget allocations are made yearly. Before a congressional hearing, Gunn answered a demand by leading Amtrak critic Arizona Senator John McCain to eliminate all operating subsidies by asking the Senator if he would also demand the same of the commuter airlines, upon whom the citizens of Arizona are dependent.

McCain, usually not at a loss for words when debating Amtrak funding, did not reply. Gunn's tenure was punctuated by successes in reducing layers of management overhead in Amtrak. He eliminated almost all of the controversial express business. His policy was that continued deferred maintenance would become a safety issue, which Amtrak would not tolerate.

The policies improved labour relations to some extent, even as Amtrak's ranks of unionized and salaried workers have been reduced. November 9, 2005, David Hughes, Amtrak's Chief Engineer, succeeded Gunn as interim president. Given Gunn's solid performance, many Amtrak supporters feared that Gunn's removal was Amtrak's death knell. On August 29, 2006, Alexander Kummant was named as Gunn's permanent replacement effective September 12, 2006. Kummant has expressed a commitment to see that Amtrak continues to operate a national rail network. He does not envision separating the Northeast corridor under separate ownership. He has said that shedding the system's long distance routes would amount to selling off national assets that are on par with national parks, and that Amtrak's abandonment of these routes would be irreversible.

He has recommended annual congressional funding of Amtrak in the amount of $1 billion for ten years. He said that this investment is moderate, in light of Federal investment in other modes of transportation. He compared the cost of four or five highway interchanges with the costs of providing one hundred mile-per-hour high-speed rail service for several hundred miles.

PUBLIC FUNDING

Amtrak commenced operations in 1971 with $40 million in direct Federal aid, $100 million in Federally insured loans, and a somewhat larger private contribution. Officials expected that Amtrak would break even by 1974, but those expectations proved unrealistic and annual direct Federal aid reached a 17-year high in 1981 of $1.25 billion. During the Reagan administration, appropriations were halved. By 1986, Federal support fell to a decade low of $601 million, almost none of which were capital appropriations.

In the late 1980s and early 1990s, Congress continued the reductionist trend even while Amtrak expenses held steady or rose. Amtrak was forced to borrow to meet short-term operating needs, and by 1995 Amtrak was on the brink of a cash crisis and was unable to continue to service its debts. In response, in 1997 Congress authorized $5.2 billion for Amtrak over the next five years—largely to complete the Acela capital project—on the condition that Amtrak submit to the ultimatum of self-sufficiency by 2003 or liquidation.

Amtrak made financial improvements during the period, but ultimately did not achieve self sufficiency. In the aftermath of the September 11, 2001, terrorist attacks, during which Amtrak kept running while airlines were grounded, the value of a national passenger rail service was briefly acknowledged in Washington. But when Congress returned to work following the attacks, the airlines received a $15 billion bailout package, and inattention towards Amtrak resumed. In 2004, a stalemate in Federal support of Amtrak forced cutbacks in services and routes as well as resumption of deferred maintenance. In fiscal 2004 and 2005, Congress appropriated about $1.2 billion for Amtrak, $300 million more than President George W.

Bush had requested. However, the company's board requested $1.8 billion through fiscal 2006, the majority of which would be used to bring infrastructure, rolling stock, and motive power back to a state of good repair. In Congressional testimony, the Department of Transportation's inspector-general confirmed that Amtrak would need at least $1.4 billion to $1.5 billion in fiscal 2006 and $2 billion in fiscal 2007 just to maintain the status quo. In 2006, Amtrak received just under $1.4 billion, with the condition that Amtrak would reduce food and sleeper service losses.

Thus, dining service were simplified and now require two fewer on-board service workers. Only Auto Train and Empire Builder services continue regular made onboard meal service. State governments have partially filled the breach left by reductions in Federal aid. Several states have entered into operating partnerships with Amtrak, notably California, Pennsylvania, Illinois, Michigan, Oregon, Washington, North Carolina, Oklahoma, Wisconsin and Vermont, as well as the Canadian province of British Columbia, which provides some of the resources for the operation of the Cascades route.

CONTROVERSY

Aid to Amtrak by government was controversial from the beginning. Formation of Amtrak in 1971 was criticized as a bailout serving corporate rail interests and union railroaders, not the traveling public. Critics assert that Amtrak has proven incapable of operating as a business and does not provide valuable transportation services meriting public support, a "mobile money-burning machine." They argue that subsidies should be ended, national rail service terminated, and the Northeast Corridor turned over to private interests. "To fund a Nostalgia Limited is not in the public interest." Proponents point out that the government heavily subsidizes the Interstate Highway System and many aspects of passenger aviation. Massive government aid of those forms of travel was a primary factor in the decline of passenger service by privately owned railroads in the 1950s and 60s. Amtrak still, indirectly, through fees to host railroads, pays property taxes that highway users do not pay.

Advocates assert that Amtrak only should be expected to be as self-sufficient as those competing modes. In other words, it should not be expected to be self sufficient at all. Proponents also argue that rail passenger service merits public support because it is safer and more energy efficient than competitors, and often more convenient and comfortable. Amtrak serves many communities which have no air service or other public transportation.

If rail operations received favourable treatment and capital support on par with automobile infrastructure and air transport, proponents argue that rail passenger service in America would not be so humble and would be more relevant to a greater number of transportation needs.

LABOUR ISSUES

Intractable positions staked out by labour leaders were blamed for part of the decline of passenger rail service in the early to middle 20th century, and labour union clout was widely credited with facilitating the creation of Amtrak in 1971. Many trade union jobs were saved by the bailout. In recent times, efforts at reforming passenger rail have addressed labour issues. In 1997, Congress released Amtrak from a prohibition on contracting for labour outside of the corporation, opening the door to privatization. Since that time, many of Amtrak's employees have been working without a contract. The most recent contract, signed in 1999, was mainly retroactive. New Amtrak president Kummant seems poised to follow a cooperative posture with Amtrak's trade unions. He has ruled out plans to privatize large parts of Amtrak's unionized workforce.

AMTRAK OPERATIONS AND SERVICES

Amtrak no longer is required by law to operate a national route system, although it nonetheless is encouraged to strive to do so. At the present time, Amtrak has some presence in all but two of the 48 contiguous states. Service on the Northeast Corridor between Washington, DC and Boston, Massachusetts, and between Philadelphia, Pennsylvania and Harrisburg, Pennsylvania is powered by overhead wires. Across the rest of the system, diesel locomotion is utilized.

Frequency of service on routes varies widely, from three trips weekly on the Sunset Limited from Los Angeles, California to New Orleans, Louisiana, to service several times per hour weekdays on the Northeast Corridor from New York

City to Washington, DC. Amtrak also operates a captive bus service, Thruway Motorcoach, that provides connections to train routes. The most popular and heavily-used routes are those on the Northeast Corridor, which include the Acela Express, and Regional. Those routes serve Boston, Massachusetts, New York City, Philadelphia, Pennsylvania, Washington, DC, and many communities in between.

Four of the six busiest stations by boardings are located on the corridor: New York; Washington; Philadelphia, and Boston. The remaining members of the top six are: Chicago and Los Angeles. Amtrak trains have both names and numbers. Train routes are named to reflect the rich and complex history of the route itself, or of the area traversed by the route.

Each individual scheduled run of the route is assigned a number. As a general rule, even-numbered routes run north and east while odd-numbered routes run south and west. Some routes, such as the Pacific Surfliners, use the opposite numbering system, inherited from the previous operators of similar routes, such as the Santa Fe Railroad.

INTERMODAL CONNECTIONS

Intermodal connections between Amtrak trains and other transportation are available at many stations. With few exceptions, Amtrak rail stations that are located in downtown areas have connections to local public transit. Amtrak also code shares with Continental Airlines, providing service between Newark Liberty International Airport and Philadelphia 30th St, Wilmington, Stamford, and New Haven. In addition, Amtrak serves airport stations at Milwaukee and Baltimore. Amtrak coordinates Thruway Motorcoach service to extend many of its routes, particularly in California.

GAPS IN SERVICE

Outside the Northeast Corridor, Amtrak was a niche player. In 2003, Amtrak accounted for 0.1% of US intercity passenger miles. In fiscal year 2004, Amtrak routes served over 25 million passengers, while in calendar year 2004 commercial airlines served over 712 million passengers. Amtrak provides some rail service in 46 states. The only states that are not served by Amtrak are Hawaii, Alaska, and South Dakota. Wyoming lost rail service in the 1997 cuts, but is still served by Amtrak's Thruway Motorcoaches.

Amtrak serves many states only nominally through stations along borders and/or away from major population areas. Many major cities in the Midwest, West, and South have two or fewer trains per day, such as Atlanta, Denver, Cincinnati, Indianapolis, and Minneapolis/Saint Paul. Amtrak's reliance on freight railroads has also been a cause for its elimination of service. Passenger rail service was entirely discontinued to Phoenix, Arizona in 1997, after the Union Pacific Railroad, which owns the tracks that served Phoenix, announced it was abandoning the right of way.

Amtrak did not have the funds to maintain the trackage thus today the city is only served only by Thruway Motorcoach. In 1983 the Palmetto was truncated from Saint Petersburg to Tampa due to Amtrak not being able to take on the costs of maintaning the Seaboard Coast Line drawbridge that took the train over Tampa Bay. Damage to railroad track caused by Hurricane Katrina interrupted service on the Sunset Limited. Originally the train departed from Orlando, Florida, but the track damage along the Gulf coast caused the train to originate at New Orleans, Louisiana. The track's owner, CSX, completed repairs by early 2006 but Amtrak service has not resumed over one year later, leaving the intermediate stations between Orlando and New Orleans without any Amtrak service. Several significant Amtrak routes have been eliminated due to lack of funding since 1971, creating other gaps. The east-west train feeding Kansas City with New York and Washington D.C. known as the National Limited was cut, leaving the only direct links between the Midwest and East through Chicago.

The North Coast Hiawatha between Chicago and Seattle provided only reduced service between Chicago and the Pacific Northwest. The last link with the vaunted Chicago-Florida services of such trains as the City of Miami, the Dixie

Flagler, and the South Wind, was broken when the Floridian was discontinued in October 1979. In 1997, the Desert Wind and Pioneer were discontinued, along with service to Las Vegas, Boise, and all of Wyoming.

In 2003 and 2005 Amtrak also discontinued the Kentucky Cardinal ending all service to Louisville, and the Three Rivers which provided another direct and daily New York to Chicago service through Pennsylvania. Also throughout the seventies Amtrak had also provided many secondary cities in Pennsylvania such as Reading and Bethlehem with service, yet has since discontinued it. All these gaps in service remain major concerns in the Amtrak system.

GUEST REWARDS

Amtrak operates a loyalty programme called Guest Rewards, which is similar to the frequent flyer programmes offered by many airlines. Guest Rewards members accumulate points by riding Amtrak and through other activities. Members can redeem these points for free or discounted Amtrak tickets and other awards.

FREIGHT

Amtrak Express provides small package and less-than-truckload shipping services between more than 100 cities. Amtrak Express also offers station-to-station shipment of human remains to many express cities. At smaller stations, funeral directors must load and unload the shipment onto and off the train. Amtrak hauled mail for the United States Postal Service and time-sensitive freight, but discontinued these services in October 2004. On most parts of the few lines that Amtrak owns, trackage rights agreements allow freight railroads to use its trackage.

COMMUTER SERVICES

Through various commuter services, Amtrak serves an additional 61.1 million passengers per year in conjunction with state and regional authorities in California, Washington, Maryland, Connecticut, and Virginia. Amtrak's Pacific

Surfliner, Capitol Corridor, and San Joaquins are mostly funded by a state transit authority, Caltrans, and not the Federal government.

TRAINS AND TRACKS

Most tracks on which Amtrak operates are owned by freight railroads. Amtrak operates over all seven Class I railroads in the United States, as well as several short lines—the Guilford Rail System, New England Central Railroad and Vermont Railway. Other parts are owned by terminal railroads jointly controlled by freight companies or by commuter rail agencies. The arrangement has two notable impacts on Amtrak operations.

The host railroad is responsible for maintenance and occasionally Amtrak has suffered service disruptions from untimely track rehabilitation. When host railroads have simply refused to maintain their tracks to Amtrak's needs, Amtrak occasionally has been compelled to pay the host to maintain the tracks. Also, Amtrak enjoys priority over the host's freight traffic only for a specified window of time. When a passenger train misses that window, host railroads may direct passenger trains to follow lumbering freight traffic, severely exacerbating even minor delays.

TRACKS OWNED BY AMTRAK

Along the Northeast Corridor and in several other areas, Amtrak owns 730 route-miles of track, including 17 tunnels consisting of 29.7 miles of track and 1,186 bridges consisting of 42.5 miles of track. Amtrak owns and operates the following lines:

Northeast Corridor

The Northeast Corridor between Washington, D.C. and Boston via Baltimore, Philadelphia, Newark and New York is largely owned by Amtrak, working cooperatively with several state and regional commuter agencies. Amtrak's portion was acquired in 1976 as a result of the Railroad Revitalization and Regulatory Reform Act.

- Boston to the Massachusetts/Rhode Island state line
- 118.3 miles, Massachusetts/Rhode Island state line to New Haven, Connecticut
- 240 miles, New Rochelle, New York to Washington, D.C.

The part of the line from New Haven to the New York/ Connecticut border is owned by the state of Connecticut, while the portion from Port Chester to New Rochelle is owned by the state of New York. The Connecticut Department of Transportation and the Metropolitan Transportation Authority operate this line through Metro-North Railroad.

Philadelphia to Harrisburg Main Line

This line runs from Philadelphia to Harrisburg, Pennsylvania. As a result of a successful investment partnership with the commonwealth of Pennsylvania, signal and track improvements were completed in October 2006, and now allow all-electric service with a top speed of 110 mph to run along the corridor.

Empire Corridor

- 11 miles, New York Penn Station to Spuyten Duyvil, New York
- 35.9 miles, Stuyvesant to Schenectady, New York
- 8.5 miles, Schenectady to Hoffmans, New York

New Haven-Springfield Line

- 60.5 mi, New Haven to Springfield

Other Tracks

- *Chicago-Detroit Line*: 98 miles, Porter, Indiana to Kalamazoo, Michigan
- *Chicago-Detroit Line*: 4 miles in Detroit, Michigan, CP Townline to CP West Detroit
- *Post Road Branch*: 12.42 miles, Post Road Junction to Rensselaer, New York

Amtrak also owns station and yard tracks in Chicago; Hialeah; Los Angeles; New Orleans; New York City; Oakland;

Orlando; Portland, Oregon; Saint Paul, Minnesota; Seattle; and Washington, D.C. Amtrak owns the Chicago Union Station Company and Penn Station Leasing. It has a 99.7% interest in the Washington Terminal Company and 99% of 30th Street Limited. Also owned by Amtrak is Passenger Railroad Insurance.

INDIAN RAILWAYS

Indian Railways, abbreviated as IR, is a Department of the Government of India, under the Ministry of Railways, and is tasked with operating the rail network in India. The Ministry is headed by a cabinet rank Railways Minister, while the Department is managed by the Railway Board. Indian Railways is not a private corporate body; however, of late IR has been trying to adopt a corporate management style. Indian Railways has a total state monopoly on India's rail transport. It is one of the largest and busiest rail networks in the world, transporting sixteen million passengers and more than one million tonnes of freight daily.

IR is the world's largest commercial or utility employer, with more than 1.6 million employees, and is second to the Chinese Army in highest number of employees. The railways traverse the length and breadth of the country; the routes cover a total length of 63,140 km. As of 2002, IR owned a total of 216,717 wagons, 39,263 coaches and 7,739 locomotives and ran a total of 14,444 trains daily, including about 8,702 passenger trains. Railways were first introduced to India in 1853. By 1947, the year of India's independence, there were forty-two rail systems. In 1951 the systems were nationalized as one unit, becoming one of the largest networks in the world. Indian Railways operates both long distance and suburban rail systems.

HISTORY

A plan for a rail system in India was first put forward in 1832, but no further steps were taken for more than a decade. In 1844, the Governor-General of India Lord Hardinge allowed private entrepreneurs to set up a rail system in India. Two new railway companies were created and the East India Company was asked to assist them. Interest from investors in the UK led to the rapid creation of a rail system over the next few years. The first train in India became operational on 1851-12-22, and was used for the hauling of construction material in Roorkee.

A year and a half later, on 1853-04-16, the first passenger train service was inaugurated between Bori Bunder, Bombay and Thana. Covering a distance of 34 km, it was hauled by three locomotives, Sahib, Sindh and Sultan. This was the formal birth of railways in India. The British government encouraged new railway companies backed by private investors under a scheme that would guarantee an annual return of five per cent during the initial years of operation. Once established, the company would be transferred to the government, with the original company retaining operational control.

The route mileage of this network was about 14,500 km by 1880, mostly radiating inward from the three major port cities of Bombay, Madras and Calcutta. By 1895, India had started building its own locomotives, and in 1896 sent engineers and locomotives to help build the Uganda Railway. Soon various independent kingdoms built their own rail systems and the network spread to the regions that became the modern-day states of Assam, Rajasthan and Andhra Pradesh. A Railway Board was constituted in 1901, but decision-making power was retained by the Viceroy, Lord Curzon. The Railway Board operated under aegis of the Department of Commerce and Industry and had three members: a government railway official serving as chairman, a railway manager from England and an agent of one of the company railways.

For the first time in its history, the Railways began to make a tidy profit. In 1907, almost all the rail companies were taken over by the government. The following year, the first electric locomotive appeared. With the arrival of the First World War, the railways were used to meet the needs of the British outside India. By the end of the First World War, the railways had suffered immensely and were in a poor state. The government took over the management of the Railways and removed the link between the financing of the Railways and other governmental revenues in 1920, a practice that continues to date with a separate railway budget.

The Second World War severely crippled the railways as trains were diverted to the Middle East, and the railway workshops were converted into munitions workshops. At the time of independence in 1947, a large portion of the railways went to the then newly formed Pakistan. A total of forty-two separate railway systems, including thirty-two lines owned by the former Indian princely states, were amalgamated as a single unit which was christened as the Indian Railways. The existing rail networks were abandoned in favour of zones in 1951 and a total of six zones came into being in 1952. As the economy of India improved, almost all railway production units were indigenised.

By 1985, steam locomotives were phased out in favour of diesel and electric locomotives. The entire railway reservation system was streamlined with computerisation in 1995.

PASSENGER SERVICES

Indian Railways operates 8,702 passenger trains and transports 15 million daily across twenty-five states and three union territories. Sikkim, Arunachal Pradesh and Meghalaya are the only states not connected. The passenger division is the most preferred form of long distance transport in most of the country.

A standard passenger train consists of eighteen coaches, but some popular trains can have up to 24 coaches. Coaches are designed to accommodate anywhere from 18 to 72 passengers, but may actually accommodate many more during the holiday seasons and on busy routes. The coaches in use are vestibules, but some of these may be dummied on some trains for operational reasons. Freight trains use a large variety of wagons.

Each coach has different accommodation class; the most popular being the sleeper class. Up to nine of these type coaches are usually coupled. Air conditioned coaches are also attached, and a standard train may have between three and five air-conditioned coaches. Online passenger ticketing, introduced in 2004, is expected to top 100,000 per day by 2008, while ATMs in many stations will be equipped to dispense long-distance tickets by the end of 2007.

PRODUCTION SERVICES

The Indian Railways manufactures a lot of its rolling stock and heavy engineering components. This is largely due to historical reasons. As with most developing economies, the main reason is import substitution of expensive technology related products. This was relevant when the general state of the national engineering industry was immature. Production Units, the manufacturing plants of the Indian Railways, are managed directly by the ministry. The General Managers of the PUs report to the Railway Board.

The Production Units are:

- Diesel Locomotive Works, Varanasi
- Chittaranjan Locomotive Works, Chittaranjan
- Diesel-Loco Modernisation Works, Patiala
- Integral Coach Factory, Chennai
- Rail Coach Factory, Kapurthala
- Rail Wheel Factory, Bangalore
- Rail Spring Karkhana, Gwalior
- Bharat Earth Movers Limited, Bangalore

BEML is not part of railways, but they do manufacture the coaches for IR and Metro coaches for DMRC and going forward for Bangalore Metro also.

SUBURBAN RAIL

Many cities have their own dedicated suburban networks to cater to commuters. Currently, suburban networks operate in Mumbai, Chennai, Kolkata, Delhi, Hyderabad and Pune. Hyderabad, and Pune do not have dedicated suburban tracks but share the tracks with long distance trains. New Delhi, Chennai and Kolkata have their own metro networks, namely the New Delhi Metro, the Chennai MRTS- Mass Rapid

Transport System, same as other local EMU suburban service as in Mumbai and Kolkata etc., but with dedicated tracks mostly laid on a flyover and the Kolkata Metro, respectively. Suburban trains that handle commuter traffic are mostly electric multiple units.

They usually have nine coaches or sometimes twelve to handle rush hour traffic. One unit of an EMU train consists of one power car and two general coaches. Thus a nine coach EMU is made up of three units having one power car at each end and one at the middle.

The rakes in Mumbai run on direct current, while those elsewhere use alternating current. A standard coach is designed to accommodate 96 seated passengers, but the actual number of passengers can easily double or triple with standees during rush hour.

The Kolkata metro has the administrative status of a zonal railway, though it does not come under the seventeen railway zones. The Suburban trains in Mumbai handle more rush then any other suburban network in India.

The network has three lines viz, western, central and harbour. It's considered to be the lifeline on Mumbaia Central Lines start from Chhatrapati Shivaji Terminus and runs for more than 100 km till Kasara and Western Line starting from Churchgate runs again for more than 100 km till Dahanu Road. It is thus longest suburban rail in the world. So also, it is busiest suburban network in the world, in the sense that it carries more than 5 million passengers each day. On 11 July 2006 six bombs were set off on these trains, targeted at the general public.

FREIGHT

IR carries a huge variety of goods ranging from mineral ores, fertilizers and petrochemicals, agricultural produce, iron and steel, multimodal traffic and others. Ports and major urban areas have their own dedicated freight lines and yards. Many important freight stops have dedicated platforms and independent lines. Indian Railways makes 70% of its revenues and most of its profits from the freight sector, and uses these profits to cross-subsidise the loss-making passenger sector.

However, competition from trucks which offer cheaper rates has seen a decrease in freight traffic in recent years. Since the 1990s, Indian Railways has switched from small consignments to larger container movement which has helped speed up its operations. Most of its freight earnings come from such rakes carrying bulk goods such as coal, cement, food grains and iron ore. Indian Railways also transports vehicles over long distances.

Trucks that carry goods to a particular location are hauled back by trains saving the trucking company on unnecessary fuel expenses. Refrigerated vans are also available in many areas. The "Green Van" is a special type used to transport fresh food and vegetables. Recently Indian Railways introduced the special 'Container Rajdhani' or CONRAJ, for high priority freight. The highest speed notched up for a freight train is 100 km/h for a 4,700 metric tonne load. Recent changes have sought to boost the earnings from freight.

A privatization scheme was introduced recently to improve the performance of freight trains. Companies are being allowed to run their own container trains. The first length of an 11,000 km freight corridor linking India's biggest cities has recently been approved. The railways has increased load limits for the system's 220,000 freight wagons by 11%, legalizing something that was already happening. Due to increase in manufacturing transport in India that was augmented by the increase in fuel cost, transportation by rail became advantageous financially. New measures such as speeding up the turnaround times have added some 24% to freight revenues.

NOTABLE TRAINS AND ACHIEVEMENTS

The Darjeeling Himalayan Railway, a narrow gauge railway that still regularly uses steam as well as diesel locomotives is classified as a World Heritage Site by UNESCO. The route started earlier at Siliguri and now at New Jalpaiguri in the plains in West Bengal and traverses tea gardens en route to Darjeeling, a hill station at an elevation of 2,134 metres. The highest station in this route is Ghum. The Nilgiri Mountain

Railway, in the Nilgiri Hills in southern India, is also classified as a World Heritage Site by UNESCO. It is also the only rack railway in India.

The Chatrapati Shivaji Terminus railway station in Mumbai is another World Heritage Site operated by Indian Railways. The Palace on Wheels is a specially designed train, frequently hauled by a steam locomotive, for promoting tourism in Rajasthan. The Maharashtra government did try to introduce the Deccan Odyssey along the Konkan route, but it did not enjoy the same success as the Palace on Wheels. The Samjhauta Express is a train that runs between India and Pakistan. However, hostilities between the two nations in 2001 saw the line being closed. It was reopened when the hostilities subsided in 2004. Another train connecting Khokhrapar and Munabao is the Thar Express that restarted operations on February 18, 2006; it was closed down after the 1965 Indo-Pak war. The Kalka Shimla Railway till recently featured in the Guinness Book of World Records for offering the steepest rise in altitude in the space of 96 kilometres.

The Lifeline Express is a special train popularly known as the "Hospital-on-Wheels" which provides healthcare to the rural areas. This train has a carriage that serves as an operating room, a second one which serves as a storeroom and an additional two that serve as a patient ward. The train travels around the country, staying at a location for about two months before moving elsewhere. Among the famous locomotives, the Fairy Queen is the oldest running locomotive on the mainline in the world today, though the distinction of the oldest surviving locomotive that has recently seen service belongs to John Bull.

Kharagpur railway station also has the distinction of being the world's longest railway platform at 1072 m. The Ghum station along the Darjeeling Toy Train route is the second highest railway station in the world to be reached by a steam locomotive. Indian Railways operates 7,566 locomotives; 37,840 Coaching vehicles and 222,147 freight wagons.

There are a total of 6,853 stations; 300 yards; 2,300 goodssheds; 700 repair shops and a total workforce of 1.54 million.

The shortest named station is Ib and the longest is Sri Venkatanarasimharajuvaripeta. The Himsagar Express, between Kanyakumari and Jammu Tawi, has the longest run in terms of distance and time on Indian Railways network. It covers 3,745 km in about 74 hours and 55 minutes. The Trivandrum Rajdhani, between Delhi's Nizamuddin Station and Trivandrum, travels non-stop between Vadodara and Kota, covering a distance of 528 km in about 6.5 hours, and has the longest continuous run on Indian Railways today.

The Bhopal Shatabdi Express is the fastest train in India today having a maximum speed of 140 km/h on the Faridabad-Agra part. The fastest speed attained by any train is 184 km/h in 2000 during test runs. This speed is much lower than fast trains in other parts of the world. The difference in these speeds could be in part attributed to the fact that the trains run on existing tracks, which were not designed for such high speeds.

ORGANISATIONAL STRUCTURE

Indian Railways is a department of the Government, being owned and controlled by the Government of India, via the Ministry of Railways rather than a private company. As of 2007, the Railway Ministry is currently headed by Laloo Prasad Yadav, the Union Minister for Railways and assisted by two junior Ministers of State for Railways, R. Velu and Naranbhai J. Rathwa. Indian Railways is administered by the Railway Board, which has six members and a chairman. Each of the sixteen zones is headed by a General Manager who reports directly to the Railway Board. The zones are further divided into divisions under the control of Divisional Railway Managers.

The divisional officers of engineering, mechanical, electrical, signal and telecommunication, accounts, personnel, operating, commercial and safety branches report to the respective Divisional Manager and are in charge of operation and maintenance of assets. Further down the hierarchy tree are the Station Masters who control individual stations and the train movement through the track territory under their stations' administration. In addition to the zones, the six production units are each headed by a General Manager, who also reports directly to the Railway Board. In addition to this the Central Organisation for Railway Electrification, Metro Railway, Calcutta and construction organisation of N F Railway are also headed by a General Manager. CORE is located at Allahabad.

This organisation undertakes electrification projects of Indian Railway and monitors the progress of various electrification projects all over the country. Apart from these zones and production units, a number of Public Sector Undertakings are under the administrative control of the ministry of railways.

These PSU units are:

- Container Corporation Limited
- Dedicated Freight Corridor Corporation of India
- Indian Railway Finance Corporation
- Indian Railways Catering and Tourism Corporation
- IRCON International Ltd.–Construction Division
- Konkan Railway Corporation
- Mumbai Rail Vikas Corporation
- Rail Vikas Nigam Limited
- Railtel Corporation of India–Telecommunication Networks
- RITES Ltd.–Consulting Division of Indian Railways

Centre for Railway Information Systems is an autonomous society under Railway Board, which is responsible for developing the major software required by Indian Railways for its operations.

RAIL BUDGET AND FINANCES

The Railway Budget deals with the induction and improvement of existing trains and routes, the modernisation and most importantly the tariff for freight and passenger travel. The Parliament discusses the policies and allocations proposed in the budget. The budget needs to be passed by a simple majority in the Lok Sabha. The comments of the Rajya Sabha are non binding.

Indian Railways are subject to the same audit control as other government revenue and expenditures. Based on the anticipated traffic and the projected tariff, the level of resources required for railway's capital and revenue expenditure is worked out. While the revenue expenditure is met entirely by railways itself, the shortfall in the capital expenditure is met partly from borrowings and the rest from Budgetory support from the Central Government. Indian Railways pays dividend to the Central Government for the capital invested by the Central Government. As per the Separation Convention, 1924, the Railway Budget is presented to the Parliament by the Union Railway Minister, two days prior to the General Budget, usually around 26 February.

Though the Railway Budget is separately presented to the Parliament, the figures relating to the receipt and expenditure of the Railways are also shown in the General Budget, since they are a part and parcel of the total receipts and expenditure of the Government of India. This document serves as a balance sheet of operations of the Railways during the previous year and lists out plans for expansion for the current year.

The formation of policy and overall control of the railways is vested in Railway Board comprising the Chairman, Financial Commissioner and other functional Members for Traffic, Engineering, Mechanical, Electrical and Staff matters. As per the 2006 budget, Indian Railways earned ₹54,600 crores. Freight earnings increased by 10% from ₹30,450 cr in the previous year. Passenger earnings, other coaching earnings and sundry other earnings increased by 7%, 19% and 56% respectively over previous year.

Its year end fund balance is expected to stand at ₹11,280 cr. Around 20% of the passenger revenue is earned from the upper class segments of the passenger segment. The overall passenger traffic grew 7.5% in the previous year. In the first two months of India's fiscal year 2005–06, the Railways registered a 10% growth in passenger traffic, and a 12% in passenger earnings. A new concern faced by Indian Railways is competition from low cost airlines that has recently made its début in India. In a cost cutting move, the Railways plans to minimise unwanted cessations, and scrap unpopular routes. Indian railways suffer from deteriorating finances and lack the funds for future investment. Last year, India spent $28 billion, or 3.6% of GDP, on infrastructure. The main problem plaguing the Railways is the high accident rate which stands at about three hundred a year. Although accidents such as derailment and collisions are less common in recent times, many are run over by trains, especially in crowded areas. Indian Railways have accepted the fact that given the size of operations, eliminating accidents is an unrealistic goal, and at best they can only minimize the accident rate.

Human error is the primary cause blamed for mishaps. The Konkan Railway route suffers from landslides in the monsoon season, which has caused fatal accidents in the recent past. Contributing to the Railways' problems are the antiquated communication, safety and signaling equipment. One area of upgrading badly required is an automated signaling system to prevent crashes. A number of train accidents happened due to a manual system of signals between stations.

However, the changeover to a new system would require a substantial investment. It is felt that this would be required given the gradual increase in train speeds and lengths, that would make accidents more dangerous. In the latest instances of signaling control by means of interlinked stations, failure-detection circuits are provided for each track circuit and signal circuit with notification to the signal control centres in case of problems. However, this is available in a very small subset of the total Railways.

Aging colonial-era bridges and century-old tracks also require regular maintenance and upgrading. In recent years Indian Railways has claimed that it has achieved a financial turnaround, with operating profits expected to improve by 83.7%. Credit for this achievement has been claimed by current Indian Railway Minister, Mr Lalu Prasad Yadav who claims to have brought a significant improvement in operating efficiency of goods traffic after he took over as Railway Minister in May 2004. The Rajdhani Express and Shatabadi Express are the fastest and most luxurious trains of Indian Railways, though they face increasing pressure from air travel, as the trains travel only 80 km per hour and their food and service is not competitive.

To modernize Indian Rail and to bring it at par with the developed world, would require a massive investment of about US$100 billion. Sixth Pay Commission has been constituted in India to review the pay structure of the Government employees and its recommendations are expected by the end of 2008 and based on its recommendations, the salaries of all Railways officers and staff are expected to be revised with retrospective effect. If previous Pay Commissions are taken as indicator then this revision will not be less than 50% upwards and it may hit Railways bottomlines severely and possibly mitigate all the good work of the Railways.

Sanitation and use of modern technology in that area has been a problem. Although Indian Rail has announced the introduction of dry toilets in the trains, so far not much headway has been made and the train toilets continue to drop the wastes on the rail tracks. Plans to upgrade stations, coaches and services are on track. Twenty-two of the largest stations are due for an overhaul when a private company is picked for the job. New LHB German coaches, manufactured in India, were scheduled to be introduced in 2007 on the daily run of the prestigious East Central Railway Patna-New Delhi Radjhani Express. These coaches will enhance the safety and riding comfort of passengers, and in time will eventually replace thousands of old model coaches throughout Indian Railways. Three new manufacturing units will be set up to produce state-of-the-art locomotives and coaches. Channel music, TV screens showing the latest films, and optional menus from five-star hotels are soon to be introduced on the Rajdhani and Shatabdi Express. Base kitchens and food services across the system are also slated for a makeover. More importantly, a whole new IT management infrastructure will be developed to better handle ticketing, freight, rolling stock, terminals, and rail traffic.

PALACE ON WHEELS

The Palace on Wheels is a special heritage tourist train,

which has been modified to incorporate fourteen saloons, two restaurant cum kitchen cars, one Bar cum Lounge, a library and four service cars. The cabins of each saloon are attached with bath and shower. This train is a complete example of luxury travel and has all the facilities of a five star hotel or resort. It is a seven-day trip. The train departs from Delhi Cantt station and arrives at Jaipur, Rajasthan on second day; the third day is in Jaisalmer, the fourth in Jodhpur, fifth in Ranthambore Tiger Sanctuary and Chittaurgarh Fort and the sixth day is spent in Jaipur.

On the seventh day the train goes to Agra before concluding the journey at Delhi Cantt Station on the eighth day. This train journey is a source of attraction for tourists from all over the world. The train chugs out of Delhi cantonment on a week-long run through Rajasthan every Wednesday night, with a trip also inbuilt to Agra and the Taj Mahal. Turban-wearing attendants take over from the moment you arrive at the platform, assigning you your coupes and detailing all the facilities that are on board. The train moves by night and arrives each morning at a new destination, where new experiences await you. If you are an early riser, you will see the sun rise over the horizon of the desert, a golden orb that flames in pastel colour before it ignites into brilliant orange as it mounts higher. So it has done for million years, and so it has been watched on its journey by thousands of them, residents of the desert; Suryavanshi and Chandravanshi, descended from the Sun and the Moon–incredible! It is not easy it is to believe but it is all true!

ROYAL ORIENT TRAIN

The Royal Orient train is one of the world's most exotic trains. The journey by the Royal orient train is a rare delight. It is an experience that takes you back to the times of Rajas and Maharajas. As you embark on your journey by the Royal Orient train, you get to explore two of the most fascinating and culturally rich states of India, Gujarat and Rajasthan. The journey by the Royal Orient train is a memorable experience as you get to see different facets of Indian culture. A joint venture of the Tourism Corporation of Gujarat and the Indian Railways, the Royal Orient promises you to showcase the best of Indian culture and heritage. Your experience on the Royal Orient will be unique and unforgettable; in a luxurious setting with personalized services from liveried attendants. There are thirteen coaches and saloons, named after erstwhile kingdoms of Rajputana. So get ready to experience the journey of lifetime as we promise to explore the rich cultural heritage of Rajasthan and Gujarat! The Royal Orient train is fitted with all the modern conveniences you would expect in five star hotels. Every cabin is clean, comfortable and furnished tastefully.

The cabins have spacious baths attached to them, equipped with running hot and cold water. In addition to this there are multi-cuisine restaurants that offer you the dishes of your choice. The Royal Orient train also has a bar on board. And if you are a book lover and passionate about reading, there's a library on the Royal Orient train to pass off time in your favourite way.

THE DECCAN ODYSSEY

This Luxury Maharaja Train is a joint venture between Indian Railways and Maharashtra Tourism and onboard services are managed by staff of internationally renowned Taj Group of Hotels. This Royal train tries to recreate the Era of Peshwas-medieval time Feudal Lords of Western India and there are additional facilities of Presidential Suite Cabins, Spa and Massage treatments, Conference Lounge Car, Business Centre etc. The 7 Nights Deccan Odyssey Train Tour operates Annually from October to April Ex. Mumbai every Wednesday and highlight of the Luxury Train Tour are the Golden beaches of Goa and World Heritage Cave sites of Ajanta Ellora. The Air-Conditioned Luxury Train Tour offers combination of richly furnished Deluxe Cabins and Presidential Suites; and All Passenger Cabins have private attached toilets with shower cubicles and daily refurbished with 5 Star hotel quality toiletries. There are Two Dining Cars, One Bar Saloon with smoking lounge area, Conference Area/recreation saloon with small Business Centre, Spa Saloon with mini-gym. Each passenger Saloon has four Deluxe Cabins and is serviced by a private attendant/butler, who looks after tea/coffee service and housekeeping.

TOY TRAIN OF DARJEELING

Trains came to India in the early part of the last century—among the very first and most novel, is the famous Toy Train of Darjeeling. It is 117 years old having made its maiden trip in the September of 1881. Officially known as the Darjeeling Himalayan Railway, it is as much a pioneering work of achievement, projecting not only its engineering ingenuity but also a historic development of the 19th century British convalescent centre in the remote north eastern Himalayas.

In 1870, an agent working for the Eastern Bengal Railway came up with a brilliant idea to reduce the costs of transport. His name Franklyn Prestage—the idea—the Toy Train. It took eight long years for Prestage to submit his scheme to Lt. Governor Sir Ashley Eden, who gave it immediate sanction. Named the Darjeeling Steam Tramway Co., it was changed to The Darjeeling Himalayan Railway Co. on September 15th 1881. It remained as such till it was taken over by the Indian Government on Oct. 20, 1948.

The construction had begun in 1879 and with the zeal shown by the workers, the first 20 miles from Siliguri to Tindharia station was opened in March 1880 for the Viceroy's special train only. After a further 11 miles to Kurseong were completed, it was opened to the public on August 23 of that year. Sonada was reached on February 1, 1881, the summit of Ghoom on April 14th, 1881 and finally on July 4th 1881 the baby locomotive and three coaches puffed right through to Darjeeling-a total of 50.75 miles. In 1914, the Darjeeling Himalayan Railway was further extended down south towards Kishanganj and close to the Nepalese frontier for jute traffic and in 1915. Meantime the DHR was extended from Siliguri towards Sevoke by 10 miles and further to the north 16 miles on Kalimpong road. Until 1878, the journey from Calcutta to Darjeeling took from 5 to 6 days by the East Indian Railway from Howrah to Sahebganj, then by steam ferry across the

Ganges to Charcoal, then by bullock carts on the river opposite Danger Hat, after crossing again by bullock cart or 'palki' to Purnea, Kishanganj, Titalya and Siliguri whence the ascent commenced via the Punkhabari road which finally joins the present cart road at Kurseong. In 1878, Siliguri was put on the map of the railway, the journey was cut to two days and another six to seven hours to Darjeeling.

INDIARAIL PASS

Foreign tourists, who wish to experience India by train, can enjoy special facilities earmarked for them. These are explained in greater details below.

- *Special Quota*: Several important trains have a special quota for foreign tourists. This can be availed on payment of US Dollars or Pound Sterling. Tourists without foreign currency will be allotted the special quota on production of the exchange certificates issued by any nationalized bank. At the time of reservation, the passport number and the country of origin should be mentioned.
- *Assistance Cells*: Major Reservation Centres have special Cells to help foreign tourists plan their itinerary, reserve their tickets and render any assistance required.
- *The International Tourist Bureau*: situated on the first floor of New Delhi Railway station provides personalized service and assistance to foreign tourists and NRIs regarding reservations, itinerary planning and other inquiries. This Bureau is manned by trained staff and tourist guides, fluent in foreign languages for any assistance.
- *Indrail Pass*: This travel ticket has been created especially for foreign tourists and Indian nationals residing abroad. This ticket is available for a special time period from 1/2 day to 90 days. Indrail Passes should be used within one year of issue. Validity period starts from the date of the first train journey and ends on the midnight of the last journey.

AVAILABILITY OF INDRAIL PASSES

- *In India, Indrail Passes are available for sale in Railway Offices at*: Agra Cantt, Agra City, Ahmedabad, Amritsar, Aurangabad, Bangalore City, Calcutta, Chandigarh, Chennai, Gorakhpur, Hyderabad, Jaipur, Mumbai, New Delhi, Puttaparthi Town Booking Agency, Rameswaram, Secundrabad, Trivandrum Central, Vadodara, Varanasi, Vasco da Gama and Vijayawada.
- Certain recognized Travel Agents are also authorized to sell these passes in Delhi, Mumbai, Calcutta and Chennai.

BENEFITS ON INDRAIL PASS

Travel as you like. Priority on Rail Reservation from Foreign Tourist Quota. Children below 5 years travel free and those between 5 and 12 years are charged half fares. Free meals on Rajdhani Express/Shatabdi Express trains. No sleeper surcharge on Night journey. No extra charge for Travel by Superfast Trains. No reservation fee for berths and seats. Free bedrolls on 1st AC/2nd AC/3 Tier AC.

TIPS FOR BUYING INDRAIL PASS

- For Single Journey you should purchase Half Day/ One Day pass as the validity of these passes are for 12 hours and 24 hours respectively from the time of you begin the journey.
- For Half Day/One Day pass in case of Rajdhani, you are eligible to use one class lower than you pay for the class. *E.g.* If you pay for AC class, then you will be eligible to travel by First Class/AC-2tier, AC-3 Tier/AC Chair Car.

WATER TRANSPORT

Water transportation is the intentional movement of water over large distances. Methods of transportation fall into three categories: Aqueducts, which include pipelines, canals, and tunnels; container shipment, which includes transport by truck and tanker; and towing, where a tugboat is used to pull an iceberg or a large water bag along behind it. Due to its weight, the transportation of water is very energy intensive. Unless it has the assistance of gravity, a canal or long-distance pipeline will need pumping stations at regular intervals. In this regard, the lower friction levels of the canal make it a more economical solution than the pipeline. Water transportation is also very common along rivers and oceans.

SHIP TRANSPORT

Ship transport is primarily used for the carriage of people and non-perishable goods, generally referred to as cargo. Although the historic importance of sea travel has lost much importance due to the rise of commercial aviation, it is still very effective for short trips and pleasure cruises. Nonetheless, sea transport remains the largest carrier of freight in the world. While slower than air transport, modern sea transport is a highly effective method of moving large quantities of non-perishable goods. More than 6 billion tons of cargo were delivered by sea in 2005. In addition to cargo carriage, one can consider scientific voyages and races as forms of ship transport. Transport by water is significantly less costly than transport by air for trans-continental shipping. Ship transport is often international by nature, but it can be accomplished by barge, boat, ship or sailboat over a sea, ocean, lake, canal or river. This is frequently undertaken for purposes of commerce, recreation or military objectives.

When a cargo is carried by more than one mode, the transport is termed intermodal. Ships have long been used for warfare, with applications from naval supremacy to piracy, invasions and bombardment. Aircraft carriers can be used as bases of a wide variety of military operations.

Ship transport is used for a variety of unpackaged raw materials ranging from chemicals, petroleum products, and bulk cargo such as coal, iron ore, cereals, bauxite, and so forth. So called "general cargo" covers goods that are packaged to some extent in boxes, cases, pallets, barrels, and so forth. Since the 1960s containerization has revolutionized ship transport.

CRUISE SHIP

A cruise ship or a cruise liner is a passenger ship used for pleasure voyages, where the voyage itself and the ship's amenities are considered an essential part of the experience. Cruising has become a major part of the tourism industry, with millions of passengers each year as of 2006. The industry's rapid growth has seen nine or more newly built ships catering to a North American clientele added every year since 2001, as well as others servicing European clientele.

Smaller markets such as the Asia-Pacific region are generally serviced by older tonnage displaced by new ships introduced into the high growth areas. Cruise ships operate on a mostly set roundabout courses, returning with their passengers to their originating port. In contrast, ocean liners do "line voyages" in open seas, are strongly built to withstand the rigors of transoceanic voyages, and typically ferry passengers from one point to another, rather than on round trips. Some liners also engage in longer trips which may not lead back to the same port for many months.

FERRY

A ferry is a form of transport, usually a boat or ship, but also other forms, carrying passengers and sometimes their vehicles. Ferries are also used to transport freight and even railroad cars. Most ferries operate on regular, frequent, return services.

A foot-passenger ferry with many stops, such as in Venice, is sometimes called a water bus or water taxi. Ferries form a part of the public transport systems of many waterside cities and islands, allowing direct transit between points at a capital cost much lower than bridges or tunnels.

6

Marketing: Concepts and Practices

DEFINITION OF MARKETING

The concept of marketing can be viewed from social and managerial perspectives. At its simplest, marketing can be defined as exchange transactions that take place between the buyer and the seller.

Marketing is the management function, which organizes and directs all those business activities involved in assessing and converting customer purchasing power into effective demand. Philip Kotler defines marketing as "a social process by which individuals and groups obtain what they need and want through creating, offering and freely exchanging products and services of value with others".

ASPECTS OF MARKETING CONCEPT

The important aspects of marketing concept are:

- *Creation of demand*: Marketing tries to create demand through various means. The producers first ascertain what the customers want and then produce goods just as to the needs of the customers. There is a systematic effort to sell goods and services just as to the needs of the customers.
- *Customer Orientation*: Marketing involves undertaking a range of business activities directed at the creation of customer satisfying products and services.
- *Integrated Marketing*: The customer orientation alone is not enough on the part of management. To be effective must be backed by an appropriate set up

within the country. The responsibility of marketing department is to ensure coordination of the various departments of the company *i.e.,* finance, purchase, research and development.

- *Profitable sales volume through customer satisfaction*: Marketing tries to realise long-term goals of profitability, growth and stability through satisfying customers' wants. All the basic activities of a company are planned to meet the wants of customers and still making reasonable profits. Modern marketing thus begins with the customer and ends with the customer.

MARKETING MIX

Marketing concepts had been originally developed in the context of tangible consumer goods. Marketing mix refers to the ingredients or the tools, which the marketer mixes in order to interact with a particular market. Kotler defines marketing mix as "set of marketing tools that the firm uses to pursue its marketing objectives in the target market". Each of the elements in the marketing mix is important and has an influence on the customer.

4 P'S OF MARKETING MIX

McCarthy has classified the main elements of a marketing programme in terms of 4 Ps- Product, Price, Promotion and Place.

- Product includes design, features, quality, range, size, models, appearance, packaging, and warranties. It also includes pre-sales and post-sale services like training for use, repairs, maintenance or replacements.
- Price includes concessions on basic price, discounts, rebates, credits, installation facilities and delivery terms.
- Promotion includes advertising, publicity media choices, messages, and frequency of exposure, campaigns, sales promotion, point-of-purchase, displays and merchandising.

- Place or channels of distribution includes retail outlets, wholesalers, transportation, warehousing, inventory levels, order processing procedures, etc.

Consumers generally form their perceptions of products and services based on prices. Pricing products and services is a complex process. It is based on the uniqueness of product attributes and the perceived value, which the consumer is willing to pay. Pricing strategies are planned just as to consumers' cultural norms and the political, legal and social environment of the place where the tourist product is located.

Example of Price: Indian Airlines has offered Super Saver tickets in January 2006, a multicoupon ticket is being offered with each coupon valid for travel between any two domestic destinations connected by a direct flight. The offer gives two options, one is about four-ticket option priced at ₹20000 in Economy class and the other is ₹28000 in Executive class. This is an example of good Bargain. There is also the option of buying additional ticket at incredibly low prices. Such convenience of booking provides the comforts of flying with wide choice of travel. Distribution systems or channels serve as the intermediary between consumers and suppliers and are an essential part of the travel and hospitality marketing strategy.

Many companies such as hotels or airlines use their central reservation systems to facilitate sales directly to customers. Example of Channels of Distribution: It is estimated that in the year 2004, out of a total 730 million Internet users, only 35.8 per cent use English language websites. Therefore, local language should be part of the distribution strategy and many hospitality companies also provide localized websites with several languages.

Let us understand how a marketer uses the tools of marketing mix by taking the example of a product like 'Tanishq' watches by Titan Industries. The watch is packed in plastic box, has a design, features, quality and company ensures warranty. It has list price but at times the dealer permits discount or rebate. The company distributes the watch through exclusive retail outlets. The company promotes it by using advertising and sales force. All the activities of Titan are the ingredients that have gone into the making of 'Tanishq' for the purpose of creating exchanges with the potential customers.

TARGET MARKET

The term 'market' refers to the collective of existing and prospective customers for the product. People who need to stay outside their usual residence use a hotel. A person may not have such a need but if such a need arises later, he is a prospective customer. The marketing effort is aimed at such prospective customers who would choose to buy the marketer's hotel services. However, all persons who need to stay outside are not prospective customers for the 5-star hotels. They may stay at budget hotels.

Hence, the market for the five star hotels is only part of the total market of total hotel users. Such parts are called segments of the market. The customers of the hotel are those who come to stay as well as users of other facilities. They are different groups and each group constitutes different segments since the needs and expectations of each one of these groups are different. For example, segmentation is possible on the basis of usage of swimming pool. The segments using the pools for training are different from regular guests in terms of age, behaviour, attention required, hours spent in the pool or cleanliness demanded and so on.

MARKET SEGMENTATION

Market segmentation is the process of identifying groups of buyers of the total market with different desires. Most markets are too large for an organization to provide all the products and services needed by all buyers in that market. This leads organizations selecting target markets necessitating market segmentation.

Market segmentation has certain obvious advantages in that the organization is:

- Better placed to spot and compare marketing opportunities,

- Cater to the specific needs of the buyers,
- Develop marketing programmes for specific market segments.

In tourism, market segmentation is very important. The strategy of market segmentation in tourism is to divide the present and the potential market on the basis of some characteristic and then concentrate marketing efforts like pricing, supply and promotion efforts to the target markets.

BASES FOR MARKET SEGMENTATION

Segmentation is usually done on the basis of one or more of the following characteristics:

- Buying behaviour- volumes of purchase, delivery requirements.
- Demographic- family size, religion, gender, income, occupation, language, education.
- Geographic- region, district, density of population, climate, urbanrural.
- Psychographics- value system, lifestyles, and personality types.

Usually the tourist market is segmented in terms of demographic, geographic, psychographic, social and economic criteria. For example the market for a particular area might be the businessmen in the age group of 40-60 years who have an income of over $100,000 per year and who live in southern parts of Germany.

The tourist market may be segmented on the basis of:

- Destinations.
- Economic status and spending tendencies.
- Place or origin of tourists.
- Preferences of staying, like camping, luxury hotels, caravans, etc.
- Preferences of travel, like air, sea, road, or rail.
- Purpose of tour like holidays, pilgrimage, sightseeing, shopping, etc.

Each segment of the market differs in terms of needs and expectations. No one organization can cater to the needs of all segments. Each organization has to decide on the particular segment or segments it would cater to. The segment so identified is called the target segment. Having identified the market, all activities will have to be planned keeping this target market in mind.

The services being offered, the messages in communication, the media used for communication, the pricing policies, the arrangements have to be consistent with the preferences and behaviour patterns of the target market. For example, if the hotel is targeting on the domestic tourists at religious places, then providing foreign food or advertising in business magazines would be the waste of resources. Instead, provide vegetarian thali food and advertise in religious magazines and on channels like Aastha and Sanskar.

TOURISM MARKETING

It is a well known fact that as long as the inherent sense of curiosity and adventure dwells in the hearts of human beings, the desire to travel in order to see new sights and experience new things, to live under different environments will always grows.

The marketing in tourism industry has evolved as part of the process initiated by the desire for travel in people. Without exception, all human beings will always nurture a desire to travel in order to see places.

The question arises that if the desire is ever present in people to travel and experience new things, why then would the tourism industry need marketing efforts at all? The marketing problems in tourism is quite different from marketing problems in other industries, and this justifies making marketing in tourism, a subject for separate and specialized enquiry.

The concepts and principles, the techniques and methods of marketing can be equally applied to tourism. The concept of tourism marketing can be better understood by identifying and considering the differences between markets for physical, tangible goods on the one hand and the market for tourism on the other. Tourism marketing could be defined as the systematic and coordinated efforts exerted by tourist enterprises at international, national and local levels to optimize the satisfaction of tourists, groups and individuals, in view of a sustained tourism growth. Krippendorf, "Marketing in tourism is to be understood as the systematic and coordinated execution of business policy by tourist undertakings, whether private or state owned, at local, regional, national or international levels to achieve the optimal satisfaction of the needs of identifiable consumer groups, and in doing so to achieve an appropriate return."

Tourism is a very complex industry because of its multifaceted activities, which together produce the tourist products otherwise considered as independent industry. Besides, its complexity lies mostly in the fact that tourists are located in different places, have different socio-economic structures, different needs, tastes, attitudes, expectations, and behaviour patterns.

The marketing concept helps the tourist organization to establish a consistent and effective communication system with actual and potential tourists in the selected markets. It also helps them to know their customers' wishes, needs, motivations, likes and dislikes.

SPECIAL FEATURES OF TOURISM MARKETING

From ancient times when travel was a prerogative of a select few who travelled in search of adventure to the present day jet travel, there have been many changes. Travel in ancient times was a simple affair. The type of facilities that were required by the people to travel was provided by a handful of suppliers of such services. In the present scenario of travel expansion, markets necessitated the application of marketing techniques. Marketing of tourist products has certain peculiarities.

The difference arises due to peculiar nature of tourist products:

- *A tourist product is assembled by many producers*: The tourist product cannot be provided by a single enterprise. In tourism, airline provides 'seat' to travel, hotels provide 'accommodation', a travel agent 'bookings' while a museum provides 'place of experience'. So, the tourist product is an amalgamation of many components, which together make a complete product.

- Intermediaries play a dominant role: In tourism, sales intermediaries like tour operators, travel agents, reservation services and hotel brokers play a dominant role. They determine to a large extent which services will be sold and to whom.
- *Production and consumption of tourist services are closely Interrelated*: The travel agent who sells his product cannot store it since there is a close link between production and consumption of tourist services. Production can only take place or can only be completed if the customer is actually present.
- *Tourism demand is highly unstable*: Tourism demand is influenced by seasonal, economic, political and other such factors. For example, political unrest affects inflow of tourist to a particular destination.
- *Tourism is an intangible, non-material product*: Unlike a tangible product, no transfer of ownership of goods is involved in tourism. Instead certain facilities are made available for a specified time and for a specified use like a seat in an aeroplane or room in a hotel.
- *Travel motivations are diverse in nature*: The reasons, expectations, and desires, which influence tourists' choice for certain holiday destinations, types of accommodation and vacation activities are varied. Very often people make exactly the same choice for entirely different reasons.

To a considerable extent, tourism marketing depends on various market factors. Therefore, marketing of tourism as compared to other industries needs a somewhat different approach.

PRODUCT IN TOURISM

The needs of the tourist relate to comfort and pleasure in travel, stay, food arrangements and visiting spots of interest and attraction.

Hence, the tourist expectations are:

- Able to experience the new places–their life-styles, food, culture, heritage, etc. as per one's own choice.
- Be able to visit places of interest, spend adequate time at such places.
- Facility of transportation available.
- Facing no risk to one's person or belongings, etc.
- Getting suitable food to one's tastes and health.
- Not to be hurried or hustled against the preferred place.
- To be looked after and cared for.

The three basic components of a tourist product are:

- Attractions,
- Facilities, and
- Accessibility.

Attractions constitute an important feature of the product. Attractions are those elements in the tourist product, which determine the choice of the particular tourist product, to visit one particular destination rather than another. These are things to see and enjoy like cultural sites, historical buildings, beaches, mountains, national parks, or events like trade fairs, exhibitions, music festivals, etc. Facilities are those elements in the tourist product, which are a necessary aid to the tourist centre. The facilities complement the attractions. These include accommodation, food, communications, guides and so on.

Accessibility is a means by which a tourist can reach the areas where attractions are located. Tourists' attractions are of little importance if their locations are inaccessible by the normal means of transport. It also relates to the formalities in reaching the places like visas, customs, bookings etc.

In Tourism, the products are varied. A travel agent may arrange for itineraries and airline bookings and may also help in getting passport, visas, foreign exchange clearances, embarkation facilities at airport and so on. Similarly attractions are added to a destination. For example, 18 rooms of Buckingham Palace have been opened to visitors, which are a major tourist attraction to visitors. Apart from the Throne Room, Drawing Room and the Picture Gallery, the Souvenir shop selling white china mugs with Buckingham Palace written on it or Crystal Balls with details from the State Dining Room is also a part of the attraction. A product in tourism is the place of destination and what one may experience while proceedings to and staying at that destination.

For example,

- Sentose islands of Singapore, is packaged as a place where there are no shops, no skyscrapers, no offices- a place of quiet and tranquility, to relax and be with nature, so different from Singapore. Travelling by cable car to the island is also a part of the package.
- Places in Rajasthan like Jaisalmer are being offered as tourism products to experience the life-style of Maharajas, living in real palaces with kingly comforts, travelling on ' Palace on Wheels', the luxuriously fitted railway train, going hunting on elephant back and so on. The product is not merely the city of Jaisalmer and what it may offer as historical and cultural importance. The product is the total experience of travel and other attractions, all related to the royalty of Jaisalmer.

The tourism product may be developed with emphasis on art, architecture, culture, religion, history, sports, leisure, temples, life-styles, etc.

- Himalayas are a product not only for sports and adventure tourism, but also for nature lovers and spirituality.
- Varanasi is a product based on religion, the Ganges capturing the essence of Oldest Hindu heritage.
- The accommodation provided, is as much a part of the safari in the African forests as the prospect of seeing wild-life. Many prefer and pay more to live in the open country 'with nature' instead of in five-star comfort.

CHARACTERISTICS OF TOURISM PRODUCTS

A product is something that a producer makes and offers to consumers to provide satisfaction of needs. Like all products, tourism also needs marketing and it is different from marketing of manufactured goods since tourism product has different characteristics.

INTANGIBLE

Manufactured goods are tangible in the sense that they have physical dimensions and attributes and can be seen, felt, or tasted. The tourism product is an intangible product. Take for example, an aviation industry. One can see the airplane, the facilities provided within, etc. But none of these would determine the nature and quality of services imparted by the airline. One cannot see, feel, smell, touch or measure a service performed. It can only be experienced from the effects produced during the journey.

INSEPARABILITY

A physical product is produced in the factory, bought in the shop and consumed in the customer's premises at his convenience. But when the customer buys a service like travelling in an airline, the production and consumption of the services takes place at the same time. The experience of the tourist product exists when it is produced as well as consumed. The service in the airline is the promptness of delivery of baggage or courtesy of the airhostess or safety of travel.

PERISHABILITY

A manufacturer of a physical product can anticipate the demand in advance and store the goods in warehouse and deliver them to the customers at the time of need. But the supply of the tourism product cannot be stored because tourism products are highly perishable. A seat in the plane or a room in the hotel not used today is a total waste. If an advertisement placed in the media channel is not seen or read, it is a waste. If the supply is not used, it perishes. So, the seats in an aircraft, the rooms in the hotels, the space in the ship, the services of a tourist guide, the time of the travel agency, etc. all perish if not utilized when available. What is not sold cannot be carried forward like stocks to be sold the next day or at any other time.

OWNERSHIP

No ownership passes from seller to buyer in a service. The buyer only acquires the right to certain benefits of what the seller offers. One may have the right to use a hotel room or a railway berth for a period of time, but the ownership of the room or berth remains with the hotel or the railways.

MARKETING MIX IN TOURISM MARKETING

Tourist marketing mix is largely a complex group of factors to achieve the 'end products', which helps the marketing manager to understand the demand in relation to supply and marketing investments. A balanced mix is necessary to reach this targeted result.

The tourist marketing mix can include the following elements:

The Product:

- Image, reputation, positioning
- Size and facilities offered
- Staff members and their attitudes
- The characteristics of the product

The Price:

- Corporate
- Discounted
- Normal
- Promotional
- Seasonal
- Wholesaler rates

The Promotion:

- Advertising
- Direct mail
- Public relations
- Sales promotion

The Distribution:

- Airlines
- Channels of distribution
- Clubs/Associations

- Intermediaries
- Reservation systems

'Marketing mix' has both short-term as well as long-term aspects. Long-term plans are based on study of natural, economic, social and technological aspects of the markets and customers. The short-term aspects relate to price reduction, aggressive promotion, or introduction of a new product in the market.

TOURISM MARKETING STRATEGY

One of the basic considerations for successful marketing strategy is the need for research. It provides the information base for effective marketing. It relates to providing answers to various questions pertaining to the marketing activities. Market research can be defined as the "systematic collection of information relating to supply and demand for the product in such a way that the information may be used to make decisions about its policies and objectives". In order to formulate any marketing strategy, it is essential for a tourist organization and others engaged in marketing of tourist products to know the answer of following questions:

- Who are the persons engaged in tourism and where do they live?
- Who are the potential customers and where do they come from?
- What are their likes and dislikes?
- What are their travel preferences and interests?
- What do they buy and where do they stay?
- What mode of transport do they use?
- What are their entertainment preferences?
- What are the trends in competition?
- What type of marketing programmes would be needed?

Market research provides answers to all the above questions. To make the overall marketing efforts effective and successful, as in the case of manufactured products, the tourist organization has to be totally aware of the trends in travel habits, vacation habits and complete knowledge about potential customers. It is very important to have detailed information on all aspects of a market. Results of such research will work as a guideline for designing and launching a successful marketing programme. A lot of data can be collected through publications, commercial analysis, trade information, press cuttings, previous studies etc.

Other ways to obtain data are:

- Tourism Departments,
- Discussion with tourists,
- Observation of customers at premises,
- Observations and discussions with visitors in exhibitions and trade shows,
- Attitudes, image perceptions and awareness studies,
- Advertisement and other media response studies,
- Studies of usage pattern.

7

Understanding Tourism Planning

AN OVERVIEW

Tourism is one of many activities in a community or region that requires planning and coordination. Here we provide a simple structure and basic guidelines for comprehensive tourism planning at a community or regional level. Planning is the process of identifying objectives and defining and evaluating methods of achieving them. By comprehensive planning we mean planning which considers all of the tourism resources, organizations, markets, and programmes within a region. Comprehensive planning also considers economic, environmental, social, and institutional aspects of tourism development.

TWO SIDES OF TOURISM PLANNING

Tourism planning has evolved from two related but distinct sets of planning philosophies and methods. On the one hand, tourism is one of many activities in an area that must be considered as part of physical, environmental, social, and economic planning. Therefore, it is common to find tourism addressed, at least partially, in a regional land use, transportation, recreation, economic development, or comprehensive plan.

The degree to which tourism is addressed in such plans depends upon the relative importance of tourism to the community or region and how sensitive the planning authority is to tourism activities. Tourism may also be viewed as a business in which a community or region chooses to engage.

Individual tourism businesses conduct a variety of planning activities including feasibility, marketing, product development, promotion, forecasting, and strategic planning. If tourism is a significant component of an area's economy or development plans, regional or community-wide marketing plans are needed to coordinate the development and marketing activities of different tourism interests in the community. A comprehensive approach integrates a strategic marketing plan with more traditional public planning activities. This ensures a balance between serving the needs and wants of the tourists versus the needs and wants of local residents. A formal tourism plan provides a vehicle for the various interests within a community to coordinate their activities and work towards common goals. It also is a means of coordinating tourism with other community activities.

STEPS IN THE PLANNING PROCESS

Like any planning, tourism planning is goal-oriented, striving to achieve certain objectives by matching available resources and programmes with the needs and wants of people. Comprehensive planning requires a systematic approach, usually involving a series of steps. The process is best viewed as an iterative and on-going one, with each step subject to modification and refinement at any stage of the planning process.

There are six steps in the planning process:

- Define goals and objectives.
- Identify the tourism system.
  - Resources
  - Organizations
  - Markets
  - Generate alternatives.
- Evaluate alternatives.
- Select and implement.
- Monitor and evaluate.

STEP ONE

Obtaining clear statements of goals and objectives is

difficult, but important. Ideally, tourism development goals should flow from more general community goals and objectives. It is important to understand how a tourism plan serves these broader purposes. Is the community seeking a broader tax base, increased employment opportunities, expanded recreation facilities, better educational programmes, a higher quality of life? How can tourism contribute to these objectives? If tourism is identified as a means of serving broader community goals, it makes sense to develop plans with more specific tourism development objectives.

These are generally defined through a continuing process in which various groups and organizations in a community work together towards common goals. A local planning authority, chamber of commerce, visitors bureau, or similar group should assume a leadership role to develop an initial plan and obtain broad involvement of tourism interests in the community. Public support for the planning process and plan is also important. Having a good understanding of tourism and the tourism system in your community is the first step towards defining goals and objectives for tourism development.

The types of goals that are appropriate and the precision with which you are able to define them will depend upon how long your community has been involved in tourism and tourism planning. In the early stages of tourism development, goals may involve establishing organizational structures and collecting information to better identify the tourism system in the community. Later, more precise objectives can be formulated and more specific development and marketing strategies evaluated.

STEP TWO

Identifying Your Tourism System When planning for any type of activity, it is important to first define its scope and characteristics. Be clear about exactly what your plan encompasses. A good initial question is, "What do you mean by tourism?" Tourism is defined in many ways. Generally, tourism involves people traveling outside of their community for pleasure. Definitions differ on the specifics of how far people must travel, whether or not they must stay overnight, for how long, and what exactly is included under traveling for "pleasure".

Do you want your tourism plan to include day visitors, conventioneers, business travellers, people visiting friends and relatives, people passing through, or seasonal residents? Which community resources and organizations serve tourists or could serve tourists? Generally, tourists share community resources with local residents and businesses.

Many organizations serve both tourists and locals. This complicates tourism planning and argues for a clear idea of what your tourism plan entails. You can begin to clarify the tourism system by breaking it down into three subsystems:

- Tourism resources,
- Tourism organizations, and
- Tourism markets.

An initial task in developing a tourism plan is to identify, inventory, and classify the objects within each of these subsystems.

Tourism Resources are any:

- Natural,
- Cultural,
- Human, or
- Capital resources that either are used or can be used to attract or serve tourists.

A tourism resource inventory identifies and classifies the resources available that provide opportunities for tourism development. Conduct an objective and realistic assessment of the quality and quantity of resources you have to work with. Some data suggested classification to help obtain a broad and organized picture of your tourism resources. Tourism Organizations combine resources in various proportions to provide products and services for the tourist. A partial list and classification of organizations that manage or coordinate tourism-related activities. It is important to recognize the diverse array of public and private organizations involved with tourism. The most difficult part of tourism planning is to get these groups to work towards common goals. You should develop a list of these organizations within your own community and obtain their input and cooperation in your tourism planning efforts.

Setting up appropriate communication systems and institutional arrangements is a key part of community tourism planning.

TOURISM RESOURCES

Natural Resources:

- Climate-seasons
- Fauna-fish and wildlife
- Flora-forests, flowers, shrubs, wild edibles
- Geological resources-topography, soils, sand dunes, beaches, caves, rocks and minerals, fossils
- Scenery-combinations of all of the above
- Water resources-lakes, streams, waterfalls

Cultural Resources:

- Anthropological resources
- Cuisine
- Ethnic cultures
- Historic buildings, sites
- Industry, government, religion, etc.
- Local celebrities
- Monuments, shrines

Human Resources:

- Craftsman and artisans
- Hospitality skills
- Local populations
- Management skills
- Other labour skills from chefs to lawyers to researchers
- Performing artists-music, drama, art, storytellers, etc.
- Seasonal labour force

Capital:

- Availability of capital, financing
- Infrastructure-transportation roads, airports, railroads, harbors and marinas, trails and walkways

- Infrastructure: utilities water, power, waste treatment, communications.

Tourism Management Organizations and Services

Off-Site

Coordination, planning, technical assistance, research, regulation:

- Educational organizations and consultants, *e.g.*, Travel and Tourism Research Association; U.S. Travel Data Centre; Travel Reference Centre, Univ. of Colorado, Boulder; Travel, Tourism, and Recreation Resource Centre, Michigan State University.
- Federal and state departments of commerce, transportation, and natural resources
- Federal, state, regional, and local tourism associations
- Travel information and reservation services

On-Site

Development, promotion and management, of tourism resources:

- Federal agencies, NB. departments of commerce, transportation, and land management agencies.
- Local government organizations, *e.g.*, visitor information, chamber of commerce, convention and visitor's bureaus, parks.
- State agencies, NB. departments of commerce, transportation, and land/facility management agencies

Businesses:

- *Accommodations*: Hotels, motels, Lodges, resorts, bed and breakfast cabins and cottages, Condominiums, second homes, Campgrounds
- *Food and Beverage*: Restaurants, Grocery, Bars, nightclubs, Fast food, Catering services
- *Information*: Travel agencies, Information and reservation services, Automobile clubs
- Transportation: Air, rail, bus; Local transportation: taxi, limo, Auto, bicycle, boat rental; Local tour services

Recreation Facilities and Services

Winter sports: Ski, skating, snowmobile areas; Golf courses, miniature golf; Swimming pools, water slides, beaches; tennis, handball, racquetball courts, bowling alleys; Athletic clubs, health spas; Marinas, boat rentals and charters; hunting and fishing guides; Horseback enterprises; Sporting goods sales and rentals:

- *Entertainment*: Nightclubs, amusement parks, spectator sport facilities; Gambling facilities: casinos, horse racing, bingo; video arcades; art galleries and studios, craft shops, studios, demonstrations; performing arts: theater, dance, music, film; historic and prehistoric sites; museums: art, history, science, technology; arboreta, zoos, nature centres,
- *Support services*: Auto repair, gasoline service stations; boat and recreation vehicle dealers and service; retail shops: sporting goods, specialties, souvenirs, clothing; health services: hospitals, clinics, pharmacies; laundry and dry cleaning; beauty and barber shops; babysitting services; pet care; communications: newspaper, telephone; banking and financial services

Tourism Markets

Tourists makeup the third, and perhaps most important subsystem. Successful tourism programmes require a strong market orientation. The needs and wants of the tourists you choose to attract and serve must be the focus of much of your marketing and development activity. Therefore, it is important to clearly understand which tourism market segments you wish to attract and serve. Tourists fall into a very diverse set of categories with quite distinct needs and wants. You should identify the different types of tourists, or market segments that you presently serve or would like to serve. This may involve one or more tourism market surveys.

A visitor survey identifies the size and nature of the existing market and asks the following questions:

- How did they find out about your community?
- How satisfied are they with your offerings?

- What are the primary market segments you presently attract?
- What attracted them to the community?
- What local businesses and facilities do they use?
- Where do they come from?

A market survey (usually a telephone survey) also can be conducted among households in regions from which you wish to attract tourists. This type of study helps identify potential markets, and means of attracting tourists to your area.

Tourism Market Segments

In a general tourism plan, some clear target tourism market segments should be identified. You might begin by defining the market area from which you will draw most of your visitors. The size of your market area depends upon the uniqueness and quality of your "product", transportation systems, tastes and preferences of surrounding populations, and your competition. Identifying the market area will help target information and promotion and define transportation routes and modes, competition, and characteristics of your market.

Next, divide your travel market into the following trip length categories:

- Day trips from 50 to 200 miles away,
- Day trips from a 50 mile radius,
- Extended overnight vacation trips.
- Overnight trips of 1 or 2 nights (most likely weekends), and
- Pass-through travellers,

After you have an idea of your market area and kinds of trips you will be serving, begin defining more specific market segments like vehicle campers, downhill skiers, sightseers, family vacationers, single weekenders, and the like. These segments can be more clearly tied to particular resources, businesses, and facilities in your community. What kinds of products and services are likely to attract each of these groups? Tourist needs as well as their impact on the local community are quite different for day tourists versus overnight tourists.

Areas catering primarily to weekend traffic will experience large fluctuations in use. In deciding the relative importance of these different segments, communities need to assess both their ability to provide required services (do you have enough rooms?), as well as the demand for different types of trips relative to the supply and your competition.

THE ENVIRONMENT

A tourism plan is significantly affected by many factors in the broader environment. Indeed, one of the complexities of tourism planning is the number of variables that are outside of the control of an individual tourism business or community. These include such things as tourism offerings and prices at competing destinations, federal and state policy and legislation, currency exchange rates, the state of the economy, and weather. These factors are discussed more fully in Extension bulletin E-1959 as part of the market environment analysis. Local populations also must be considered in tourism planning. As they compete with tourists for resources, they can be significantly affected by tourism activity, and they are an important source of support in getting tourism plans implemented. A survey of local residents can be conducted to assess community attitudes towards tourism development, identify impacts of tourism on the community, and obtain local input into tourism plans. Public hearings, workshops, and advisory boards are other ways to obtain public involvement in tourism planning. Local support and cooperation is important to the success of tourism programmes and should not be overlooked.

STEP THREE

Generating alternative development and marketing options to meet your goals requires some creative thinking and brainstorming. The errors made at this stage are usually thinking too narrowly or screening out alternatives prematurely. It is wise to solicit a wide range of options from a diverse group of people. If tourism expertise is lacking in your community, seek help and advice outside the community.

Tourism planning involves a wide range of interrelated development and marketing decisions.

The following development questions will get you started:

- How much importance should be assigned to tourism within a community or region?
- What are the relative roles of public and private sectors?
- Which general community goals is tourism development designed to serve?
- Which organization(s) will provide the leadership and coordination necessary for community tourism planning?

Tourism marketing decision questions include:

- *Place*: Where should tourism facilities be located?
- *Price*: What prices should be charged for which products and services. Who should capture the revenue?
- *Product*: What kinds of tourism products and services should be provided? Who should provide what?
- *Promotion*: What kinds of promotion should be used, by whom, in which media, how much, when? What community tourism theme or image should be established?
- *Segments*: Which market segments should be pursued; geographic markets, trip types, activity or demographic subgroups?

STEP FOUR

Tourism development and marketing options are evaluated by assessing the degree to which each option will be able to meet the stated goals and objectives. There are usually two parts to a systematic evaluation of tourism development and marketing alternatives:

- Feasibility analysis, and
- Impact assessment.

These two tasks are interrelated, but think of them as trying to answer two basic questions:

- Can it be done?, and
- What are the consequences?

A decision to take a specific action must be based both on feasibility and desirability. Feasibility Analysis: First, screen alternatives and eliminate those that are not feasible due to economic, environmental, political, legal, or other factors. Evaluate the remaining set of alternatives in more paying particular attention to the market potential and financial plan. Make a realistic assessment of your community's ability to attract and serve a market segment or segments. This requires a clear understanding of the tourism market in your area and how this market is changing.

Also carefully identify your competition and evaluate your advantages and disadvantages compared to the competition. Plan towards the future because it takes time to implement decisions and for your actions to take effect. Therefore, look at the likely market and competition for several years to come. Review forecasts for the travel market in your area, if available. Careful tracking of tourism trends in your own community can help identify changes in the market that you will have to adapt to.

Impact Assessment

When evaluating alternative development and marketing strategies it is important to understand the impacts, both positive and negative, of proposed actions. A classification of economic, environmental, and social impacts associated with tourism development. The types of impacts and their importance vary across different communities and proposed actions.

Generally, the size, extent, and nature of tourism impacts depend upon:

- Degree of concentration/dispersal of tourist activity in the area
- How well tourism is planned, controlled, and managed.
- Length and nature of tourist contacts with the community
- Similarities or differences between local populations and tourists

- Stability/sensitivity of local economy, environment, and social structure
- Volume of tourist activity relative to local activity

Look at both the benefits and costs of any proposed actions. While tourism development can increase income, revenues, and employment, it also involves costs. Evaluate benefits and costs of tourism development from the perspectives of local government, businesses, and residents.

IMPACTS OF TOURISM

Economic Impacts:

- Economic base and structure
- Employment
- Fiscal impact-taxes, infrastructure costs
- Prices
- Sales, revenue, and income

Environmental Impacts:

- Air
- Flora and fauna
- Infrastructure
- Lands
- Waters

Social Impacts:

- Community spirit and cohesion
- Congestion and crowding
- Education
- Occupations
- Population structure and distribution
- Quality of life
- Safety and security
- Values and attitudes

Impacts on Local Government

Local government provides most of the infrastructure and many of the services essential to tourism development, including highways, public parks, law enforcement, water and sewer, garbage collection and disposal. Evaluate tourism decisions with a clear understanding of the capacity of the local infrastructure and services relative to anticipated needs, and take into account both the needs of local populations and tourists.

A fiscal impact analysis evaluates the impact of tourism on the community's tax base and local government costs. It entails predicting the additional infrastructure and service requirements of tourism development, estimating their costs, deciding who will pay for/provide them, and how. Will tourism generate increased local government revenue through fees and charges, local sales or use taxes, increased property values or property tax rates, or larger local shares of federal and state tax revenues?

Impacts on Business and Industry

Businesses that are directly serving tourists benefit from sales to tourists. Through secondary impacts, tourism activity also benefits a wide range of businesses in a community. For example, a local textile industry may sell to a linen supply firm that serves hotels and motels catering primarily to tourists. A local forest products industry sells to a lumberyard where local woodcarvers or furniture makers buy their supplies.

They in turn sell to tourists through various retail outlets. All of these businesses benefit from tourism. If most products and services for tourists are bought outside of the local area, much of the tourist spending "leaks" out of the local economy. The more a community is "self-sufficient" in serving tourists, the larger the local impact.

Impacts on Residents

Local residents may experience a broad range of both positive and negative impacts from tourism development. Tourism development may provide increased employment and income for the community. Although tourism jobs are primarily in the service sectors and are often seasonal, part time, and low-paying, these characteristics, are neither universal nor always undesirable. Residents may value opportunities for part time and seasonal work. In particular, employment opportunities and work experiences for students or retirees may be desired. Residents may also benefit from local services that otherwise would not be available.

Tourism development may mean a wider variety of retailers and restaurants, or a better community library. It may also mean more traffic, higher prices, and increases in property values and local taxes. The general quality of the environment and life in the community may go up or down due to tourism development. This depends on the nature of tourism development, the preferences and desires of local residents, and how well tourism is planned and managed.

STEPS FIVE AND SIX

As suggested, not attempt a complete discussion of decision making, plan implementation, and monitoring, but these are critical steps in the success of a tourism plan. A set of specific actions should be prescribed with clearly defined responsibilities and timetables.

Monitor progress in implementing the plan and evaluate the success of the plan in meeting its goals and objectives on a regular basis. Plans generally need to be adjusted over time due to changing goals, changing market conditions, and unanticipated impacts. It is a good idea to build monitoring and evaluation systems into your planning efforts.

CONCLUDING REMARKS

Successful tourism planning and development means serving both tourists and local residents. The bulletins in this series stress the importance of a market orientation for attracting and serving tourists. This market orientation must be balanced with a clear view of how tourism serves the broader community interest and an understanding of the positive and negative impacts of tourism development. Remember, tourism should serve the community first and the tourist second. Tourism development must be compatible with other activities in the area and be supported by the local population. Therefore, the tourism plan should be closely coordinated with other local and regional planning efforts, if not an integral part of them.

NATIONAL AND REGIONAL TOURISM PLANNING

The importance of effective tourism planning in ensuring economic benefit and sustainability is now widely recognized. Here we introduce concepts of national and regional tourism planning and look at the basic approaches, techniques and principles applied at this level. It is now recognized that tourism must be developed and managed in a controlled, integrated and sustainable manner, based on sound planning. With this approach, tourism can generate substantial economic benefits to an area, without creating any serious environmental or social problems. Tourism's resources will be conserved for continuous use in the future.

There are numerous examples in the world where tourism has not been well planned and managed. These uncontrolled developments may have brought some short-term economic benefits. Over the longer term, however, they have resulted in environmental and social problems and poor quality tourist destinations. This has been detrimental to the area's residents, and tourist markets have been lost to better planned destinations elsewhere. Many of these places are now undergoing redevelopment. It is obviously better to plan for controlled development initially, and prevent problems from arising in the first place.

Tourism planning is carried out at all levels of development-international, national, regional and for specific areas and sites. National and regional planning lays the foundation for tourism development of a country and its regions. It establishes the policies, physical and institutional structures and standards for development to proceed in a logical manner. It also provides the basis for the continuous and effective management of tourism which is so essential for the long-term success of tourism. This publication is divided into two parts. The first part briefly explains planning concepts and describes planning and marketing methodologies. Emphasis is placed on the integrated approach, balancing economic, environmental and socio-cultural factors, and achieving sustainable development. Importance is also given to techniques that need to be used in implementing plans.

Without adopting and applying these techniques, tourism plans cannot be realised.

The second part presents case studies of tourism policies and plans which have actually been prepared and, for the most part, are being implemented. The case studies have been selected to represent the several different elements of plans that must be considered in integrated development. Most of the case studies are ones that have been prepared by the WTO for several countries and regions during the past decade. One of the important functions of the WTO is its technical cooperation activities. The organization has assisted many countries throughout the world in preparing planning, marketing, economic and other types of tourism studies, advising on all aspects of tourism development, and training local tourism-related personnel.

Both Parts I and II of this publication reflect the WTO's basic approach to planning for the integrated and sustainable development of tourism in its global technical cooperation activities. The WTO hopes that this publication will provide tourism officials, planners and others involved in tourism with an understanding of national and regional tourism planning. Their application of sound planning practice can then provide the basis for their countries to achieve successful tourism development.

THE IMPORTANCE OF PLANNING TOURISM

Planning tourism at all levels is essential for achieving successful tourism development and management. The experience of many tourism areas in the world has demonstrated that, on a long-term basis, the planned approach to developing tourism can bring benefits without significant problems, and maintain satisfied tourist markets. Places that have allowed tourism to develop without the benefit of planning are often suffering from environmental and social problems. These are detrimental to residents and unpleasant for many tourists, resulting in marketing difficulties and decreasing economic benefits. These uncontrolled tourism areas cannot effectively compete with planned tourist destinations elsewhere. They usually can be redeveloped, based on a planned approach, but that requires much time and financial investment. Tourism is a rather complicated activity that overlaps several different sectors of the society and economy. Without planning, it may create unexpected and unwanted impacts. Tourism is also still a relatively new type of activity in many countries. Some governments and often the private sector have little or no experience in how to develop tourism properly.

For countries that do not yet have much tourism, planning can provide the necessary guidance for its development. For those places that already have some tourism, planning is often needed to revitalize this sector and maintain its future viability. First, tourism should be planned at the national and regional levels. At these levels, planning is concerned with tourism development policies, structure plans, facility standards, institutional factors and all the other elements necessary to develop and manage tourism. Then, within the framework of national and regional planning, more detailed plans for tourist attractions, resorts, urban, rural and other forms of tourism development can be prepared. There are several important specific benefits of undertaking national and regional tourism planning.

These advantages include:

- Developing tourism so that its natural and cultural resources are indefinitely maintained and conserved for future, as well as present, use.
- Establishing the guidelines and standards for preparing detailed plans of specific tourism development areas that are consistent with, and reinforce, one another, and for the appropriate design of tourist facilities.
- Establishing the overall tourism development objectives and policies -what is tourism aiming to accomplish and how can these aims be achieved.
- Integrating tourism into the overall development policies and patterns of the country or region, and establishing dose linkages between tourism and other economic sectors.

- Laying the foundation for effective implementation of the tourism development policy and plan and continuous management of the tourism sector, by providing the necessary organizational and other institutional framework.
- Making possible the coordinated development of all the many elements of the tourism sector. This includes inter-relating the tourist attractions, activities, facilities and services and the various and increasingly fragmented tourist markets.
- Offering a baseline for the continuous monitoring of the progress of tourism development and keeping it on track.
- Optimizing and balancing the economic, environmental and social benefits of tourism, with equitable distribution of these benefits to the society, while minimizing possible problems of tourism.
- Providing a physical structure which guides the location, types and extent of tourism development of attractions, facilities, services and infrastructure.
- Providing a rational basis for decision-making by both the public and private sectors on tourism development.
- Providing the framework for effective coordination of the public and private sector efforts and investment in developing tourism.

The planned approach to developing tourism at the national and regional levels is now widely adopted as a principle, although implementation of the policies and plans is still weak in some places. Many countries and regions of countries have had tourism plans prepared. Other places do not yet have plans, but should consider undertaking planning in the near future.

In some countries, plans had previously been prepared but these are now outdated. They need to be revised based on present day circumstances and likely future trends. Founded on accumulated experience, the approaches and techniques of tourism planning are now reasonably well understood. There is considerable assurance that, if implemented, planning will bring substantial benefits to an area.

APPROACHES TO TOURISM PLANNING

It is important to understand the basic approaches to planning and managing tourism development.

PLANNING TOURISM AS AN INTEGRATED SYSTEM

An underlying concept in planning tourism is that tourism should be viewed as an inter-related system of demand and supply factors. The demand factors are international and domestic tourist markets and local 'residents who use the tourist attractions, facilities and services. The supply factors comprise tourist attractions and activities, accommodation and other tourist facilities and services. Attractions include natural, cultural and special types of features-such as theme parks, zoos, botanic gardens and aquariums-and the activities related to these attractions. Accommodation includes hotels, motels, guest houses and other types of places where tourists stay overnight.

The category of other tourist facilities and services includes tour and travel operations, restaurants, shopping, banking and money exchange, and medical and postal facilities and services. These supply factors are called the tourism product. Other elements also relate to supply factors. In order to 'make the facilities and services usable, infrastructure is required. Tourism infrastructure particularly includes transportation (air, road, rail, water, etc.), water supply, electric power, sewage and solid waste disposal, and telecommunications.

Demand Factors:

- Domestic tourist markets
- International tourist markets
- Residents' use of tourist attractions, facilities and services

Supply Factors:

- Attractions and activities Ïper cent Accommodation
- Institutional elements

- Other infrastructure
- Other tourist facilities and services Ïper cent Transportation

Provision of adequate infrastructure is also important to protect the environment. It helps maintain a high level of environmental quality that is so necessary for successful tourism and desirable for residents. The effective development, operation and management of tourism requires certain institutional elements.

These elements include:

- Availability of financial capital to develop tourist attractions, facilities, services and infrastructure, and mechanisms to attract capital investment.
- Education and training programmes, and training institutions to prepare persons to work effectively in tourism.
- Marketing strategies and promotion programmes to inform tourists about the country or region, and induce them to visit it, and tourist information facilities and services in the destination areas.
- Organizational structures, especially government tourism offices and private sector tourism associations such as hotel associations.
- Tourism-related legislation and regulations, such as standards and licensing requirements for hotels and tour and travel agencies.
- Travel facilitation of immigration (including visa arrangements), customs and other facilities and services at the entry and exit points of tourists.

The institutional elements also include consideration of how to enhance and distribute the economic benefits of tourism, environmental protection measures, reducing adverse social impacts, and conservation of the cultural heritage of people living in the tourism areas. As an inter-related system, it is important that tourism planning aim for integrated development of all these parts of the system, both the demand and supply factors and the physical and institutional elements. The system will function much more effectively and bring the desired benefits if it is planned in an integrated manner, with coordinated development of all the components of the system. Sometimes, this integrated system approach is also called the comprehensive approach to tourism planning because all the elements of tourism are considered in the planning and development process.

Just as important as planning for integration within the tourism system is planning for integration of tourism into the overall development policies, plans and patterns of a country or region. Planning for this overall integration will, for example, resolve any potential conflicts over use of certain resources or locations for various types of development. It also provides for the multi-use of expensive infrastructure to serve general community needs as well as tourism. Emphasis is given to formulating and adopting tourism development policies and plans for an area in order to guide decision-making on development actions.

The planning of tourism, however, should also be recognized as a continuous and flexible process. Within the framework of the policy and plan recommendations, there must be flexibility to allow for adapting to changing circumstances. Planning that is too rigid may not allow development to be responsive to changes. There may be advancements in transportation technology, evolution of new forms of tourism and changes in market trends.

Even though allowed to be flexible, the basic objectives of the plan should not be abrogated although the specific development patterns may be changed. Sustainable development must still be maintained. Planning for tourism development should make recommendations that are imaginative and innovative, but they must also be feasible to implement. The various techniques of implementation should be considered throughout the planning process.

This approach ensures that the recommendations can be accomplished, and provides the basis for specifying the implementation techniques that should be applied. Implementation techniques can also be imaginative and not only rely on established approaches. It is common practice for a tourism plan to include specification of implementation techniques, and sometimes a separate manual on how to achieve the plan recommendations.

PLANNING FOR SUSTAINABLE DEVELOPMENT

The underlying approach now applied to tourism planning, as well as to other types of development, is that of achieving sustainable development. The sustainable development approach implies that the natural, cultural and other resources of tourism are conserved for continuous use in the future, while still bringing benefits to the present society The concept of sustainable development has received much emphasis internationally since the early 1980s, although tourism plans prepared even before that period often were concerned with conservation of tourism resources. The sustainable development approach to planning tourism is acutely important because most tourism development depends on attractions and activities related to the natural environment, historic heritage and cultural patterns of areas. If these resources are degraded or destroyed, then the tourism areas cannot attract tourists and tourism will not be successful. More generally, most tourists seek destinations that have a high level of environmental quality-they like to visit places that are attractive, clean and neither polluted nor congested.

It is also essential that residents of the tourism area should not have to suffer from a deteriorated environment and social problems. One of the important benefits of tourism is that, if it is properly developed based on the concept of sustainability, tourism can greatly help justify and pay for conservation of an area's natural and cultural resources. Thus, tourism can be an important means of achieving conservation in areas that otherwise have limited capability to accomplish environmental protection and conservation objectives. A basic technique in achieving sustainable development is the environmental planning approach.

Environmental planning requires that all elements of the environment be carefully surveyed, analysed and considered in determining the most appropriate type and location of development. This approach would not allow, for example, intensive development in flood plain and steep hillside areas. An important aspect of sustainable development is emphasizing community-based tourism. This approach to tourism focuses on community involvement in the planning and development process, and developing the types of tourism which generate benefits to local communities. It applies techniques to ensure that most of the benefits of tourism development accrue to local residents and not to outsiders.

Maximizing benefits to local residents typically results in tourism being better accepted by them and their actively supporting conservation of local tourism resources. The communitybased tourism approach is applied at the local or more detailed levels of planning, but it can be set forth as a policy approach at the national and regional levels. The benefits accruing to local communities are also beneficial to the country, through the income and foreign exchange earned, employment generated and support that local communities give to national tourism development and conservation policies. Also related to sustainable development is the concept of quality tourism.

This approach is being increasingly adopted for two fundamental reasons-it can achieve successful tourism from the marketing standpoint and it brings benefits to local residents and their environment. Quality tourism does not necessarily mean expensive tourism. Rather, it refers to tourist attractions, facilities and services that offer 'good value for money', protect tourism resources, and attract the kinds of tourists who will respect the local environment and society. Quality tourism development can compete more effectively in attracting discriminating tourists. It is also more environmentally and socially self-sustaining. Achieving quality tourism is the responsibility of both the public and private sectors. This concept should be built into the tourism planning, development and management process.

LONG-RANGE AND STRATEGIC PLANNING

Long-range comprehensive planning is concerned with

specifying goals and objectives and determining preferred future development patterns. Tourism development policies and plans should be prepared for relatively long-term periods-usually for 10 to 15 and sometimes 20 years-depending on the predictability of future events in the country or region. These may seem to be long planning periods, but it commonly requires this length of time to implement basic policy and structure plans. Even development of specific projects, such as major resorts or national park-based tourism, can require a long time.

A planning approach which has received considerable attention in recent years, and is applicable to some tourism areas, is strategic planning. While the outcomes of strategic and long-range comprehensive planning may be very similar, strategic planning is somewhat different. It focuses more on identification and resolution of immediate issues. Strategic planning typically is more oriented to rapidly changing future situations and how to cope with changes organizationally. It is more action oriented and concerned with handling unexpected events.

Applied only by itself, strategic planning can be less comprehensive in its approach. By focusing on immediate issues, it may deviate from achieving such long-term objectives as sustainable development. But if used within the framework of integrated long-range policy and planning, the strategic planning approach can be very appropriate.

PUBLIC INVOLVEMENT IN PLANNING

Planning is for the benefit of people, and they should be involved in the planning and development of tourism in their areas. Through this involvement, tourism development will reflect a consensus of what the people want. Also, if residents are involved in planning and development decisions-and if they understand the benefits the tourism can bring-they will more likely support it.

At the national and regional levels of preparing tourism plans, the common approach to obtaining public involvement is to appoint a steering committee. This committee offers guidance to the planning team and reviews its work, especially the draft reports and policy and planning recommendations that are made. A planning study steering committee is typically composed of representatives of the relevant government agencies involved in tourism, the private sector, and community, religious and other relevant organizations. Also, open public hearings can be held on the plan. These hearings provide the opportunity for anybody to learn about the plan and express their opinions. Another common approach, when the plan is completed, is to organize a national or regional tourism seminar.

This meeting informs participants and the general public about the importance of controlled tourism development and the recommendations of the plan. Such seminars often receive wide publicity in the communications media. In a large country or region, the usual procedure is for the tourism plan to be prepared by the central authority with public involvement. This can be termed the 'top-down' approach. Another procedure sometimes used is the 'bottom-up' approach. This involves holding meetings with local districts or communities to determine what type of development they would like to have. These local objectives and ideas are then fitted together into a national or regional plan. This approach achieves greater local public involvement in the planning process. But it is more time consuming and may lead to conflicting objectives, policies and development recommendations among the local areas. These conflicts need to be reconciled at the national and regional levels in order to form a consistent plan.

It is important that the development patterns of the local areas complement and reinforce one another, but also reflect the needs and desires of local communities. Often a combination of the 'top-down' and 'bottom-up' approaches achieves the best results.

THE TOURISM PLANNING PROCESS

The first step in the planning process is careful preparation of the study so that it provides the type of development guidance that is needed. Study preparation involves formulating the project terms of reference, selecting the technical team to carry out the study, appointing a steering committee, and organizing the study activities. The terms of reference (TOR) for the planning study should be carefully formulated so that the study achieves its desired results and outputs.

The TOR for a national or regional plan indicates the outputs and activities that are necessary to prepare the development policy and plan. The special considerations to be made in planning-such as economic, environmental or social issues and the critical institutional elements-should be specified in the TOR. Identification of implementation techniques are also specified. The TOR format typically follows the planning process explained here, but it is tailored to the specific characteristics and needs of the planning area. Many places already have some limited tourism development, and these existing patterns must be considered in formulating the TOR. Other countries or regions will have considerable existing tourism development, but it may be declining or not be in a form that generates optimum benefits.

The TOR will therefore emphasize how to rejuvenate and improve existing development, along with how to provide guidance on the future expansion of tourism. It is common for a single study include various levels of tourism planning, such as national and regional plans along with detailed planning for priority development areas and projects. The planning for all these levels will need to be specified in the TOR.

BUDDHIST CIRCUIT

India is the birthplace of one of the most widely accepted religions in the world-Buddhism. The four holy places associated with Gautam Buddha in India are-Lumbini, his birthplace, which now lies in Nepal; Bodhgaya, where he attained enlightenment; Sarnath, near Varanasi, where he preached his first sermon; Kushinagar, near Gorakhpur, where he achieved Mahanirvana. The other important tourist places associated with Buddhism are: Sanchi, Vaishali, Nalanda, Amravati and Nagargunakonda.

All these places together are known as the famous Buddhist circuit in India. Bodhgaya is the most important Buddhist pilgrimage amongst all these places in India. Apart from being a significant archaeological site, it is renowned for the Mahabodhi Temple, which houses a 50 metre high pyramidal spire and an image of the Buddha. Sarnath near Varanasi is a vital centre of the Buddhist world where he delivered his first sermon and set in motion the wheel of law, the Dharmachakra. Buddhism germinated in Sarnath amidst the deer park. Nalanda is the famous education centre of Buddhism where the Chinese scholar and traveller Hiuen Tsang stayed in the 7th century to explore the roots of Buddhism.

Vaishali is significant to Buddhists as Lord Buddha announced his impending Nirvana here. One of the famous pillars erected by Ashoka to propagate Buddhism also stands here in Nalanda. Sanchi in Madhya Pradesh is known for its numerous stupas, monasteries, temples and pillars dating from the 3rd century B.C. to the 12th century A.D. Amaravati on the bank of river Krishna in the South India, is famous for its temple, dedicated to Lord Amarewara. The temple is the dilapidated 2000-year-old Buddhist stupa that draws millions of archaeologists and pilgrims every year. Named after the great scholar of Buddhism, Nagarjunakonda, located on the banks of river Krishna retains its status as the greatest centre of Buddhist learning in the South of Vindhyas. Earlier known as Vijayapuri, Nagarjunakonda was the venue of the massive congregation of monks and scholars during the bygone era.

The Buddhist circuit in India thus introduces you with the major townships in India that mark the evolution, development and propagation of Buddhism. After Gautam Buddha, it was Emperor Ashoka followed by his daughter and son Sanghmitra and Mahindra, who took the charge of propagating Buddhism in India as well as the South Asian countries like Burma, Nepal, China, Japan, Malaysia, Sri Lanka etc.

8

Information and Communication Technologies

INTRODUCTION

"Atithi Devo Bhava"—Lets welcome tourists as guests and send them back as friends." The new advertisement by the Ministry of Tourism has been seen by all of us. Using Information Technology, this message, is being sent out for Tourists, Tour operators, Travel agents, public at large for the following two basic purposes.

- To create a sense of security amongst Tourists.
- To change the attitude towards Tourists in India.

ICT Information Communication Technologies have been transforming tourism globally. The ICT driven re-engineering has gradually generated a new paradigm-shift completely changing the Industry structure and developing a whole range of opportunities and threats. The new technologies enable the customers to customise, purchase and select the tourism products with pace and ease.

In fact the information technologies are undergoing a revolution world over. They are a key determinant for maximizing the gains. However the success of ICT deployment requires constant improvement and innovative management. The customer's decision risk has increased manifold because he has only information to rely on as he neither sees or inspects or tries out tourist services before deciding to use them. He can rely on the Internet, which is the latest product of Information Technology. It is possible once the customer has access to Internet site; he gets various opportunities out of which E-mail is one. The latest one to be used is video-conferencing, which is fast being identified as a powerful means of communication between the service providers of Tourism and the users of such services. In fact the communication technologies have completely revolutionized the Tourism Industry. Role of Communication Technologies is vital to any business and particularly to the tourism business. They are important for cost savings and improved communications that arise from an internal network. They help in reaching out and connecting with customers, suppliers and collaborators, which, in the case of Tourism Industry are:

- Airways, Railways and Roadways
- Hotels and all the other types of accommodation
- Tour operators and Travel agents
- Tourists and Travellers

To be precise, following benefits are offered by telecommunication to Tourism as well as other businesses:

- Enables sharing and dissemination of information of all tourism partners.
- Helps geographically separate persons to come together.
- Promotes new ways of tourism partnership.
- Restructure relationship with partners.

However the communication technologies are also prone to following limitations:

- High initial set-up cost
- Practical difficulties
- Security Risks

Inspite of the limitations, Information Communication Technologies are being used in a big way by the Tourism Industry. In fact, it will not be wrong to say that no successful Tour operator or Travel Agent can function without using information technologies. It is, therefore, extremely significant to the Tourism Industry. It will be appropriate here to extend the following quote. "A Journey of a thousand miles must begin with a single step" Lao Tzu. "No single step by a tourist can be taken without using Information Technologies".

OBJECTIVES

So far you have learnt about the concept of marketing and understood that Tourism marketing stands apart from marketing of other products and their advertising techniques and Public relations are also unique. After having this basic knowledge, with respect to tourism marketing, this session will deal with the basic concepts of information technologies in tourism marketing.

After having gone through this session, you should be able to:

- Define and explain different information technologies.
- Know various sectors of Tourism that require information technologies.
- Realise the benefits of information technologies for the user as well as Tour and Travel agents.
- Understand how the use of information technology has led to the growth of Tourism world over.
- Understand the role of Information Technologies in Information Centres.
- Understand Tourism with respect to changing communication technologies.

COMMUNICATION TECHNOLOGY: SIGNIFICANCE

The communication technology is significant in tourism industry in following ways:

- Allows organizations to use their resources more wisely and profitably.
- Creates a sense of security amongst tourists and also provides a friendly environment.
- Develops new avenues and new tourist spots.
- Enables central control and outsourcing of non-core functions.
- Helps in development of extensive growth between partner organizations and between employees, consumers and organizations.
- Helps in sustaining and promoting the existing ones.
- Information technology devices help in linking and sharing data and processes electronically, to build

complementary services, expand, reach and enhance collaboration.

- Most devices result in information power storage and profitability.
- Possibility of handling complex details with increase in speed.
- Results in enhancement of processing capabilities.

Davis and Meyer state "Almost instantaneous communication and computation, for example, are shrinking time and focusing us on speed. Connectivity is putting everybody and everything on line in one way or the other and has led to the "the death of distance", a shrinking of space. Intangible value of all kinds, like services and information is growing explosively reducing the importance of tangible mass". The opinion clearly highlights the importance and impact of emerging communication technologies in this highly dynamic industry. The concept of "Global Village" would be very appropriate in this scenario because it is growing communication technologies, which have opened doors for tourists .and travellers and have made availability of information only with the press of a button, with the help of several new Information Technologies.

NEW INFORMATION TECHNOLOGIES

- Cable Television Technology
- Computer Technology
- Internet and Travel and Tourism
- Satellite Television
- Sky Track Technology
- Telecopy Technology
- Telefax Technology
- Teletex Technology
- Videotex Technology
- Websites

COMPUTER TECHNOLOGY

Computer is a tool, which is capable of processing a very large amount of data rapidly, or it is any device capable of processing information to produce a desired result. No matter how large or small they are, computers typically perform their work in three well-defined steps:

- Accepting input
- Processing the input just as to predefined rules
- Producing output

Computer is a multi-function electronic device that can execute instructions to perform a task. Therefore an electronic device that performs pre-defined or programmed computations at a high speed and with great accuracy; a machine that is used to store, transfer, and transform information is known as "Computer" to us. It has made its entry in the field of tourism in a big way. In fact, computers are in use in some way or the other in various branches of tourism since the early sixties.

Be it travel agencies, hotels, Airlines or recently even in the Railways, Computers have played a key role in making the task of providers of travel services an easy affair. Not only this, through home terminals, computers are undertaking, among other jobs, the planning of vacations for an individual and his family.

Computer applications are used in:

- Airlines
- Cargo
- Hotels
- Terminals
- Travel Agency
- Railways

In the year 1983–Thompson Holidays first used computers using online programmes and introduced reservations via Prestel. Several other big tour operators, since then used similar to sell their various programmes.

SATELLITE TELEVISION

Satellite television is television operated by means of orbiting communication satellites located 37,000 km above the earth's surface. The first satellite television signal was relayed from Europe to the Telstar satellite over North America in 1962.

The first domestic North American satellite to carry television was Canada's Anik 1, which was launched in 1973. Satellite can also be described as a television system in which the signal is transmitted to an orbiting satellite that receives the signal and amplifies it and transmits it back to earth.

Therefore, it refers to courses that are broadcast, usually live, by an electronic signal sent to a satellite orbiting the earth and then retrieved by a satellite dish. The satellite dish broadcasting the programme is called an "uplink", and the receiving dish is called a "downlink". For Tour operators, as well as Travel agents it serves as a linking device for making available the information of one corner of world to the other corner and Tourists are also, accordingly, benefitted by this linking device.

CABLE TELEVISION TECHNOLOGY

Cable television or Community Antenna Television is a system of providing television, FM radio programming and other services to consumers via radio waves transmitted directly to people's televisions through fixed coaxial cables as opposed to the over-the-air method used in traditional television broadcasting in which a television antenna is required. Cable system covering defined areas, such as the UK's franchise to install and operate a cable system granted by the Cable Authority and Department of Trade and Industry, offering TV channel output and, increasingly, local loop digital telephony services. The Cable Television Association is the CATV industry's representative organization.

Therefore it is a transmission system that distributes and broadcasts television signals and other services by means of a coaxial cable. Cable Television Technology has also greatly helped in information transfer and information sharing. Therefore, it has brought the tourists, the tour operators and the destinations close. It immensely helps in advertising and marketing of Tourism products.

VIDEOTEX TECHNOLOGY

Videotex is a system for sending of pages of text to a user

in computer form, typically to be displayed on a television. It is computer technology of the 1980s that uses ordinary television sets, or similar low-cost monitors, to display computer information.

Videotex systems, such as Canada's Telidon, were a complete commercial failure in North America, but achieved a modicum of success in Europe–*e.g.* France's Teletel and, to a much lesser degree, the UK's Prestel. Therefore, it is a form of electronic publishing consisting of computer-generated text distributed through telecommunications and received and viewed on home television.

It occupies a special position among the 'new media'. It plays a key role in the link between telecommunication and the computer sciences. Its advantage lies in the possibility it provides for linking computers and also in its interactive dialogue capabilities. Using Videotex, information and communication systems can be converted into interactive systems capable of communicating with one another. In fact, Videotex is a multipurpose instrument with multiplicity of uses.

It serves as:

- An instrument for data processing
- An information medium
- An organizational aid
- A communication system
- A marketing instrument

This relatively new service connects various forms of use of the facilities and at the same time offers some other possibilities. To operate this service, a television set with a decoder and telephone is necessary, without which the service cannot operate. In Europe, nearly all the households have television sets and a telephone and with the help of Vedeotex, separate households can be reached in large areas. Members of German BTX service as well as Members of France Telecom services can now obtain all kinds of information from external computers or use data bank all through their television sets. In many other European countries and USA, similar systems are in use.

It is being used in a big way in Tourism, also in India because:

- It allows rapid message transmission
- Fast and inexpensive data collection
- Keeps up-to-date information, which is crucial for advertising

It has been found that Videotex is the most advantageous means of Communication, taking into account its low cost and wider range of applications. This technology enables the tour operators and travel agents or hoteliers to send complete pages of information text to the tourist to assist him in deciding and finalizing his tour plans. Satellite, Cable and Videotex technologies are very important because of their wider coverage and their technical methods of transmission, however, they have one shortcoming that none can be directed to one specific person. In addition, the person receiving information is only partially informed. The receiver of information cannot also start a dialogue or communicate. However, the following gives possibility of direct transmission of information to a single consumer:

TELETEX TECHNOLOGY

Teletex is a text and document communications service that could be provided over telephone lines. Teletex allows for the transmission and outing of Group 4 facsimile documents. It is neither like Telex nor like Teletex. Although it may not be as versatile a technology as some others that have been mentioned earlier in this session, but helps in transmitting information which is required by a tourist from a tour operator, Travel agent or a Hotel. Computer information and even copies of documents can be transferred to the tourist with efficiency. It is an improvement over telex and has in fact developed from it. The receiver for Teletex is an electronic 'typewriter', which can send electronically enriched 'letters' to owners of ordinary telex equipment. The transmission of message time is usually shorter in comparison with time taken with telex. Besides, it is also possible to transmit more office typewriters, symbols. A normal electronic typewriter can also be used as a receiver for telefax.

TELEFAX TECHNOLOGY

It is an electronic post office box system. Each member of the system has his or her 'post office box' in the computer, where other members can leave their message. The owner of each box can electronically contact the others. All the means discussed permit the exchange of information electronically through a data 'network'. The exchange of information between the members with the assistance of electronic transmission is very fast. The data is also available in written form in printouts.

'Network' is a system of transmission linking facilities for automatic data processing. In this way, different computers are connected, permitting data exchange and processing over long distances. Telecommunication is possible only when there is such a network available. Telephone is the simplest and best communication network. In addition there is also separate clear data network for the exchange of data, which works digitally. In this way, a high transmission speed is achieved and there is a very low ratio of errors during transmission. There are different types of networks, which can be used for telecommunication purposes either separately or combined. In Tourism, in addition to travel agents, tour operators, hoteliers, airlines, travel journalist's etc. use this technology.

TELECOPY

It provides the possibility of exchanging photocopies through a data network. Information, in the form of either written document or technical drawing, is remote copied. This means that two facilities for copying are connected. One at the sender's end and the other at the receiver's end. Transmission time is only a few minutes. Usually the details of packages, booking details or list of itineraries are sent to this tourist by the Tour operator, Travel agent or the Hotel.

INTERNET AND TRAVEL AND TOURISM

So far the information technology dealt with has been of the kind where intermediaries, travel agents, tour operators etc. are an indispensable part in the distribution and marketing of travel and tourism products, and as an important point of sale or product outlets. This is an information technology where the producer and the consumer are directly communicating, by putting the indispensability of travel intermediaries in question. As has been discussed earlier, the intangibility of the product where risk and uncertainty for the customer is higher, his need for reliable prepurchase information is stronger. Through Internet, which is the latest product of information technology, this need is fulfilled.

This interactive information-supplying medium is user friendly and gives enormous information of all kinds related to travel. Apart from supplying information about the world's leading and emerging tourist destination of all kinds, it is now possible to book and buy holidays through Internet using plastic money. It gives information on all Airlines, Hotels and Car hire companies, which are in its database. Microsoft is a travel agent. Its Internet site branded Expedia is one of the most important examples of the new generation of travel intermediaries.

Distribution of travel and tourism products using the Internet has a substantial cost reduction advantage for providers of tourism services. The cost incurred by suppliers in receiving a customer booking is the one, which is costly. So, Internet gives a practical aid both in supplying information and receiving bookings or selling tourism products on the principal's behalf. Marketing tourism products on the Internet is also possible. This is done through the page of the company's Internet site.

Once the company gets access to the Internet, it gets various opportunities. Of these, Electronicmail is one. As a tourism product supplier, especially with business travel as a selected target market, it can communicate with the person through his/her e-mail address wherever the client is. Unlike telephone communication, there is no need for the presence of the receiver of the message during message transmission. It also gives a typed copy of the message. E-mail communication medium is very cheap yet efficient and effective. On the other hand, marketing on the Internet has an advantage of being used by all company's of all sizes as long as they can establish their Web Site on the Internet.

WEBSITES

A website is a collection of all pages under one domain. Sometimes, the subdirectories of large ISP(s) are also referred to as websites as they have been designed by different users and with different interests in mind.

Benefits of Websites

No matter how small or large a business is, one can profit enormously from a website in following ways.

- Reduces advertising costs.
- Information remains on line and always up-to-date.
- Pictures, product description, newly won awards, customer questions and instruction videos are possible on the web-site.
- Announcement of a package, deal, and sale can be promptly updated on the website.
- Customers find it simpler to surf the net and log-on to the websites for desired information.
- Websites almost eliminate waste of time in travelling for the desired information centre.

The tourist can make use of the websites, sitting back at home for making tour plans. Accordingly enormous websites are there by tour operators, travel agents, Hotels etc, some of which are given below.

- Luxury Resortsindia.com
- Destinations India.com
- Jaipur JodhpurUdaipur.com
- India Tours and Travels.com
- Asia Tours and Travel.com
- TravelinIndia.com

SKY TRACK

It is an automated airline reservation system, which enables travel agents to make bookings on hundreds of world's airlines using standard Prestel Television set and a keyboard.

Possibility of direct transmission between tourists, tour operators and travel agents. This system invented by British Telecom is a way of providing computerized information terminal. The only requirement is a Telephone line and a standard colour Television set with an Adapter to link it to a decoder and keyboard. The information is transmitted quickly and accurately via ordinary telephone lines. The required information is rapidly transmitted through this technology and is very helpful in providing desired information to tourists.

INFORMATION TECHNOLOGY IN THE TRANSPORT SECTOR

Transport provides the essential link between tourism origin and destination areas and facilitates the movement of holidaymakers, business travellers, people visiting friends and relatives and those undertaking educational and health tourism. Before setting out on a journey of any kind, every traveller makes sure which Transport Company has a good safety record. To this effect, airplane coaches and even taxis are equipped with good communication equipment. An Airplane flies with the help of modern information technology equipment, which provides information ranging from weather, altitude and other information to the pilot, to communication made during emergency by the pilot with other airplanes and air traffic control stations.

In-flight entertainment is also a product of information technology, video games, video films are examples. In the case of buses/coaches and taxis, in many countries with developed tourism business, they are equipped with radio communication systems for various uses. For example, the driver or the tour guide updates the Tour Company headquarters about the progress of the tour throughout the touring period. This communication ensures the safety of tourists. Fast and easy information flow is of paramount importance to build confidence in the travelling public. In recent years, the confidence built due to the use of modern IT has been demonstrated by a tremendous increase in the number of travellers worldwide.

INFORMATION TECHNOLOGY IN THE ACCOMMODATION SECTOR

In the accommodation sector also the contribution of information technology is prominent. Any individual or group wishing to travel to any part of the world now has an easy access to the accommodation service providers. A visitor can access information about the kind of hotels at the destination, their ranges of product, the price and other relevant information without leaving his/her office or home. What one has to do is to ring up a travel agency and get the expert advice. This will help any visitor greatly as to where to stay during any kind of trip away from home. Here the information can be obtained aided by still or moving pictures in order to give an exact feature of an accommodation, facilities and services of one's choice. At a destination also visitors are at ease during their stay in every respect, in getting information about their business, family or other information back home. They are also at ease to relaxing with the videos and television entertainment programmes, which nowadays are part and parcel of many accommodation units.

INFORMATION TECHNOLOGY IN THE ATTRACTION SECTOR

In the case of attractions, both man-made and natural the owners need to communicate or inform their customers and potential customers about their product. Information about the kind of attraction, where it is located and how to get there is of vital importance. The attraction owners, particularly the national tourist offices, discharge their duty of promoting their country's tourist attractions using the information technology products. Information through promotional videos, Internet web Sites, television advertisements and travel documentaries are the main information dissemination tools. There is, in fact, competition amongst tour operation to create better and better sites for the user to enable the tourist to decide in their favour. More and more people around the Globe are getting computer literate or so to say computer savvy, due to which, they have increasingly become information seekers.

Before deciding on the desired destination, they not only rely on the sites of tour operators or travel agents, they even take feedback from other travellers to find out about their experiences. In the Attraction Sector communication technologies are thus very significant.

INFORMATION CENTRES AND COMMUNICATION TECHNOLOGIES

Several information centres and tourist offices of Government of India are currently located at India and abroad. Overseas offices are located in Australia, Canada, France, Germany, Italy, Japan, Netherlands, Singapore, Spain, Sweden, UAE, U.K., U.S.A., New York, Israel, the Russian Federation and South Africa.

INFORMATION TECHNOLOGY AND GROWTH OF TOURISM WORLD OVER

It was in 1908 that the first move was made for promoting tourism by only three countries namely Spain, France and Portugal who founded the France Hispano Portuguese. Federation of Tourist Association is considered the first international tourist organization. After first the World War, several other countries realised the need as well, but due to lack of communication technologies, the endeavour could not take off inspite of setting up the International Union of National Tourist Propaganda Organization in 1925.

After the Second World War, this endeavour was revived from the year 1963. With the revolution in the Information Communication Technologies the world Tourism, as a joint effort gained momentum. It was in the 1980s that the Tourist did not feel lost or insecure due to lack of information. Interestingly, during the same period, India was perceived as a country, which was backward and inhabited with wildlife and natives because India lagged far behind in growth of communication technologies.

It was only the late 1980s due to the advent of computer technology in a big way and satellite network that India could change that perception among foreigners. India also saw tourism increasing due to changed perceptions, advertising, marketing and attracting the tourists using information technologies. Currently, tourist arrivals are predicted to grow by an average 4.3% a year over the next two decades, while receipts from international tourism will climb by 6.7% a year.

Tourism: Mega Trends for the 21st century:

- Globalization versus localization
- Electronic technology will become all-powerful in influencing destination choice and distribution
- Fast track travel–emphasis will be placed on facilitation and the speeding up of the travel process
- Customers 'call the shots' through technology such as CDROM atlases, internet, internet inspection of hotels and other facilities, brokers offering discounted rooms on websites, last minute e-mails, low fares etc.
- The tourist world shrinking by the day, due to technology, the tourist is nearly reaching 'space tourism'
- Growing impact of technologies, helping aggressive campaign is kindling the urge for travel consumption.

However, growth and related benefits of tourism cannot be taken for granted. The competition among countries, tour operators, destinations, etc. is becoming so fierce, that, in order to be a winner the following imperatives will have to be kept in mind by every country,

- Development focused on quality and responsibility
- Value for money
- Full utilization of information technology to identify and communicate effectively with market segments and niches.

9

Tourism Promotion

PROMOTION

Promotion means activities that communicate the merits of the product and persuade target customers to buy it. Ford spends about $2.3 billion each year on advertising to tell consumers about the company and its many products. The franchised dealers and salespeople assist potential buyers to buy a Ford car. Ford and its dealers offer promotions- sales, cash rebates and low financing rates as purchase incentives.

The promotion activities of marketing are concerned with communication with the customers that the product is available at the right price and at the right place. The promotional communication aims at informing and persuading the actual and potential customers into actual purchase of the product.

An effective marketing programme moulds all the marketing mix elements–product, price, place and promotion to achieve the marketing objectives.

PROMOTIONAL OBJECTIVES

Effective promotion starts from an analysis and formulation of clear-cut objectives.

These include:

- Identification of the target audience to be reached;
- Identification of the purpose of the communication;
- Formulation of message to achieve the goal;
- Choice of media for delivering the message to the target audience;

- Allocation of the budget to achieve the desired purpose;
- Evaluation in terms of sales and feedback obtained from the customers.

The more carefully objectives are set the better promotion works.

Promotional planning can be done with a view:

- To create new ideas and attitudes: The purpose could be to create awareness of completely new tourism products such as Spa and Spirituality in Himalayas.
- To change the image: The purpose could be to change the unfavourable image of an existing tourism product in the minds of customers. For example New York, in late seventies changed the image of the city to promote tourism.
- To reinforce the image: Larger firms try to reinforce the attitude of customers to retain their existing market like visit to Disneyland and destinations like Goa, Uttaranchal and Singapore.

INTEGRATING COMMUNICATION PROCESS WITH PROMOTION PROGRAMMES

Every consumer goes through various stages of the decision- making process to arrive at a satisfactory decision.

The process of decision-making is a sequence of various steps:

- Need recognition
- Information search
- Evaluation of various alternatives
- Choice of product/services
- Post-purchase evaluation

The marketing communicator needs to effectively design the promotion programme in order to help the consumer in making a proper decision. The good communication strategy should address target consumers needs and wants and help them to choose a particular tourism product. Steps in Developing Effective Market for Tourism Product The marketer needs to address various issues while designing the programme to effectively market the tourism product.

IDENTIFYING THE TARGET MARKET

A tourist organization needs to know their target market consisting of actual and potential customers. The target audience will determine the promotional campaign on what to say, how to say, when to say, where to say and who will say.

DETERMINING THE PROMOTIONAL OBJECTIVE

Once the target market has been identified, the marketer must decide about the purpose of promotional activity.

- *Awareness*: The target market may be totally unaware of the product. The communicator needs to make them aware and knowledgeable about the tourism product.
- *Preference*: If consumers know the product, they need to be made to feel favourably about the product and then moved to the stage of being convinced about preferring such a product to other products.
- *Purchase*: Some members of the target market might be convinced about the product, they need to be taken to the action stage of making an actual purchase of the product. Offering special promotional prices or rebates can persuade them.

DESIGNING A MESSAGE

It is an important step after deciding upon the promotional objective. The communicator needs to develop an effective message to decide what to say and how to say it. "Incredible India' campaign on television is aimed at capturing the attention of viewers about various tourist places all over the India.

CHOOSING THE MEDIA

The communicator must select between personal and non-personal channels of communication.

- Personal communication channels include face-to-face interaction, telephone or mail and are effective channels of influencing the customers of target market.

- Non-personal communication channels include media such as newspapers, magazines, radio, television, billboards, posters and websites. They are a major source to influence, create and reinforce the image of a product among consumers.

FEEDBACK

After deciding and sending the message, the marketing communicator needs to obtain feedback on its promotional efforts. They need to know about target consumers' attitudes towards the product and company. Such feedback facilitates changes in the promotion programme or in the product itself. For example, most of the Airlines and 5-star hotels ask consumers about their experience after the flight or stay in the hotel.

THE PROMOTIONAL MIX

After knowing about the main objectives of promotion, let us understand the four main elements of the promotional mix. A company's total marketing communication mix- also called its promotion mix consists of the specific blend of advertising, sales promotion, public relations, and personal selling that the company uses to pursue its advertising and marketing objectives.

The four major promotional tools of promotion are as follows:

- *Advertising*: Any paid form of nonpersonal presentation and promotion of ideas, goods, or services by an identified sponsor.
- *Sales Promotion*: Short term incentives to encourage the purchase or sale of a product or service.
- *Public Relations*: Building a good reputation of the company with the public by obtaining favourable publicity, good corporate image, and handling unfavourable events if any.
- *Personal Selling*: The sales force of the company makes personal presentations to make sales.

ADVERTISING

Advertising has been defined as any non-personal

presentation by an identified sponsor for the promotion of ideas, goods, or services in exchange for value. While in designing the advertising programme, the target audience and message requirements should be analysed carefully. Advertising in tourism has many uses.

They include:

- Creating awareness;
- Advertising a special offer;
- Providing information on seasonal deals;
- Informing about special services;
- Direct selling;
- Soliciting consumer information;
- Overcoming negative attitudes;
- Reaching a new target audience;
- Providing a new use.

CERTAIN COMMON TERMS USED IN ADVERTISING

A number of technical concepts are needed to be understood in media planning. While selecting media channel as a tool of promotion, the advertising planner has to decide on

- *Media Class*: The basic medium to be used, *e.g.* T.V, radio or press.
- *Media Vehicle*: The individual medium within each selected class *e.g.* Aastha channel or Discovery channel within T.V.
- *Media Unit*: The specific time or space to be utilized within a vehicle *e.g.* a 30 second commercial or half space advertisement.
- *Frequency*: An estimate of how many times the advertising campaign is exposed to target audience over a period of time.
- *Reach*: The total percentage of people in the target market who are exposed to the ad campaign during a given period of time.
- *Impact*: The advertiser must decide on the desired media impact of a message through a given medium.

For example, the visual impact of "Incredible India" campaign has more impact on audience if advertised on T.V as compared to print media.

- *Circulation and Readership*: These two concepts are often confused. Circulation is the number of copies of a print medium sold. Readership is the number of the people who actually read it. Readership of the newspaper is often 2-3 times higher than its circulation.

DEVELOPMENT OF ADVERTISING PROGRAMMES

Marketing management must make four important decisions when developing an advertising programme:

- Setting advertising objectives
- Setting the advertising budget
- Selecting advertising Media
- Evaluating Advertising Campaigns

SETTING ADVERTISING OBJECTIVES

The advertising objectives should be set with a view to define the job and task to be accomplished with target audience during a specific period of time. Advertising objectives can de done with the purpose to inform, persuade, or remind.

Informative Advertising is used when:

- Introducing a new product category,
- Suggesting new uses for a product,
- Informing the market of a price change,
- Describing available services, and
- Building a company image.

Persuasive Advertising is done to influence the customer to actual purchase of the product and is done while:

- Building brand preference,
- Persuading consumer to purchase now,
- Changing consumer's perception about product, and
- Encouraging consumer to switch to your brand.

Reminder Advertising results in consumer recalling the product again and again and is done while:

- Reminding consumer where to buy it,

- Reminding consumer during off-season, and
- Reminding consumer that the product may be needed in future.

SETTING THE ADVERTISING BUDGET

In general, marketing of products can be done with a variety of media options available but certain particular features exist with relation to advertising of travel and tourism in media:

- Tourism has a large and highly fragmented advertising market, consisting of few big enterprises with huge advertising budgets and a large number of small firms with less to spend on advertising.
- Print is the dominant medium in travel and tourism advertising. The higher cost of advertising on TV has made press a more economical medium to reach the target audience.
- Much of the expenditure on travel and tourism is done on brochures, destination guides, and point- of-sales displays. Tourist Boards, tour operators, and tourist information centres provide large amounts of information through printed material to prospective customers.

These specific factors should be kept in mind while setting the advertising budget for a tourism product.

SELECTING ADVERTISING MEDIA

The media planner has to essentially choose the most economical combination of media channels to reach desired target audience. There are various factors to be considered while appraising the media options.

Some of the main factors in media selection are:

- Readership or audience size;
- Geographical reach;
- Repetition and frequency of advertisement;
- Segment target market size;
- Unit cost and cost per thousand:
- Seasonal/period discounts available;

- Availability of medium;
- Reproduction quality.

EVALUATING ADVERTISING

The evaluation of advertising programmes is done to measure the:

- Communication effect, and
- Sales effect.

The communication effect is measured to know whether the advertisement has resulted in consumer product awareness, knowledge and preference. It can be done by placing the ad before the consumers and asking them specific question how they like it and whether it has changed their attitude.

Sales effect is measured by knowing what sales are caused by an ad by comparing sales with advertising expenditure. However, the sales effect of advertising is more difficult to measure than the communication effects.

SOME ADVERTISING TECHNIQUES IN TOURISM MARKETING

The advertiser creates the message in such a manner that will capture the target market's attention and interest. In tourism marketing some techniques of message presentation have been extensively used by advertisers over the years such as following:

SLICE OF LIFE

This technique shows some characters using or discussing the product's uses/benefits. For example, husband and wife recalling their experiences to a particular destination and decide to visit the place again.

LIFESTYLE

This style shows how a particular product fits in with a particular lifestyle. For example, Uttaranchal Tourism prints advertisement exhorting adventurous people to come for river rafting in Rishikesh.

TESTIMONY

The method of selling the product is through the testimony of satisfied customers. A single person, a number of people or a famous celebrity can do it.

PROBLEM SOLUTION

This method starts with a problem, introduces the product and its benefits and shows the problem resolved at the end. For example, a T.V commercial shows an Indian family that wants to go to Europe for a tour and there is a problem of choosing a holiday package that provides Indian vegetarian food during the tour. The advertisement introduces a particular package and its features and finish with a satisfied family.

DEMONSTRATION

This method uses an actual description of the product or its use. For example, an advertisement showing the interiors of a cruise ship for promotion to make an impact on customers.

DOCUMENTARY

This TV technique involves using real-life short films of destinations.

For example, Discovery channel showing a documentary on Mystic India or Geographic channel showing a documentary on wild life of India.

FANTASY

This method creates a fantasy around the product or its use. For example, ads showing a honeymoon couple enjoying a particular destination for its blissful peace and privacy.

MUSICAL

This method shows one or more people singing about the product. For example, Broadway actors sang the song 'I Love New York' to encourage tourists to visit New York. The tourist organizations often use a combination of the techniques while promoting tourist product.

SALES PROMOTION

Sales promotion can be defined as: Those marketing activities other than personal selling and advertising and publicity that stimulate purchases such as exhibitions, shows, and demonstrations. In a way they refer to short –term incentives offered to the consumer to induce a booking, reservation or sale.

OBJECTIVES OF SALES PROMOTION

The sales Promotion in tourism is done with the following objectives:

- *Creating awareness*: Sometimes companies devise special promotions like two or more companies join or tie up together to build awareness. For example, an Airline and hotel group tie-up to promote a particular destination.
- *Encouraging early bookings*: Tour operators often offer discounts at the start of the season to generate immediate bookings. For example, Deccan Airways providing airline tickets at auction to Pune, Bombay or Goa if booked in advance.
- *Increase trial*: The tourists are encouraged to try the product by giving incentives like free stays or trial coupons at much discounted prices.
- *Enhanced repeat buy*: Some promotions are done to encourage repeat stays or visits. For example, Indian Airline offers of multi-coupon discounts to frequent flyers.
- *Combating competition*: Tour operators or hotels may cut down their prices to combat any price cut by competitors or may be done to block competitors' moves in advance.
- *Promote use of tourist product during off- season*: When demand is low for hotel rooms, during low season, special season offers are used to attract customers. For example, Goa hotels offer special discounts during the rainy season; Jaipur and Agra hotels offer discounts during the summer season.

- *Motivating sales force*: The travel agencies give commission to travel agents for selling a certain number of tickets. The agents are also provided coupons, free offers, sales aids and training materials.

TECHNIQUES OF TOURISM SALES PROMOTION

Some of the sales promotion activities used in travel and tourism are as follows:

- *Rebates*: The tourist product is made available at special price less than original price for a limited period of time.
- *Discounts*: Certain percentage of price is deducted as discount from the original price to induce them to buy or buy more. For example, hotel stay for two children at discounted price for a particular package.
- *Refunds*: The seller offers to refund a part of the price paid by the customer on previous purchase of the product.
- *Contests*: These are another form of promotion. In these consumers are required to participate in some competitive event involving application of skills and winners are given some reward.
- *Quantity deals*: The tourist operator provides special package in which buyer is offered additional product at lower or no price. For example, a tourist operator coming out with the offer in family package 'two children for the price of one'.

Some other techniques of sales promotion are:

- Vouchers,
- Competitions,
- Prizes,
- Gifts and premium,
- Additional night stay,
- Slide shows,
- Point of purchase displays, and
- Posters.

Bibliography

Moilliet, D.: *Hospitality Research Journal,* London: Macmillan, 2001.

Moscardo, G.: *The Journal of Tourism Studies,* New Delhi: Penguin Books, 2000.

Payne, K.: *Tourism and Hospitality Research,* Guwahati: United Publishers, 1998.

Pearce, P.: *Locating Tourism Studies in the Landscape of Knowledge,* Calgary: University of Calgary, 1997.

Shea, L. J.: *Journal of Hospitality and Tourism Education,* Kolkata: ICSP Publication, 2001.

Sheldon, P. J.: *Training Needs Assessment in the Travel Industry,* Mumbai: Sabrang Publications, 2000.

Tao, H.: *The Development and Construction of Tourism Personnel,* London: Yale University Press, 2003.

Tribe, J.: *The Tourism Curriculum,* London: Yale University Press, 1998.

Umbreit, T.: *The Role of Education in the Tourist Industry,* Salt Lake City: University of Utah, 2002.

Vroom, J. A.: *Tourism Education: A Model Program,* New Delhi: Manas Publications, 2004.

Vukonic, B.: *Tourism as a Field of Research,* New Delhi: Oxford University Press, 2005.

Vukoniæ, B.: *Tourism in Central and Eastern Europe: Educating for Quality,* Tilberg: Tilberg University Press, 2000.

Walle, A.H.: *Journal of Hospitality and Tourism Education,* New Delhi: Indian Institute of Public Administration, 2000.

Walsh, M. E.: *Tourism Management*, New Delhi: Government of India Press, 2007.

Watson, J.: *Developing Tourism Managers*, New Delhi: Government of India Press, 2005.

Xiao, H.: *Annals of Tourism Research*, New Delhi: Oxford University Press, 2004.

Xiao, Q. H.: *Tourism and Hospitality Education*, New Delhi: Planning Commission, 2005.

Youell, R.: *Tourism Education Handbook*, London: The Tourism Society, 1996.

Zhao, J. L.: *International Journal of Hospitality Management*, New York: HRW, 1998.

Index